THE ULTIMATE
ECAA COLLECTION

UniAdmissions

Published by *RAR Medical Services Limited*
www.uniadmissions.co.uk
info@uniadmissions.co.uk
0208 068 0438

ENGAA INTENSIVE COURSE

UNIADMISSIONS

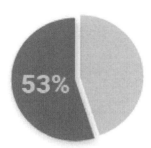

53%

UNIADMISSIONS 3-Year Oxbridge Engineering Programme Success Rate

14%

The Average Cambridge Engineering Success Rate

WHY STUDENTS SEE SUCCESS ON OUR INTENSIVE COURSE

1 **EXPERT TUTORS.**
The course is designed and led by an expert course instructor who has scored in the top 10% of their admissions cycle for this exam. You'll only be taught by the best.

2 **GUIDED THROUGH ALL SECTIONS.**
You'll be taken through each section of the exam in-depth with a tutor who truly knows the test inside out. They will teach you how to effectively approach each section of the test.

3 **LEARN KEY STRATEGIES & TIME-SAVING TIPS.**
Throughout the course, you will learn vital strategies to apply when sitting the exam. You will also be taught valuable time-saving tips that help you gain marks most students won't.

300+
Students successfully placed at Oxbridge in the last 3 years

50
Places available on our Oxbridge Engineering Programme

BOOK YOUR FREE INTENSIVE COURSE

VISIT: **uniadmissions.co.uk/exam-course/**

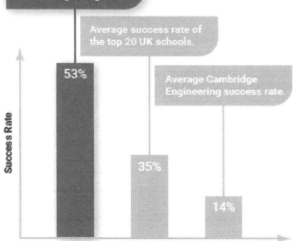

Students enrolled on an Oxbridge Programme.

Average success rate of the top 20 UK schools.

Average Cambridge Engineering success rate.

53%

35%

14%

Success Rate

UNIADMISSIONS Oxbridge Engineering Programme Average Success Rate

About the Authors

David is a **Merger & Acquisitions Associate** at The Hut Group, a leading online retailer and brand owner in the Beauty & Wellness sectors. Prior to joining The Hut Group, he worked in roles at the Professional Service firm Deloitte, the Investment Bank Greenhill and the Private Equity firm HGCapital.

David graduated with a **first class honours** in Economics from Gonville and Caius College Cambridge, where he received two college scholarships for outstanding academic performance, in addition to an Essay Prize. He is also a qualified accountant and chartered tax adviser, passing all exams first-time with multiple regional top scores. Since graduating, David has tutored & successfully provided academic coaching to hundreds of students, both in a personal capacity and for university admissions.

Rohan is the **Director of Operations** at *UniAdmissions* and is responsible for its technical and commercial arms. He graduated from Gonville and Caius College, Cambridge and is a fully qualified doctor. Over the last five years, he has tutored hundreds of successful Oxbridge and Medical applicants. He has also authored ten books on admissions tests and interviews.

Rohan has taught physiology to undergraduates and interviewed medical school applicants for Cambridge. He has published research on bone physiology and writes education articles for the Independent and Huffington Post. In his spare time, Rohan enjoys playing the piano and table tennis.

THE ULTIMATE
ECAA COLLECTION

DAVID MEACHAM

ROHAN AGARWAL

UniAdmissions

PREFACE

First of all, I'd like to thank you for trusting UniAdmissions to help you with your university application.

It's a tough and confusing process to approach in many ways. As time has passed, the application has become more competitive and convoluted with the introduction of Admissions Tests and an extremely high calibre of students applying, making differentiating yourself increasingly challenging.

When I was applying to Cambridge, there weren't any good resources that I felt I could trust my future with. Unsurprisingly, many of my peers felt the same way and UniAdmissions was born! We started in 2013 and have had an amazing response from the thousands of students we support with their applications each year. Since UniAdmissions' inception in 2013, we have made it our mission to improve our students' Oxbridge acceptance rate year on year. We've been quite successful in doing that; while the average Oxbridge acceptance rate stands at around 18%, UniAdmissions' success rate is consistently at 61% - triple the national average. Everyone here at UniAdmissions is always looking at how we can push this success rate even higher.

Overwhelmingly, our focus is on applications to highly competitive universities and courses. These are world-renowned and draw the brightest and best pupils from around to globe to their gates. To set yourself apart from this exceptional group of applicants, you must show yourself to be truly remarkable. Over the years, we have made great headway to cracking this formula – as evidenced with our success rates, which we're extremely proud of.

The purpose of this book is to help you prepare for your upcoming admissions test and, ultimately, help you gain your place to study at great universities like Oxford or Cambridge, or on your dream course. I sincerely believe this book will help you prepare, but words on a page can only take you so far.

In the past we have offered our students books, physical courses, tuition, mock interviews, online resources and much more. All of these forms of support make their mark on your application, although what we have discovered is that a holistic approach works much better. Which is why, nowadays, we have shifted our focus at UniAdmissions completely towards our Oxbridge and Medical Programmes. The Programmes each represent a structured syllabus that covers everything you need to know and practice in order to get your dream offer.

The support we provide splits broadly into four key categories: one-to-one teaching, intensive courses, materials, and enrichment seminars. Each represents a different style of learning which has its own positives and negatives. We believe in offering the very best support we can provide to each student who entrusts a portion of their application to us, as you have with this book. One of the key tenets of our support comes in the form of intensive courses. In order to help you get your dream offer, we're offering you the opportunity to **attend one of our intensive courses – completely free of charge.**

The course is a half-day affair that is led by an expert instructor for your test. You'll be taken through the ins-and-outs of the exam, learn valuable time-saving tips and vital strategies to score marks that most students won't.

The idea behind UniAdmissions was always to help each student get their dream offer. Now that we have the resources available to widen our support, we're delighted to offer you this opportunity at no cost.

All you need to do is visit uniadmissions.co.uk/exam-course/ and book your place.

All that's left is for you to read on, I hope you enjoy this book and I wish you the very best of luck!
– Dr Rohan Agarwal

HOW TO USE THIS BOOK

Congratulations on taking the first step to your ECAA preparation! First used in 2008, the ECAA is a difficult exam and you'll need to prepare thoroughly in order to make sure you get that dream university place.

The *Ultimate ECAA Collection* is the most comprehensive ECAA book available – it's the culmination of three top-selling ECAA books:
- *The Ultimate ECAA Guide*
- *ECAA Practice Papers*
- *ECAA Past Paper Solutions*

Whilst it might be tempting to dive straight in with mock papers, this is not a sound strategy. Instead, you should approach the ECAA in the three steps shown below. Firstly, start off by understanding the structure, syllabus and theory behind the test. Once you're satisfied with this, move onto doing the 300 practice questions found in *The Ultimate ECAA Guide* (not timed!). Then, once you feel ready for a challenge, go through the two ECAA Mock Papers found in *ECAA Practice Papers* under timed conditions. Finally, once you've exhausted these, start with the 2016 paper and work chronologically; check your solutions against the model answers given in *ECAA Past Paper Worked Solutions* – these are a final boost to your preparation.

As you've probably realised by now, there are well over 500 questions to tackle meaning that this isn't a test that you can prepare for in a single week. From our experience, the best students will prepare anywhere between four to eight weeks (although there are some notable exceptions!).

Remember that the route to a high score is your approach and practice. Don't fall into the trap that "you can't prepare for the ECAA"– this could not be further from the truth. With knowledge of the test, some useful time-saving techniques and plenty of practice you can dramatically boost your score.

Work hard, never give up and do yourself justice. Good luck!

THE ULTIMATE ECAA GUIDE

What is the ECAA?

The Economics Admissions Assessment (ECAA) is a two-hour written exam for prospective Cambridge Economics applicants.

What does the ECAA consist of?

Section	Skills Tested	Questions	Timing
1A	Mathematics	20 MCQs	60 minutes
1B	Advanced Mathematics	20 MCQs	(recommended 30 minutes for each)
2	Writing Task	One Long Essay	60 minutes

Why is the ECAA used?

Cambridge applicants tend to be a bright bunch and therefore usually have excellent grades. The majority of economics applicants score in excess of 90% in their A level subjects. This means that competition is fierce – meaning that the universities must use the ECAA to help differentiate between applicants.

When do I sit ECAA?

The ECAA normally takes place in the first week of November every year, normally on a Wednesday Morning.

Can I resit the ECAA?

No, you can only sit the ECAA once per admissions cycle.

Where do I sit the ECAA?

You can usually sit the ECAA at your school or college (ask your exams officer for more information). Alternatively, if your school isn't a registered test centre or you're not attending a school or college, you can sit the ECAA at an authorised test centre.

Who has to sit the ECAA?

All applicants for Cambridge Economics need to sit the test.

Do I have to resit the ECAA if I reapply?

Yes, each admissions cycle is independent - you cannot use your score from any previous attempts.

How is the ECAA Scored?

In section 1, each question carries one mark and there is no negative marking. Both sections 1A + 1B are equally weighted. In section 2, your answer will be assessed based on the argument and also its clarity.

How is the ECAA used?

Different Cambridge colleges will place different weightings on different components so it's important you find out as much information about how your marks will be used by emailing the college admissions office.

In general, the university will interview a high proportion of realistic applicants so the ECAA score isn't vital for making the interview shortlist. However, it can play a huge role in the final decision after your interview

GENERAL ADVICE

Start Early

It is much easier to prepare if you practice little and often. Start your preparation well in advance; ideally by mid-September but at the latest by early October. This way you will have plenty of time to complete as many papers as you wish to feel comfortable and won't have to panic and cram just before the test, which is a much less effective and more stressful way to learn. In general, an early start will give you the opportunity to identify the complex issues and work at your own pace.

Prioritise

Some questions in sections 1 + 2 can be long and complex – and given the intense time pressure you need to know your limits. It is essential that you don't get stuck with very difficult questions. If a question looks particularly long or complex, mark it for review and move on. You don't want to be caught 5 questions short at the end just because you took more than 3 minutes in answering a challenging multi-step question. If a question is taking too long, choose a sensible answer and move on. Remember that each question carries equal weighting and therefore, you should adjust your timing in accordingly. With practice and discipline, you can get very good at this and learn to maximise your efficiency.

Positive Marking

There are no penalties for incorrect answers in the ECAA; you will gain one mark for each right answer and will not get a mark for each wrong or unanswered one. This provides you with the luxury that you can always guess should you absolutely be not able to figure out the right answer for a question or run behind time. Since each question provides you with 4 to 6 possible answers, you have a 16-25% chance of guessing correctly. Therefore, if you aren't sure (and are running short of time), then make an educated guess and move on. Before 'guessing' you should try to eliminate a couple of answers to increase your chances of getting the question correct. For example, if a question has 5 options and you manage to eliminate 2 options- your chances of getting the question increase from 20% to 33%!

Avoid losing easy marks on other questions because of poor exam technique. Similarly, if you have failed to finish the exam, take the last 10 seconds to guess the remaining questions to at least give yourself a chance of getting them right.

Practice

This is the best way of familiarising yourself with the style of questions and the timing for this section. Practising questions will put you at ease and make you more comfortable with the exam. The more comfortable you are, the less you will panic on the test day and the more likely you are to score highly. Initially, work through the questions at your own pace, and spend time carefully reading the questions and looking at any additional data. When it becomes closer to the test, **make sure you practice the questions under exam conditions**.

Past Papers

The ECAA is a very new exam so there aren't many sample papers available. Past and Specimen papers are freely available online at https://www.undergraduate.study.cam.ac.uk/courses/economics#entry-requirements. Once you've worked your way through the questions in this book, you are highly advised to attempt them.

Repeat Questions

When checking through answers, pay particular attention to questions you have got wrong. If there is a worked answer, look through that carefully until you feel confident that you understand the reasoning, and then repeat the question without help to check that you can do it. If only the answer is given, have another look at the question and try to work out why that answer is correct. This is the best way to learn from your mistakes, and means you are less likely to make similar mistakes when it comes to the test. The same applies for questions which you were unsure of and made an educated guess which was correct, even if you got it right. When working through this book, **make sure you highlight any questions you are unsure of**, this means you know to spend more time looking over them once marked.

> ***Top tip!*** In general, students tend to improve the fastest in section 2 and slowest in section 1A; section 1B usually falls somewhere in the middle. Thus, if you have very little time left, it's best to prioritise section 2.

No Calculators

You aren't permitted to use calculators in the ECAA – thus, it is essential that you have strong numerical skills. For instance, you should be able to rapidly convert between percentages, decimals and fractions. You will seldom get questions that would require calculators but you would be expected to be able to arrive at a sensible estimate. Consider for example:

Estimate 3.962×2.322

3.962 is approximately 4 and 2.323 is approximately $2.33 = \frac{7}{3}$.

Thus, $3.962 \times 2.322 \approx 4 \times \frac{7}{3} = \frac{28}{3} = 9.33$

Since you will rarely be asked to perform difficult calculations, you can use this as a signpost of if you are tackling a question correctly. For example, when solving a question, you end up having to divide $8,079$ by 357- this should raise alarm bells as calculations in the ECAA are rarely this difficult.

Section 1A & 1B: An Overview

What will you be tested on?	No. of Questions	Duration
The ability to apply mathematical knowledge up to A Level	40 MCQs	60 Minutes

Section 1B of the exam involves short MCQ questions relating to Mathematics that are designed to see if you can quickly apply the principles that you have learnt in school in a time pressured exam. Assuming you split your time evenly between sections 1A + 1B (30 minutes each), you will have on average 90 seconds per question so it vital to work very quickly- some questions later tend to be harder so you should be doing the initial questions in under 50 seconds. I cannot emphasise enough that the limiting factor in this test is time not your ability. Practice is therefore crucial to learn the technique, skills and tricks to answer section 1 questions quickly. A quick summary of the syllabus is included below:

- **Number**- you should be confident performing a wide range of numerical calculations without the use of a calculator. As this is a MCQ exam, producing order of magnitude estimates will be very useful
- **Algebra & Functions**- you should be competent at basic algebra taught up to AS maths. You will already be at this standard but the key is to practice lots of questions so you use your algebra at the required speed The inequalities can be challenging to do under to time pressure so we recommend quickly drawing out the xy plane and identifying the region of interest. The factor/remainder theorem from A2 maths also appear in the syllabus so you may be tested on this.
- **Measure**- this is linked to "number" but we recommend that you become fully confident when dealing with scale factors. A question can often be simplified by working with this approach.
- **Statistics**- a very basic knowledge of GCSE statistics is all that is necessary. It is however important to know how to combine different statistics together and not get bogged down in long calculations
- **Probability**- a basic GCSE level of knowledge of probability but you will need to work through these questions quickly. We recommend that you practice drawing out 'tree diagrams' quickly to solve these problems
- **Coordinate Geometry** in the (x,y) plane- This is also content covered in AS Level maths and the challenge will be completing questions under time pressure. Practise converting equations to a standard form and then sketching them on the xy plane- this will often help you spot the solution. As this is a MCQ exam, you will not need to provide geometric proofs.
- **Trigonometry** - Basic trigonometry covering material tested in AS level maths. You are expected to know two basic trig formulae as well as the values of sine, cosine and tangent for the angles 0°, 30°, 45°, 60°, 90°. As you will not have a calculator, it is crucial to memorise these values. This will also be very useful for interviews.
- **Exponential and Logarithms**- be confident at using the log formulae that you learnt in AS level maths. Using the formula will often simplify a question and with practice you will be able to determine whether to solve an equation in exponential form or logarithmic form
- **Differentiation**- when sitting your ENGAA exam, you will likely have covered advanced topics in differentiation including the product, chain and quotient rule. However, the exam itself only tests very basic differentiation taught in AS maths so try not to overcomplicate these questions.
- **Integration**- this once again contains the basic integration taught as part of AS level maths. It will be important to practice definite integration without a calculator as it is very easy to make a simple mistake.
- **Graphs of Functions**- this is a very important topic as it provides a lot of tricks to solve maths questions. We recommend you know the C3 transformations of graphs inside out and draw out sketches of common functions

Section 2: An Overview

What will you be tested on?	No. of Questions	Duration
Your ability to write an essay under timed conditions, your writing technique and your argumentative abilities	No Choice – Only one question	60 Minutes

Section 2 is usually what students are more comfortable with – after all, many GCSE and A Level subjects require you to write essays within timed conditions. It does not require you to have any particular legal knowledge – the questions can be very broad and cover a wide range of topics.

Here are some of the topics that might appear in Section two:

- Science
- Politics
- Religion
- Technology
- Ethics
- Morality
- Philosophy
- Education
- History
- Geopolitics

As you can see, this list is very broad and definitely non-exhaustive, and you do not get many choices to choose from (you have to write one essay out of three choices). Many students make the mistake of focusing too narrowly on one or two topics that they are comfortable with – this is a dangerous gamble and if you end up a topic you are unfamiliar with, this is likely to negatively impact your score.

You should ideally focus on at least four topics to prepare from the ECAA, and you can pick and choose which topics from the list above are the ones you would be more interested in. Here are some suggestions:

Economics Science

An essay that is related to science might relate to recent technological advancements and their implications, such as the rise of Bitcoin and the use of blockchain technology and artificial intelligence. This is interrelated to ethical and moral issues; hence you cannot merely just regurgitate what you know about artificial intelligence or blockchain technology. The examiners do not expect you to be an expert in an area of science – what they want to see is how you identify certain moral or ethical issues that might arise due to scientific advancements, and how do we resolve such conundrums as human beings.

Politics

Politics is undeniably always a hot topic and consequently a popular choice amongst students. The danger with writing a politics question is that some students get carried away and make their essay too one-sided or emotive – for example a student may chance upon an essay question related to Brexit and go on a long rant about why the referendum was a bad idea. You should always remember to answer the question and make sure your essay addresses the exact question asked – do not get carried away and end up writing something irrelevant just because you have strong feelings about a certain topic.

Religion

Religion is always a thorny issue and essays on religion provide strong students with a good opportunity to stand out and display their maturity in thought. Questions can range from asking about your opinion with regards to banning the wearing of a headdress to whether children should be exposed to religious practices at a young age. Questions related to religion will require a student to be sensitive and measured in their answers and it is easy to trip up on such questions if a student is not careful.

Education

Education is perhaps always a relatable topic to students, and students can draw from their own experience with the education system in order to form their opinion and write good essays on such topics. Questions can range from whether university places should be reduced, to whether we should be focusing on learning the sciences as opposed to the arts.

Section 2: Revision Guide

SCIENCE

	Resource	What to read/do
1.	**Newspaper Articles**	• The Guardian, The Times, The Economist, The Financial Times, The Telegraph, The New York Times, The Independent
2.	**A Levels/IB**	• Look at the content of your science A Levels/IB if you are doing science subjects and critically analyse what are the potential moral/ethical implications • Use your A Levels/IB resources in order to seek out further readings – e.g., links to a scientific journal or blog commentary • Remember that for your LNAT essay you should not focus on the technical issues too much – think more about the ethical and moral issues
3.	**Online videos**	• There are plenty of free resources online that provide interesting commentary on science and the moral and ethical conundrums that scientists face on a daily basis • E.g., Documentaries and specialist science channels on YouTube • National Geographic, Animal Planet etc. might also be good if you have access to them
4.	**Debates**	• Having a discussion with your friends about topics related to science might also help you formulate some ideas • Attending debate sessions where the topic is related to science might also provide you with excellent arguments and counter-arguments • Some universities might also host information sessions for sixth form students – some might be relevant to ethical and moral issues in science
5.	**Museums**	• Certain museums such as the Natural Science Museum might provide some interesting information that you might not have known about
6.	**Non-fiction books**	• There are plenty of non-fiction books (non-technical ones) that might discuss moral and ethical issues about science in an easily digestible way

POLITICS

	Resource	What to read/do
1.	Newspaper Articles	• The Guardian, The Times, The Economist, The Financial Times, The Telegraph, The New York Times, The Independent
2.	Television	• Parliamentary sessions • Prime Minister Questions • Political news
3.	Online videos	• Documentaries • YouTube Channels
4.	Lectures	• University introductory lectures • Sixth form information sessions
5.	Debates	• Debates held in school • Joining a politics club
6.	Podcasts	• Political podcasts • Listen to both sides to get a more rounded view (e.g. listening to both left and right wing podcasts)

RELIGION

	Syllabus Point	What to read/do
1.	Newspaper Articles	• The Guardian, The Times, The Economist, The Financial Times, The Telegraph, The New York Times, The Independent
2.	Non-fiction books	• Read up about books that explain the origins and beliefs of different types of religion • E.g. Books that talk about the origins of Christianity, Islam or Buddhism, theology books etc.
3.	Talking to religious leaders	• Talking to religious leaders may be a good way of understanding different religions more and being able to write an essay on religion with more maturity and nuance • Talking to people from different religious backgrounds may also be a good way of forming a more well-rounded opinion
4.	Online videos	• Documentaries on religion • YouTube channels providing informative and educational videos on different religions – e.g. history, background
5.	Lectures	• Information sessions • Relevant introductory lectures
6.	Opinion articles	• Informative blogs and journals • Read both arguments and counter-arguments and come up with your own viewpoint

EDUCATION

Syllabus Point	What to read/do
1. **Newspaper Articles**	• The Guardian, The Times, The Economist, The Financial Times, The Telegraph, The New York Times, The Independent
2. **A Levels/IB**	• Draw inspiration from what you are studying in your A Levels or IB – do you feel like what you are studying is useful and relevant? E.g. Studying arts versus science • Compare the education you are receiving with your friends in different schools or different subjects
3. **Educational exchange**	• If you have an opportunity to go on an educational exchange, this might be a good opportunity to compare and contrast different educational systems • E.g. the approach to education in Germany versus the UK
4. **University applications**	• Have a read of how different universities promote themselves – do they claim to provide students with academic enlightenment, or better job prospects, or a good social life? • Why do different universities focus on different things?
5. **Online videos**	• Documentaries • YouTube Channels
6. **Talk to your teachers**	• Your teachers have been in the education industry for years and maybe decades – talk to them and ask them for their opinion • Talk to different teachers and compare their opinions regarding how we should approach education

Maths Revision Checklist

The material for the overviews of sections one and two have mainly been taken from the 2017 syllabus - this may change in the future. We recommend you consult the most up to date syllabus to see if there are any differences.

Syllabus Point	What to Know
1. Number	Understand and use BIDMAS
	Define; factor, multiple, common factor, highest common factor, least common multiple, prime number, prime factor decomposition, square, positive and negative square root, cube and cube root
	Use index laws to simplify multiplication and division of powers
	Interpret, order and calculate with numbers written in standard index form
	Convert between fractions, decimals and percentages
	Understand and use direct and indirect proportion; Apply the unitary method
	Use surds and π in exact calculations, simplify expressions that contain surds.
	Calculate upper and lower bounds to contextual problems
	Rounding to a given number of decimal places or significant figures
2. Algebra	Simplify rational expressions by cancelling or factorising and cancelling
	Set up quadratic equations and solve them by factorising
	Set up and use equations to solve problems involving direct and indirect proportion
	Use linear expressions to describe the nth term of a sequence
	Use Cartesian coordinates in all four quadrants
	Equation of a straight line, $y=mx+c$, parallel lines have the same gradient
	Graphically solve simultaneous equations
	Recognise and interpret graphs of simple cubic functions, the reciprocal function, trigonometric functions and the exponential function $y=kx$ for integer values of x and simple positive values of k
	Draw transformations of $y = f(x)$ **[$y=af(x)$, $y=f(ax)$, $y=f(x)+a$, $y=f(x-a)$ only]**
3. Geometry	Recall and use properties of angle at a point, on a straight line, perpendicular lines and opposite angles at a vertex, and the sums of the interior and exterior angles of polygons
	Understand congruence and similarity; Use Pythagoras' theorem in 2-D and 3-D
	Use the trigonometric ratios, between 0° and 180°, to solve problems in 2-D and 3-D
	Understand and construct geometrical proofs, including using circle theorems:
	a. **the angle subtended at the circumference in a semicircle is a right angle**
	b. **the tangent at any point on a circle is perpendicular to the radius at that point**
	Describe and transform 2-D shapes using single or combined rotations, reflections, translations, or enlargements, including the use of vector notation
4. Measures	Calculate perimeters and areas of shapes made from triangles, rectangles, and other shapes, find circumferences and areas of circles, including arcs and sectors
	Calculate the volumes and surface areas of prisms, pyramids, spheres, cylinders, cones and solids made from cubes and cuboids (formulae given for the sphere and cone)
	Use vectors, including the sum of two vectors, algebraically and graphically
	Discuss the inaccuracies of measurements; Understand and use three-figure bearings

5.	Statistics	Identify possible sources of bias in experimental methodology
		Discrete vs. continuous data; Design and use two-way tables
		Interpret cumulative frequency tables and graphs, box plots and histograms
		Define mean, median, mode, modal class, range, and inter-quartile range
		Interpret scatter diagrams and recognise correlation, drawing and using lines of best fit
		Compare sets of data by using statistical measures
6.	Probability	List all the outcomes for single and combined events
		Identify mutually exclusive outcomes; the sum of the probabilities of all these outcomes is 1
		Construct and use Venn diagrams
		Know when to add or multiply two probabilities, and understand conditional probability
		Understand the use of tree diagrams to represent outcomes of combined events

A word on timing...

"If you had all day to do your ECAA, you would get 100%. But you don't."
Whilst this isn't completely true, it illustrates a very important point. Once you've practiced and know how to answer the questions, the clock is your biggest enemy. This seemingly obvious statement has one very important consequence. **The way to improve your ECAA score is to improve your speed.** There is no magic bullet. But there are a great number of techniques that, with practice, will give you significant time gains, allowing you to answer more questions and score more marks.

Timing is tight throughout the ECAA – **mastering timing is the first key to success**. Some candidates choose to work as quickly as possible to save up time at the end to check back, but this is generally not the best way to do it. ECAA questions can have a lot of information in them – each time you start answering a question it takes time to get familiar with the instructions and information. By splitting the question into two sessions (the first run-through and the return-to-check) you double the amount of time you spend on familiarising yourself with the data, as you have to do it twice instead of only once. This costs valuable time. In addition, candidates who do check back may spend 2–3 minutes doing so and yet not make any actual changes. Whilst this can be reassuring, it is a false reassurance as it is unlikely to have a significant effect on your actual score. Therefore, it is usually best to pace yourself very steadily, aiming to spend the same amount of time on each question and finish the final question in a section just as time runs out. This reduces the time spent on re-familiarising with questions and maximises the time spent on the first attempt, gaining more marks.

It is essential that you don't get stuck with the hardest questions – no doubt there will be some. In the time spent answering only one of these you may miss out on answering three easier questions. If a question is taking too long, choose a sensible answer and move on. Never see this as giving up or in any way failing, rather it is the smart way to approach a test with a tight time limit. With practice and discipline, you can get very good at this and learn to maximise your efficiency. It is not about being a hero and aiming for full marks – this is almost impossible and very much unnecessary (even Oxbridge will regard any score higher than 7 as exceptional). It is about maximising your efficiency and gaining the maximum possible number of marks within the time you have.

Top tip! Ensure that you take a watch that can show you the time in seconds into the exam. This will allow you have a much more accurate idea of the time you're spending on a question. In general, if you've spent more than 3 minutes on question – move on regardless of how close you think you are to solving it.

Use the Options:

Some questions may try to overload you with information. When presented with large tables and data, it's essential you look at the answer options so you can focus your mind. This can allow you to reach the correct answer a lot more quickly. Consider the example below:

The table below shows the results of a study investigating antibiotic resistance in staphylococcus populations. A single staphylococcus bacterium is chosen at random from a similar population. Resistance to any one antibiotic is independent of resistance to others.

Calculate the probability that the bacterium selected will be resistant to all four drugs.

A. 1 in 10^6
B. 1 in 10^{20}
C. 1 in 10^{25}
D. 1 in 10^{35}

Antibiotic	Number of Bacteria tested	Number of Resistant Bacteria
Benzyl-penicillin	10^{11}	98
Chloramphenicol	10^9	1200
Metronidazole	10^8	256
Erythromycin	10^5	2

Looking at the options first makes it obvious that there is **no need to calculate exact values**- only in powers of 10. This makes your life a lot easier. If you hadn't noticed this, you might have spent well over 90 seconds trying to calculate the exact value when it wasn't even being asked for. In other cases, you may actually be able to use the options to arrive at the solution quicker than if you had tried to solve the question as you normally would. Consider the example below:

A region is defined by the two inequalities: $x - y^2 > 1$ and $xy > 1$. Which of the following points is in the defined region?

A. (10,3)
B. (10,2)
C. (−10,3)
D. (−10,2)
E. (−10,−3)

Whilst it's possible to solve this question both algebraically or graphically by manipulating the identities, by far **the quickest way is to use the options**. Note that options C, D and E violate the second inequality, narrowing down to answer to either A or B. For A: $10 - 3^2 = 1$ and thus this point is on the boundary of the defined region and not actually in the region. Thus, the answer is B as $10 - 4 = 6 > 1$.

In general, it pays to look at the options briefly and see if they can be help you get to the answer quicker. Get into this habit early — it may feel unnatural at first, but it's guaranteed to save time in the long run.

Keywords

If you're stuck on a question; pay particular attention to the options that contain key modifiers like "**always**", "**only**", "**all**" as examiners like using them to test if there are any gaps in your knowledge. E.g., the statement "arteries carry oxygenated blood" would normally be true; "All arteries carry oxygenated blood" would be false because the pulmonary artery carries deoxygenated blood.

SECTION 1

This is the first section of the ECAA and as you walk in, it is inevitable that you will feel nervous. Make sure that you have been to the toilet because once it starts you cannot simply pause and go. Take a few deep breaths and calm yourself down. Remember that panicking will not help and may negatively affect your marks- so try and avoid this as much as possible.

You have one hour to answer 40 questions in section 1. Whilst this section of the ECAA is renowned for being difficult to prepare for, there are powerful shortcuts and techniques that you can use to save valuable time on these types of questions.

You have one and a half minutes per question; this may sound like a lot but it can often not be enough. Some questions in this section are very tricky and can be a big drain on your limited time. **The people who fail to complete section 1 are those who get bogged down on a particular question**.

Therefore, it is vital that you start to get a feel for which questions are going to be easy and quick to do and which ones should be left till the end. The best way to do this is through practice and the questions in this book will offer extensive opportunities for you to do so.

SECTION 1A: MATHS QUESTIONS

Section 1 Maths are arguably the hardest to prepare for out of the whole ECAA. However, there are some useful techniques you can employ to solve some types of questions much more quickly:

Construct Equations

Some of the problems in Section 1 are quite complex and you'll need to be comfortable with turning prose into equations and manipulating them. For example, when you read "Mark is twice as old as Jon" – this should immediately register as $M = 2J$. Once you get comfortable forming equations, you can start to approach some of the harder questions in this book (and past papers) which may require you to form and solve simultaneous equations. Consider the example:

Nick has a sleigh that contains toy horses and clowns and counts 44 heads and 132 legs in his sleigh. Given that horses have one head and four legs, and clowns have one head and two legs, calculate the difference between the number of horses and clowns.
A. 0
B. 5
C. 22
D. 28
E. 132
F. More information is needed.

To start with, let C = Clowns and H = Horses.
For Heads: $C + H = 44$
For Legs: $2C + 4H = 132$
This now sets up your two equations that you can solve simultaneously.
$C = 44 - H$
So $2(44 - H) + 4H = 132$
Thus, $88 - 2H + 4H = 132$;
Therefore, $2H = 44$; $H = 22$
Substitute back in to give $C = 44 - H = 44 - 22 = 22$
Thus, the difference between horses and clowns $= C - H = 22 - 22 = 0$

It's important you are able to do these types of questions quickly and **without resorting to trial & error** as they are commonplace in section 1.

Diagrams

When a question asks about timetables, orders or sequences, draw out diagrams. By doing this, you can organise your thoughts and help make sense of the question.

"Mordor is West of Gondor but East of Rivendale. Lorien is midway between Gondor and Mordor. Erebus is West of Mordor. Eden is not East of Gondor." Which of the following **cannot** be concluded?

A. Lorien is East of Erebus and Mordor.
B. Mordor is West of Gondor and East of Erebus.
C. Rivendale is west of Lorien and Gondor.
D. Gondor is East of Mordor and East of Lorien
E. Erebus is West of Mordor and West of Rivendale.

Whilst it is possible to solve this in your head, it becomes much more manageable if you draw a quick diagram and plot the positions of each town:

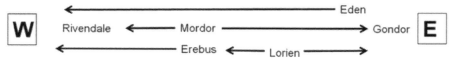

Now, it's a simple case of going through each option and seeing if it is correct according to the diagram. You can now easily see that Option E- Erebus cannot be west of Rivendale.

Don't feel that you have to restrict yourself to linear diagrams like this either – for some questions you may need to draw tables or even Venn diagrams. Consider the example:

Slifers and Osiris are not legendary. Krakens and Minotaurs are legendary. Minotaurs and Lords are both divine. Humans are neither legendary nor divine.
A.   Krakens may be only legendary or legendary and divine.
B.   Humans are not divine.
C.   Slifers are only divine.
D.   Osiris may be divine.
E.   Humans and Slifers are the same in terms of both qualities.

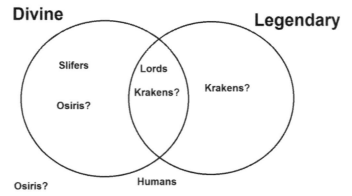

Constructing a Venn diagram allows us to quickly see that the position of Osiris and Krakens aren't certain. Thus, A and D must be true. Humans are neither so B is true. Krakens may be divine so A is true. E cannot be concluded as Slifers are divine but are humans are not. Thus, E is False.

MATHS QUESTIONS

1. Robert has a box of building blocks. The box contains 8 yellow blocks and 12 red blocks. He picks three blocks from the box and stacks them up high. Calculate the probability that he stacks two red building blocks and one yellow building block, in **any** order.

A. $\frac{8}{20}$

B. $\frac{44}{95}$

C. $\frac{11}{18}$

D. $\frac{8}{19}$

E. $\frac{12}{20}$

F. $\frac{35}{60}$

2. Solve $\frac{3x+5}{5} + \frac{2x-2}{3} = 18$

A. 12.11

B. 13.49

C. 13.95

D. 14.2

E. 19

F. 265

3. Solve $3x^2 + 11x - 20 = 0$

A. $\frac{3}{4}$ and $-\frac{4}{3}$

B. $-\frac{3}{4}$ and $\frac{4}{3}$

C. -5 and $\frac{4}{3}$

D. 5 and $\frac{4}{3}$

E. 12 only

F. -12 only

4. Express $\frac{5}{x+2} + \frac{3}{x-4}$ as a single fraction.

A. $\dfrac{15x-120}{(x+2)(x-4)}$

B. $\dfrac{8x-26}{(x+2)(x-4)}$

C. $\dfrac{8x-14}{(x+2)(x-4)}$

D. $\dfrac{15}{8x}$

E. 24

F. $\dfrac{8x-14}{x^2-8}$

5. The value of p is directly proportional to the cube root of q. When $p = 12$, $q = 27$. Find q when $p = 24$.

A. 32

B. 64

C. 124

D. 128

E. 216

F. 1728

6. Write 72^2 as a product of its prime factors.

A. $2^6 \times 3^4$

B. $2^6 \times 3^5$

C. $2^4 \times 3^4$

D. 2×3^3

E. $2^6 \times 3$

F. $2^3 \times 3^2$

7. Calculate: $\dfrac{2.302 \times 10^5 + 2.302 \times 10^2}{1.151 \times 10^{10}}$

A. 0.0000202

B. 0.00020002

C. 0.00002002

D. 0.00000002

E. 0.000002002

F. 0.000002002

8. Given that $y^2 + ay + b = (y + 2)^2 - 5$, find the values of a and b.

A. $a = -1, b = 4$
B. $a = 1, b = 9$
C. $a = -1, b = -9$
D. $a = -9, b = 1$
E. $a = 4, b = -1$
F. $a = 4, b = 1$

9. Express $\frac{4}{5} + \frac{m-2n}{m+4n}$ as a single fraction in its simplest form:

A. $\frac{6m+6n}{5(m+4n)}$

B. $\frac{9m+26n}{5(m+4n)}$

C. $\frac{20m+6n}{5(m+4n)}$

D. $\frac{3m+9n}{5(m+4n)}$

E. $\frac{3(3m+2n)}{5(m+4n)}$

10. A is inversely proportional to the square root of B. When A = 4, B = 25. Calculate the value of A when B = 16.

A. 0.8
B. 4
C. 5
D. 6
E. 10
F. 20

11. S, T, U and V are points on the circumference of a circle, and O is the centre of the circle. Given that angle SVU = 89°, calculate the size of the smaller angle SOU.

A. 89°
B. 91°
C. 102°
D. 178°
E. 182°
F. 212°

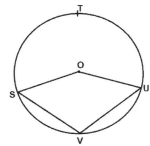

12. Open cylinder A has a surface area of 8π cm² and a volume of 2π cm³. Open cylinder B is an enlargement of A and has a surface area of 32π cm². Calculate the volume of cylinder B.

A. 2π cm³
B. 8π cm³
C. 10π cm³
D. 14π cm³
E. 16π cm³
F. 32π cm³

13. Express $\frac{8}{x(3-x)} - \frac{6}{x}$ in its simplest form.

A. $\frac{3x-10}{x(3-x)}$
B. $\frac{3x+10}{x(3-x)}$
C. $\frac{6x-10}{x(3-2x)}$
D. $\frac{6x-10}{x(3+2x)}$
E. $\frac{6x-10}{x(3-x)}$
F. $\frac{6x+10}{x(3-x)}$

14. A bag contains 10 balls. 9 of those are white and 1 is black. What is the probability that the black ball is drawn in the tenth and final draw if the drawn balls are not replaced?

A. 0
B. $\frac{1}{10}$
C. $\frac{1}{100}$
D. $\frac{1}{10^{10}}$
E. $\frac{1}{362,880}$

15. Gambit has an ordinary deck of 52 cards. What is the probability of Gambit drawing 2 Kings (without replacement)?

A. 0
B. $\frac{1}{169}$
C. $\frac{1}{221}$
D. $\frac{4}{663}$
E. None of the above

16. I have two identical unfair dice. The probability that the dice get a 6 is twice as high as the probability of any other outcome, which are all equally likely. What is the probability that when I roll both dice the total will be 12?

A. 0

B. $\frac{4}{49}$

C. $\frac{1}{9}$

D. $\frac{2}{7}$

E. None of the above

17. A roulette wheel consists of 36 numbered spots and 1 zero spot (i.e., 37 spots in total). What is the probability that the ball will stop in a spot either divisible by 3 or 2?

A. 0

B. $\frac{25}{37}$

C. $\frac{25}{36}$

D. $\frac{18}{37}$

E. $\frac{24}{37}$

18. I have a fair coin that I flip 4 times. What is the probability I get 2 heads and 2 tails?

A. $\frac{1}{16}$

B. $\frac{3}{16}$

C. $\frac{3}{8}$

D. None of the above

E. $\frac{9}{16}$

19. Shivun rolls two fair dice. What is the probability that he gets a total of 5, 6 or 7?

A. $\frac{9}{36}$

B. $\frac{7}{12}$

C. $\frac{1}{6}$

D. $\frac{5}{12}$

E. None of the above

20. Dr Savary has a bag that contains x red balls, y blue balls and z green balls (and no others). He pulls out a ball, replaces it, and then pulls out another. What is the probability that he picks one red ball and one green ball?

A. $\dfrac{2(x+y)}{x+y+z}$

B. $\dfrac{xz}{(x+y+z)^2}$

C. $\dfrac{2xz}{(x+y+z)^2}$

D. $\dfrac{(x+z)}{(x+y+z)^2}$

E. $\dfrac{4xz}{(x+y+z)^4}$

F. More information needed

21. Mr Kilbane has a bag that contains x red balls, y blue balls and z green balls (and no others). He pulls out a ball, does **NOT** replace it, and then pulls out another. What is the probability that he picks one red ball and one blue ball?

A. $\dfrac{2xy}{(x+y+z)^2}$

B. $\dfrac{2xy}{(x+y+z)(x+y+z-1)}$

C. $\dfrac{2xy}{(x+y+z)^2}$

D. $\dfrac{xy}{(x+y+z)(x+y+z-1)}$

E. $\dfrac{4xy}{(x+y+z-1)^2}$

F. More information needed

22. There are two tennis players. The first player wins the point with probability p, and the second player wins the point with probability $1-p$. The rules of tennis say that the first player to score four points wins the game, unless the score is 4 to 3. At this point the first player to get two points ahead wins. What is the probability that the first player wins in exactly 5 rounds?

A. $4p^4(1-p)$

B. $p^4(1-p)$

C. $4p(1-p)$

D. $4p(1-p)^4$

E. $4p^5(1-p)$

F. More information needed

23. Solve the equation $\frac{4x+7}{2} + 9x + 10 = 7$.

A. $\frac{22}{13}$

B. $-\frac{22}{13}$

C. $\frac{10}{13}$

D. $-\frac{10}{13}$

E. $\frac{13}{22}$

F. $-\frac{13}{22}$

24. The volume of a sphere is $V = \frac{4}{3}\pi r^3$, and the surface area of a sphere is $S = 4\pi r^2$. Express S in terms of V.

A. $S = (4\pi)^{\frac{2}{3}}(3V)^{\frac{2}{3}}$

B. $S = (8\pi)^{\frac{1}{3}}(3V)^{\frac{2}{3}}$

C. $S = (4\pi)^{\frac{1}{3}}(9V)^{\frac{2}{3}}$

D. $S = (4\pi)^{\frac{1}{3}}(3V)^{\frac{2}{3}}$

E. $S = (16\pi)^{\frac{1}{3}}(9V)^{\frac{2}{3}}$

25. Express the volume of a cube, V, in terms of its surface area, S.

A. $V = \left(\frac{S}{6}\right)^{\frac{3}{2}}$

B. $V = S^{\frac{3}{2}}$

C. $V = \left(\frac{6}{S}\right)^{\frac{3}{2}}$

D. $V = \left(\frac{S}{6}\right)^{\frac{1}{2}}$

E. $V = \left(\frac{S}{36}\right)^{\frac{1}{2}}$

F. $V = \left(\frac{S}{36}\right)^{\frac{3}{2}}$

26. Solve the equations $4x + 3y = 7$ and $2x + 8y = 12$.

A. $(x,y) = \left(\frac{17}{13}, \frac{10}{13}\right)$

B. $(x,y) = \left(\frac{10}{13}, \frac{17}{13}\right)$

C. $(x,y) = (1, 2)$

D. $(x,y) = (2, 1)$

E. $(x,y) = (6, 3)$

F. $(x,y) = (3, 6)$

G. No solutions possible.

27. Rearrange $\frac{(7x+10)}{(9x+5)} = 3y^2 + 2$, to make x the subject.

A. $\dfrac{15\,y^2}{7 - 9(3y^2+2)}$

B. $\dfrac{15\,y^2}{7 + 9(3y^2+2)}$

C. $-\dfrac{15\,y^2}{7 - 9(3y^2+2)}$

D. $-\dfrac{15\,y^2}{7 + 9(3y^2+2)}$

E. $-\dfrac{5\,y^2}{7 + 9(3y^2+2)}$

F. $\dfrac{5\,y^2}{7 + 9(3y^2+2)}$

28. Simplify $3x\left(\dfrac{3x^7}{x^{\frac{1}{3}}}\right)^3$

A. $9x^{20}$

B. $27x^{20}$

C. $87x^{20}$

D. $9x^{21}$

E. $27x^{21}$

F. $81x^{21}$

29. Simplify $2x[(2x)^7]^{\frac{1}{14}}$

A. $2x\sqrt{2\,x^4}$

B. $2x\sqrt{2x^3}$

C. $2\sqrt{2\,x^4}$

D. $2\sqrt{2x^3}$

E. $8x^3$

F. $8x$

30. What is the circumference of a circle with an area of 10π?

A. $2\pi\sqrt{10}$

B. $\pi\sqrt{10}$

C. 10π

D. 20π

E. $\sqrt{10}$

F. More information needed

31. If $a.b = (ab) + (a+b)$, then calculate the value of $(3.4).5$

A. 19
B. 54
C. 100
D. 119
E. 132

32. If $a.b = \dfrac{a^b}{a}$, calculate $(2.3).2$

A. $\dfrac{16}{3}$
B. 1
C. 2
D. 4
E. 8

33. Solve $x^2 + 3x - 5 = 0$

A. $x = -\dfrac{3}{2} \pm \dfrac{\sqrt{11}}{2}$
B. $x = \dfrac{3}{2} \pm \dfrac{\sqrt{11}}{2}$
C. $x = -\dfrac{3}{2} \pm \dfrac{\sqrt{11}}{4}$
D. $x = \dfrac{3}{2} \pm \dfrac{\sqrt{11}}{4}$
E. $x = \dfrac{3}{2} \pm \dfrac{\sqrt{29}}{2}$
F. $x = -\dfrac{3}{2} \pm \dfrac{\sqrt{29}}{2}$

34. How many times do the curves $y = x^3$ and $y = x^2 + 4x + 14$ intersect?

A. 0
B. 1
C. 2
D. 3
E. 4

35. Which of the following graphs **do not** intersect?

I. $y = x$

II. $y = x^2$

III. $y = 1 - x^2$

IV. $y = 2$

A. I and II

B. II and III

C. III and IV

D. I and III

E. I and IV

F. II and IV

36. Calculate the product of 897,653 and 0.009764.

A. 87646.8

B. 8764.68

C. 876.468

D. 87.6468

E. 8.76468

F. 0.876468

37. Solve for x: $\frac{7x+3}{10} + \frac{3x+1}{7} = 14$

A. $\frac{929}{51}$

B. $\frac{949}{47}$

C. $\frac{949}{79}$

D. $\frac{980}{79}$

38. What is the area of an equilateral triangle with side length x

A. $\frac{x^2\sqrt{3}}{4}$

B. $\frac{x\sqrt{3}}{4}$

C. $\frac{x^2}{2}$

D. $\frac{x}{2}$

E. x^2

F. x

39. Simplify $3 - \dfrac{7x(25x^2-1)}{49x^2(5x+1)}$

A. $3 - \dfrac{5x-1}{7x}$

B. $3 - \dfrac{5x+1}{7x}$

C. $3 + \dfrac{5x-1}{7x}$

D. $3 + \dfrac{5x+1}{7x}$

E. $3 - \dfrac{5x^2}{49}$

F. $3 + \dfrac{5x^2}{49}$

40. Solve the equation $x^2 - 10x - 100 = 0$

A. $-5 \pm 5\sqrt{5}$

B. $-5 \pm \sqrt{5}$

C. $5 \pm 5\sqrt{5}$

D. $5 \pm \sqrt{5}$

E. $5 \pm 5\sqrt{125}$

F. $-5 \pm \sqrt{125}$

41. Rearrange $x^2 - 4x + 7 = y^3 + 2$ to make x the subject.

A. $x = 2 \pm \sqrt{y^3 + 1}$

B. $x = 2 \pm \sqrt{y^3 - 1}$

C. $x = -2 \pm \sqrt{y^3 - 1}$

D. $x = -2 \pm \sqrt{y^3 + 1}$

E. x cannot be made the subject for this equation.

42. Rearrange $3x + 2 = \sqrt{7x^2 + 2x + y}$ to make y the subject.

A. $y = 4x^2 + 8x + 2$

B. $y = 4x^2 + 8x + 4$

C. $y = 2x^2 + 10x + 2$

D. $y = 2x^2 + 10x + 4$

E. $y = x^2 + 10x + 2$

F. $y = x^2 + 10x + 4$

43. Rearrange $y^4 - 4y^3 + 6y^2 - 4y + 2 = x^5 + 7$ to make y the subject.

A. $y = 1 + (x^5 + 7)^{\frac{1}{4}}$

B. $y = -1 + (x^5 + 7)^{\frac{1}{4}}$

C. $y = 1 + (x^5 + 6)^{\frac{1}{4}}$

D. $y = -1 + (x^5 + 6)^{\frac{1}{4}}$

44. The aspect ratio of my television screen is 4:3 and the diagonal is 50 inches. What is the area of my television screen?

A. 1,200 inches²

B. 1,000 inches²

C. 120 inches²

D. 100 inches²

E. More information needed.

45. Rearrange the equation $\sqrt{1 + 3x^{-2}} = y^5 + 1$ to make x the subject.

A. $x = \dfrac{(y^{10} + 2y^5)}{3}$

B. $x = \dfrac{3}{(y^{10} + 2y^5)}$

C. $x = \sqrt{\dfrac{3}{y^{10} + 2y^5}}$

D. $x = \sqrt{\dfrac{y^{10} + 2y^5}{3}}$

E. $x = \sqrt{\dfrac{y^{10} + 2y^5 + 2}{3}}$

F. $x = \sqrt{\dfrac{3}{y^{10} + 2y^5 + 2}}$

46. Solve $3x - 5y = 10$ and $2x + 2y = 13$

A. $(x, y) = (\frac{19}{16}, \frac{85}{16})$

B. $(x, y) = (\frac{85}{16}, -\frac{19}{16})$

C. $(x, y) = (\frac{85}{16}, \frac{19}{16})$

D. $(x, y) = (-\frac{85}{16}, -\frac{19}{16})$

E. No solutions possible.

47. The two inequalities $x + y \leq 3$ and $x^3 - y^2 < 3$ define a region on a plane. Which of the following points is inside the region?

A. $(2, 1)$
B. $(2.5, 1)$
C. $(1, 2)$
D. $(3, 5)$
E. $(1, 2.5)$
F. None of the above.

48. How many times do $y = x + 4$ and $y = 4x^2 + 5x + 5$ intersect?

A. 0
B. 1
C. 2
D. 3
E. 4

49. How many times do $y = x^3$ and $y = x$ intersect?

A. 0
B. 1
C. 2
D. 3
E. 4

50. A cube has unit length sides. What is the length of a line joining a vertex to the midpoint of the opposite side?

A. $\sqrt{2}$

B. $\sqrt{\frac{3}{2}}$

C. $\sqrt{3}$

D. $\sqrt{5}$

E. $\frac{\sqrt{5}}{2}$

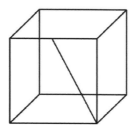

51. Solve for x, y, and z.
$$x + y - z = -1$$
$$2x - 2y + 3z = 8$$
$$2x - y + 2x = 9$$

A. $x = 2, y = -15, z = -14$
B. $x = 15, y = 2, z = 14$
C. $x = 14, y = 15, z = -2$
D. $x = -2, y = 15, z = 14$
E. $x = 2, y = -15, z = 14$
F. No solutions possible

52. Fully factorise: $3a^3 - 30a^2 + 75a$

A. $3a(a - 3)^3$
B. $a(3a - 5)^2$
C. $3a(a^2 - 10a + 25)$
D. $3a(a - 5)^2$
E. $3a(a + 5)^2$

53. Solve for x and y:
$$4x + 3y = 48$$
$$3x + 2y = 34$$

A. $x = 8, y = 6$
B. $x = 6, y = 8$
C. $x = 3, y = 4$
D. $x = 4, y = 3$
E. $x = 30, y = 12$
F. $x = 12, y = 30$
G. No solutions possible

54. Evaluate: $\dfrac{-(5^2 - 4 \times 7)^2}{-6^2 + 2 \times 7}$

A. $-\dfrac{3}{50}$
B. $\dfrac{11}{22}$
C. $-\dfrac{3}{22}$
D. $\dfrac{9}{50}$
E. $\dfrac{9}{22}$
F. 0

55. All license plates are 6 characters long. The first 3 characters consist of letters and the next 3 characters of numbers. How many unique license plates are possible?

A. 676,000
B. 6,760,000
C. 67,600,000
D. 1,757,600
E. 17,576,000
F. 175,760,000

56. How many solutions are there for $2(2(x^2 - 3x)) = -9$

A. 0
B. 1
C. 2
D. 3
E. Infinite solutions

57. Evaluate: $\left(x^{\frac{1}{2}} y^{-3}\right)^{\frac{1}{2}}$

A. $\dfrac{x^{\frac{1}{2}}}{y}$

B. $\dfrac{x}{y^{\frac{3}{2}}}$

C. $\dfrac{x^{\frac{1}{4}}}{y^{\frac{3}{2}}}$

D. $\dfrac{y^{\frac{1}{4}}}{x^{\frac{3}{2}}}$

58. Bryan earned a total of £1,240 last week from renting out three flats. From this, he had to pay 10% of the rent from the 1-bedroom flat for repairs, 20% of the rent from the 2-bedroom flat for repairs, and 30% from the 3-bedroom flat for repairs. The rent on the 3-bedroom flat costs twice as much as the 1-bedroom flat. Given that the total repair bill was £276 calculate the rent for each apartment.

	1 Bedroom	2 Bedrooms	3 Bedrooms
A	280	400	560
B	140	200	280
C	420	600	840
D	250	300	500
E	500	600	1,000

59. Evaluate: $5\left[5(6^2 - 5 \times 3) + 400^{\frac{1}{2}}\right]^{\frac{1}{3}} + 7$

A. 0
B. 25
C. 32
D. 49
E. 56
F. 200

60. What is the area of a regular hexagon with side length 1?

A. $3\sqrt{3}$
B. $\frac{3\sqrt{3}}{2}$
C. $\sqrt{3}$
D. $\frac{\sqrt{3}}{2}$
E. 6
F. More information needed

61. Dexter moves into a new rectangular room that is 19 metres longer than it is wide, and its total area is 780 square metres. What are the room's dimensions?

A. Width = 20m; Length = −39m
B. Width = 20m; Length = 39m
C. Width = 39m; Length = 20m
D. Width = −39m; Length = 20m
E. Width = −20m; Length = 39m

62. Tom uses 34 meters of fencing to enclose his rectangular lot. He measured the diagonals to 13 metres long. What is the length and width of the lot?

A. 3m by 4m
B. 5m by 12m
C. 6m by 12m
D. 8m by 15m
E. 9m by 15m
F. 10m by 10m

63. Solve $\dfrac{3x-5}{2}+\dfrac{x+5}{4}=x+1$

A. 1
B. 1.5
C. 3
D. 3.5
E. 4.5
F. None of the above

64. Calculate: $\dfrac{5.226\times10^6+5.226\times10^5}{1.742\times10^{10}}$

A. 0.033
B. 0.0033
C. 0.00033
D. 0.000033
E. 0.0000033

65. Calculate the area of the triangle shown to the right:

A. $3+\sqrt{2}$
B. $\dfrac{2+2\sqrt{2}}{2}$
C. $2+5\sqrt{2}$
D. $3-\sqrt{2}$
E. 3
F. 6

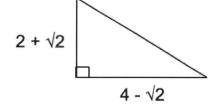

$2+\sqrt{2}$

$4-\sqrt{2}$

66. Rearrange $\sqrt{\dfrac{4}{x}+9}=y-2$ to make x the subject.

A. $x=\dfrac{11}{(y-2)^2}$
B. $x=\dfrac{9}{(y-2)^2}$
C. $x=\dfrac{4}{(y+1)(y-5)}$
D. $x=\dfrac{4}{(y-1)(y+5)}$
E. $x=\dfrac{4}{(y+1)(y+5)}$
F. $x=\dfrac{4}{(y-1)(y-5)}$

67. When 5 is subtracted from $5x$ the result is half the sum of 2 and $6x$. What is the value of x?

A. 0
B. 1
C. 2
D. 3
E. 4
F. 6

68. Estimate $\dfrac{54.98 + 2.25^2}{\sqrt{905}}$

A. 0
B. 1
C. 2
D. 3
E. 4
F. 5

69. At a pizza parlour, you can order one of three types of crust: single, double or triple cheese. You also have the option to include ham, olives, pepperoni, bell pepper, meat balls, tomato slices, and pineapples. How many different types of pizza are available at the Pizza Parlour?

A. 10
B. 96
C. 192
D. 384
E. 768
F. None of the above

70. Solve the simultaneous equations $x^2 + y^2 = 1$ and $x + y = \sqrt{2}$ for $x, y > 0$

A. $(x, y) = (\frac{\sqrt{2}}{2}, \frac{\sqrt{2}}{2})$
B. $(x, y) = (\frac{1}{2}, \frac{\sqrt{3}}{2})$
C. $(x, y) = (\sqrt{2} - 1, 1)$
D. $(x, y) = (\sqrt{2}, \frac{1}{2})$

71. How many negative roots does $f(x) = 16x^4 + 32x^3 + 24x^2 + 8x + 1$ have?

A. 0
B. 1
C. 2
D. 3
E. 4
F. 5

72. Solve the inequality $x^2 \geq 6 - x$

A. $x \leq -3$ and $x \leq 2$
B. $x \leq -3$ and $x \geq 2$
C. $x \geq -3$ and $x \leq 2$
D. $x \geq -3$ and $x \geq 2$
E. $x \geq 2$ only
F. $x \geq -3$ only

73. The hypotenuse of an equilateral right-angled triangle is x cm. What is the area of the triangle in terms of x?

A. $\frac{\sqrt{x}}{2}$
B. $\frac{x^2}{4}$
C. $\frac{x}{4}$
D. $\frac{3x^2}{4}$
E. $\frac{x^2}{10}$

74. Mr Heard derives a formula: $Q = \frac{(X+Y)^2 A}{3B}$. He doubles the values of X and Y, halves the value of A and triples the value of B. What happens to value of Q?

A. Decreases by $\frac{1}{3}$
B. Increases by $\frac{1}{3}$
C. Decreases by $\frac{2}{3}$
D. Increases by $\frac{2}{3}$
E. Increases by $\frac{4}{3}$
F. Decreases by $\frac{4}{3}$

75. Consider the graphs $y = x^2 - 2x + 3$, and $y = x^2 - 6x - 10$. Which of the following is true?

A. Both equations intersect the x-axis.

B. Neither equation intersects the x-axis.

C. The first equation does not intersect the x-axis; the second equation intersects the x-axis.

D. The first equation intersects the x-axis; the second equation does not intersect the x-axis.

76. A crocodile's tail weighs 30kg. Its head weighs as much as the tail and one half of the body and legs. The body and legs together weigh as much as the tail and head combined. What is the total weight of the crocodile?

A. 220kg

B. 240kg

C. 260kg

D. 280kg

E. 300kg

77. Evaluate the following: $\dfrac{4.2 \times 10^{10} - 4.2 \times 10^6}{2 \times 10^3}$

A. 2.09979×10^6

B. 2.09979×10^7

C. 2.09979×10^8

D. 2.09979×10^9

E. 2.09979×10^{10}

78. Calculate $a - b$

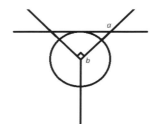

A. 0°

B. 5°

C. 10°

D. 15°

E. 20°

79. Jack has a bag with a complete set of snooker balls (15 red, 1 yellow, 1 green, 1 brown, 1 blue, 1 pink and 1 black ball) within it. Blindfolded Jack draws two balls from the bag. What is the probability that he draws a blue and a black ball in any order?

A. $\dfrac{2}{41}$

B. $\dfrac{1}{210}$

C. $\dfrac{2}{210}$

D. $\dfrac{1}{105}$

E. $\dfrac{2}{441}$

80. Which is the equivalent function to: $y = 9x^{-\frac{1}{3}}$

A. $y = \frac{1}{x}$

B. $y = \sqrt[3]{9x}$

C. $y = \frac{1}{\sqrt[3]{9x}}$

D. $y = \frac{9}{\sqrt[3]{x}}$

E. $y = \frac{3}{\sqrt[3]{x}}$

81. Make y the subject of the formula: $\frac{y+x}{x} = \frac{x}{a} + \frac{a}{x}$

A. $y = \frac{x^2}{a} + a$

B. $y = \frac{x^2 + a^2 - ax}{a}$

C. $y = \frac{-ax}{x^2 + a^2}$

D. $y = \frac{x^2}{ax} + a - x$

E. $y = a^2 - ax$

82. The graph below shows a circle with radius 5 and centre (0,0).

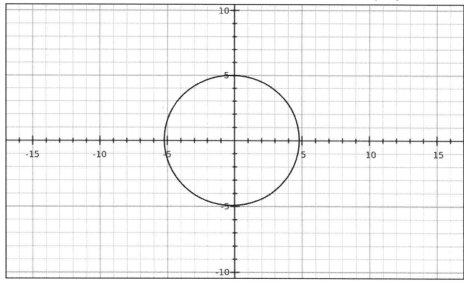

What are the values of x when the line $y = 3x - 5$ meets the circle?

A. $x = 0$ or $x = 3$

B. $x = 0$ or $x = 3.5$

C. $x = 1$ or $x = 3.5$

D. $x = 1.5$ or $x = -3$

E. $x = 1.5$ or $x = -2$

83. There are 1000 international airports in the world. If 4 flights take off every hour from each airport, estimate the annual number of commercial flights worldwide, to the nearest 1 million

A. 20 million
B. 35 million
C. 37 million
D. 40 million
E. 42 million
F. 44 million

84. How many seconds are there in 66 weeks? $[n! = 1 \times 2 \times 3 \times ... \times n]$

A. 7!
B. 8!
C. 9!
D. 10!
E. 11!
F. 12!

85. Write $\frac{\sqrt{20}-2}{\sqrt{5}+3}$ in the form: $p\sqrt{5} + q$

A. $2\sqrt{5} - 4$
B. $3\sqrt{5} - 4$
C. $3\sqrt{5} - 5$
D. $4\sqrt{5} - 6$
E. $5\sqrt{5} + 4$

86. Consider the triangle below where BE = 4cm, EC = 2cm and AC = 9cm. What is the length of side DE?

A. 4cm
B. 5.5cm
C. 6cm
D. 7.5cm
E. 8cm

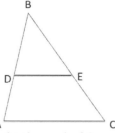

87. An investment of £500 is made in a compound interest account that compounds annually. At the end of 3 years the balance reads £1687.50. What is the interest rate?

A. 20%   B. 35%   C. 50%   D. 65%   E. 80%

88. Rupert plays one game of tennis and one game of squash. The probability that he will win the tennis game is $\frac{3}{4}$. The probability that he will win the squash game is $\frac{1}{3}$. What is the probability that he will win one game only?

A. $\frac{3}{12}$

B. $\frac{7}{12}$

C. $\frac{4}{5}$

D. $\frac{13}{12}$

E. $\frac{7}{6}$

89. Calculate the perimeter of a regular polygon each interior angle is 150° and each side is 15 cm.

A. 75 cm

B. 150 cm

C. 180 cm

D. 225 cm

E. 1,500 cm

F. More information is needed.

90. Calculate $\dfrac{1.25\times10^{10}+1.25\times10^{9}}{2.5\times10^{8}}$

A. 0

B. 1

C. 55

D. 110

E. 1.25×10^8

F. 5.5×10^7

G. 5.5×10^8

91. Solve $y = 2x - 1$ and $y = x^2 - 1$ for x and y

A. $(0, -1)$ and $(2, 3)$

B. $(1, -1)$ and $(2, 2)$

C. $(1, 4)$ and $(3, 2)$

D. $(2, -3)$ and $(4, 5)$

E. $(3, -1)$ and $(3, 1)$

F. $(4, -2)$ and $(-2, 4)$

92. Simplify fully: $\dfrac{(3x^{\frac{1}{2}})^3}{3x^2}$

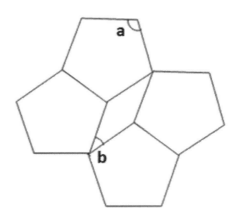

A. $\dfrac{3x}{\sqrt{x}}$

B. $\dfrac{9}{x}$

C. $3x^{\frac{1}{2}}$

D. $3x\sqrt{x}$

E. $\dfrac{9}{\sqrt{x}}$

93. Study the diagram, comprising regular pentagons. What is the product of a and b?

A. 580°
B. 1,111°
C. 3,888°
D. 7,420°
E. 9,255°
F. 15,552°

94. Tim stands at the waterfront and holds a 30 cm ruler horizontally at eye level one metre in front of him. It lines up so it appears to be exactly the same length as a cruise ship 1 km out to sea. How long is the cruise ship?

A. 299.7 m
B. 300.0 m
C. 333.3 m
D. 29,970 m
E. 30,000 m

95. Bob is twice as old as Kerry, and Kerry is three times as old as Bob's son. Their ages combined make 50 years. How old was Bob when his son was born?

A. 15
B. 20
C. 25
D. 30
E. 35

96. The mean of a set of 11 numbers is 6. Two numbers are removed, and the mean is now 5. Which of the following is not a possible combination of removed numbers?

A. 1 and 20
B. 6 and 9
C. 10 and 11
D. 15 and 6
E. 19 and 2

97. Evaluate: $\dfrac{3.4\times10^{11} + 3.4\times10^{10}}{6.8\times10^{12}}$

A. 5.5×10^{-12}
B. 5.5×10^{-2}
C. 5.5×10^{1}
D. 5.5×10^{2}
E. 5.5×10^{10}
F. 5.5×10^{12}

98. A circle has a radius of 3 m. A line passes through the circle's centre and intersects with a tangent 4 m from its tangent point. How far is this point of intersection from the centre of the circle?

A. 1 m   B. 3 m   C. 5 m   D. 7 m   E. 9 m

99. Consider A: $y = 3x$ and B: $y = \dfrac{6}{x} - 7$. At what values of x do the two equations intersect

A. $x = 2$ and $x = 9$
B. $x = 3$ and $x = -6$
C. $x = \dfrac{2}{3}$ and $x = -3$
D. $x = 6$
E. $x = -\dfrac{2}{3}$

100. Calculate the radius of a sphere which has a surface area three times as great as its volume.

A. 0.5
B. 1
C. 1.5
D. 2
E. 2.5
F. More information is needed

101. The diagram shows a series of identical rectangular sports fields, calculate the shortest distance between points A and B.

A. 100 m
B. 105 m
C. 146 m
D. 148 m
E. 154 m
F. None of the above.

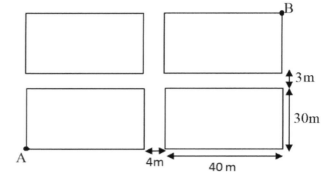

102. Simplify fully: $1 + \left(3\sqrt{2} - 1\right)^2 + \left(3 + \sqrt{2}\right)^2$

A. $30 + 6\sqrt{2} - 2\sqrt{18}$
B. $30 + 6\sqrt{2} + 2\sqrt{18}$
C. $3\left[2\left(\sqrt{2} - 1\right) + 2\right]$
D. 24
E. 29
F. 31

103. Each vertex of a square lies directly on the edge of a circle with a radius of 1cm. Calculate the area of the circle that is not occupied by the square. Use $\pi = 3$.

A. 0.25 cm²   B. 0.5 cm²   C. 0.75 cm²   D. 1.0 cm²   E. 1.25 cm²   F. 1.5 cm²

104. If $(3p + 5)^2 = 24p + 49$, calculate p

A. −5 or −9
B. −3 or −6
C. −4 or 6
D. −6 or 4
E. 4 or −2

105. Find the values of angles b and c.

A. 45° and 135°
B. 45° and 130°
C. 50° and 135°
D. 55° and 130°
E. More information needed.

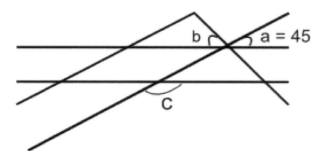

106. If the lines $y_1 = (n + 1)x + 10$ and $y_2 = (n + 3)x + 2$ are perpendicular, then n must equal which of the following?

A. 2
B. −2
C. 3
D. −3
E. 0
F. 1

107. A formula: $\frac{z(x+y)(l-m+n)}{3}$ is given. If each variable in the equation was measured in metres, what would you expect this formula to calculate?

A. A length
B. An area
C. A volume
D. A volume of rotation
E. A geometric average

108. What is the equation of the line of best fit for the scatter graph below?

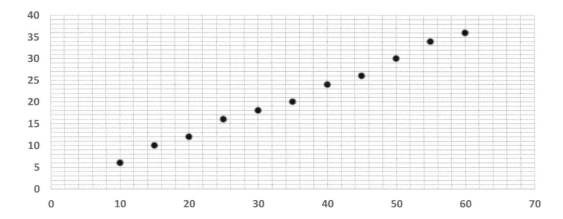

A. $y = 0.2x + 0.35$
B. $y = 0.2x - 0.35$
C. $y = 0.4x + 0.35$
D. $y = 0.4x - 0.35$
E. $y = 0.6x + 0.35$

109. What is the median of the following numbers: $\frac{7}{36}$; $0.\dot{3}$; $\frac{11}{18}$; 0.25; 0.75; $\frac{62}{72}$; $\frac{7}{7}$

A. $\frac{7}{36}$

B. $0.\dot{3}$

C. $\frac{11}{18}$

D. $\frac{62}{72}$

E. 0.75

110. The table below shows the results of a study investigating antibiotic resistance in staphylococcus populations.

Antibiotic	Number of Bacteria tested	Number of Resistant Bacteria
Benzyl-penicillin	10^{11}	98
Chloramphenicol	10^9	1200
Metronidazole	10^8	256
Erythromycin	10^5	2

A single staphylococcus bacterium is chosen at random from a similar population. Resistance to any one antibiotic is independent of resistance to others. Calculate the probability that the bacterium selected will be resistant to all four drugs.

A. 1 in 10^{12}

B. 1 in 10^6

C. 1 in 10^{20}

D. 1 in 10^{25}

E. 1 in 10^{30}

F. 1 in 10^{35}

111. Solve $y = x^2 - 3x + 4$ and $y - x = 1$ as (x, y).

A. $(-1, 2)$ and $(3, 4)$

B. $(1, 2)$ and $(3, 4)$

C. $(7, -2)$ and $(6, 5)$

D. $(2, -3)$ and $(4, -1)$

E. $(1, -1)$ and $(-7, -1)$

112. Evaluate the following: $\left(\left(\frac{6}{8}\times\frac{7}{3}\right)\div\left(\frac{7}{5}\times\frac{2}{6}\right)\right)\times 0.40\times 15\%\times 5\%\times\pi\times\left(\sqrt{e^2}\right)\times 0.20\times(e\pi)^{-1}$

A. $\dfrac{4}{55}$

B. $\dfrac{8}{770}$

C. $\dfrac{9}{4,000}$

D. $\dfrac{8}{54,321}$

E. $\dfrac{9}{67,800}$

113. Bill wants to lay down laminate flooring in his living room, which has an in-built circular fish tank that he will have to lay the flooring around. He has decided to buy planks that he can cut to fit the dimensions of his room. He must, however, buy whole planks and cut them down himself. The room's dimensions are given below, as are those of one plank. Calculate the number of planks needed to cover the whole floor. Take $\pi = 3$.

A. 30
B. 417
C. 600
D. 589
E. 43

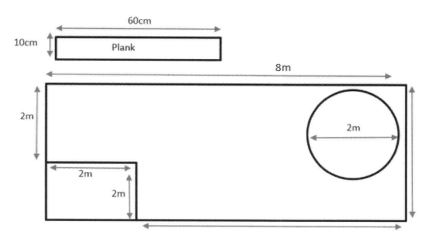

114. Rearrange $\dfrac{(16x+11)}{(4x+5)} = 4y^2 + 2$ to make x the subject

A. $x = \dfrac{20y^2-1}{[16-4(4y^2+2)]}$

B. $x = \dfrac{20y^2-8}{[16-6(4y^2+2)]}$

C. $x = \dfrac{6y^2-1}{[16-4(4y^2+2)]}$

D. $x = \dfrac{21y^2-1}{[16-4(2y^2+2)]}$

E. $x = \dfrac{7y^2-1}{[6-14(6+7)]}$

115. Four unbiased coins are tossed. What is the probability of getting at most two heads?

A. $\frac{3}{4}$

B. $\frac{7}{8}$

C. $\frac{11}{16}$

D. $\frac{1}{2}$

E. $\frac{5}{8}$

116. What is the probability of rolling the same number exactly three times with five six-sided dice?

A. $\frac{10}{36}$

B. $\frac{17}{32}$

C. $\frac{125}{648}$

D. $\frac{108}{124}$

E. $\frac{133}{648}$

117. What is the digit in the 10,000s place in the number 301^5?

A. 0

B. 9

C. 3

D. 5

E. 1

F. 2

G. 7

118. Calculate the value of $\sqrt{20 - 20\sqrt{5} + 25} + \sqrt{5 - 8\sqrt{5} + 16}$.

A. $9 - 3\sqrt{5}$

B. $1 - \sqrt{5}$

C. $\sqrt{5} - 1$

D. $3\sqrt{5} - 9$

E. $\sqrt{66 - 28\sqrt{5}}$

F. 13

G. -3

119. A hospital has two wards, one for critically ill patients called Ward A and one for general patients, called Ward B. The probability a patient in Ward A survives is $\frac{1}{9}$, and the probability a patient in Ward B survives is $\frac{3}{5}$. (Every patient is in one of the two wards). Given that there are p people in Ward A, and the overall survival rate of the hospital is $\frac{1}{4}$, what is q, the number of people in Ward B, in terms of p?

A. $\frac{3p}{45}$

B. $\frac{45p}{3}$

C. $\frac{25p}{63}$

D. $\frac{63p}{25}$

E. 50

F. $\frac{45p}{12p-45}$

G. $\frac{12p-45}{45p}$

120. A man tosses a fair coin 7 times. What is P(he gets more than 4 heads and two of the last 3 tosses are heads)?

A. $\frac{3}{16}$

B. $\frac{7}{8}$

C. $\frac{33}{128}$

D. $\frac{3}{8}$

E. $\frac{33}{64}$

F. $\frac{279}{512}$

121. I have 2 blue balls and 3 red balls which I will throw into 5 <u>indistinguishable</u> boxes. Assuming I don't miss, how many distinct situations could I be in after all the balls are thrown?

A. 14

B. 5^5

C. 32

D. 16

E. 8

F. 4

G. $5^3 + 5^2$

122. What angle is swept by the minute hand on a clock between 08:34 and 11:12?

A. 1260°
B. 948°
C. 924°
D. 720°
E. 724°

123. An inflated spherical football is packaged in the smallest possible box that it will fit inside of. What is the ratio of volume taken up by the football to the volume of the box?

A. $\frac{\pi}{12} : 1$
B. $\frac{12}{\pi} : 1$
C. $\frac{6}{\pi} : 1$
D. $\frac{\pi}{6} : 1$
E. $\frac{8}{\pi} : 1$

124. The diagram below shows a scalene triangle with a line crossing through it parallel to the base. What is the length of the base, which is marked x?

A. $6\frac{1}{7}$ m
B. $7\frac{5}{8}$ m
C. $6\frac{3}{8}$ m
D. $6\frac{6}{7}$ m
E. $7\frac{1}{6}$ m

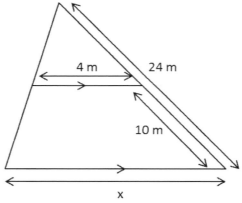

125. There are five rides in a theme park which are arranged on the corners of a regular pentagon, as shown in the diagram below. If someone wants to walk from ride 2 to ride 4, what bearing should they walk on?

A. 45°
B. 54°
C. 112°
D. 234°
E. 245°

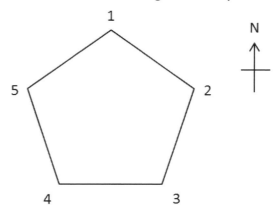

126. What is the area of the grey section in the diagram below?

A. $12\sqrt{15}$

B. $18\sqrt{10}$

C. $\frac{18}{7}\sqrt{35}$

D. $\frac{6}{5}\sqrt{15}$

E. $\frac{43}{9}\sqrt{35}$

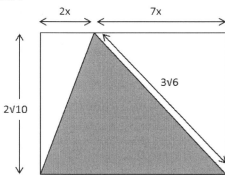

127. The diagram shows a garden, the grey area is to be covered with grass. The grass comes in rolls that are 1 m by 10 m. How many rolls are needed to cover the garden?

A. 47

B. 48

C. 49

D. 50

E. 51

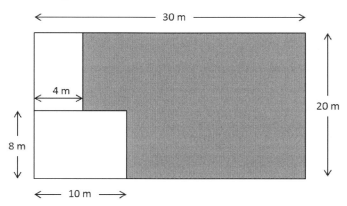

128. In a household there are 2 people with size 6 feet and 3 people with size 11 feet. Each person owns 4 pairs of shoes. All of the shoes are randomly mixed up in a large bag. If someone pulls out a left size 11 shoe, what is the probability that the next shoe that they pull out is a right size 11 shoe?

A. $\frac{1}{2}$

B. $\frac{12}{39}$

C. $\frac{3}{10}$

D. $\frac{11}{39}$

E. $\frac{16}{39}$

129. What is the surface area to volume ratio of a solid cylinder with radius 'r' and length '3r'?

A. $3:r$

B. $4\frac{1}{3}:r$

C. $8:3r$

D. $1:6r$

E. $4:1r$

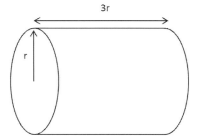

130. The volume of a cylinder is between 2 and 3 times the value of its overall surface area. If its height is 8, what values can r take? (Assuming r is non-zero)

A. $1 \leq r \leq 3$
B. $r \leq 8$
C. $8 \leq r \leq 24$
D. $r \geq 16$
E. $\frac{3}{2} \leq r \leq \frac{7}{4}$
F. $2 \leq r \leq 3$

131. On Mondays Professor X takes class A or B. The probability he picks class A is $\frac{2}{7}$. On Tuesdays, he takes class A if he took class B the day before, otherwise he picks in the same way he did on Monday. Prof. X took class A on Tuesday; what is the probability he took class A on Monday?

A. $\frac{2}{7}$
B. $\frac{5}{7}$
C. $\frac{10}{49}$
D. $\frac{10}{39}$
E. $\frac{4}{39}$
F. $\frac{7}{39}$
G. $\frac{31}{49}$

132. Every day, a man decides whether to walk his dog with probability $\frac{1}{3}$ that he does take it for a walk, independently of choices made on other days. After 4 days, what is the probability that he walked his dog at least once every 2 days?

A. $\frac{1}{27}$
B. $\frac{7}{27}$
C. $\frac{8}{27}$
D. $\frac{11}{27}$
E. $\frac{1}{9}$
F. $\frac{1}{3}$

133. There is a box that is 3m by 4m by 5m. What is the maximum length of stick that can fit in this box?

A. 6 m
B. $5\sqrt{2}$ m
C. $\sqrt{77}$ m
D. $2\sqrt{3}$ m
E. $\sqrt{39}$ m

134. Given you have already thrown a 6, what is the probability of throwing three consecutive 6s using a fair die?

A. $\frac{1}{216}$
B. $\frac{1}{36}$
C. $\frac{1}{6}$
D. $\frac{1}{2}$
E. 1

135. Three people, A, B and C play darts. The probability that they hit a bullseye are respectively $\frac{1}{5}, \frac{1}{4}, \frac{1}{3}$. What is the probability that at least two shots hit the bullseye?

A. $\frac{1}{60}$
B. $\frac{1}{30}$
C. $\frac{1}{12}$
D. $\frac{1}{6}$
E. $\frac{3}{20}$

136. If probability of having blonde hair is 1 in 4, the probability of having brown eyes is 1 in 2 and the probability of having both is 1 in 8, what is the probability of having neither blonde hair nor brown eyes?

A. $\frac{1}{2}$
B. $\frac{3}{4}$
C. $\frac{3}{8}$
D. $\frac{5}{8}$
E. $\frac{7}{8}$

SECTION 1B: ADVANCED MATHS

Section 1B tests principles of advanced mathematics. You have to answer 20 questions in 30 minutes. The questions can be quite difficult and it's easy to get bogged down. However, it's well worth spending time preparing for this section as its possible to rapidly improve with targeted preparation.

Gaps in Knowledge

You are highly advised to go through the ECAA Specification and ensure that you have covered all examinable topics. An electronic copy of this can be obtained from **uniadmissions.co.uk/ecaa.** The questions in this book will help highlight any particular areas of weakness or gaps in your knowledge that you may have. Upon discovering these, make sure you take some time to revise these topics before carrying on – there is little to be gained by attempting these questions with huge gaps in your knowledge. A summary of the major topics is given below:

Algebra:

- Laws of Indices
- Manipulation of Surds
- Quadratic Functions: Graphs, use of discriminant, completing the square
- Solving Simultaneous Equations via Substitution
- Solving Linear and Quadratic Inequalities
- Manipulation of polynomials e.g., expanding brackets, factorising
- Use of Factor Theorem and Remainder Theorem

Graphing Functions:

- Sketching of common functions including lines, quadratics, cubic, trigonometric functions, logarithmic functions and exponential functions
- Manipulation of functions using simple transformations

Exponentials & Logs:

- Graph of $y = a^x$ series
- Law of Logarithms:
  - $a^b = c \leftrightarrow b = log_a c$
  - $log_a x + log_a y = log_a(xy)$
  - $log_a x - log_a y = log_a(\frac{x}{y})$
  - $k\, log_a x = log_a(x^k)$
  - $log_a \frac{1}{x} = -log_a x$
  - $log_a a = 1$

Trigonometry:
- Sine and Cosine rules
- Solution of trigonometric identities
- Values of sin, cos, tan for 0, 30, 45, 60 and 90 degrees
- Sine, Cosine, Tangent graphs, symmetries, periodicities
  - $Area\ of\ Triangle\ = \frac{1}{2}ab\sin C$
  - $\sin^2\theta + \cos^2\theta\ = 1$
  - $\tan\theta = \frac{\sin\theta}{\cos\theta}$

Differentiation:
- First order and second order derivatives
- Familiarity with notation: $\frac{dy}{dx}, \frac{d^2y}{dx^2}, f'(x), f''(x)$
- Differentiation of functions like $y = x^n$

Integration:
- Definite and indefinite integrals for $y = x^n$
- Solving Differential Equations in the form: $\frac{dy}{dx} = f(x)$
- Understanding of the Fundamental Theorem of Calculus and its application:
  - $\int_a^b f(x)dx = F(b) - F(a), where\ F'(x) = f(x)$
  - $\frac{d}{dx}\int_a^x f(t)dt = f(x)$

Geometry:
- Circle Properties:
  - The angle subtended by an arc at the centre of a circle is double the size of the angle subtended by the arc on the circumference
  - The opposite angles in a cyclic quadrilateral summate to 180 degrees
  - The angle between the tangent and chord at the point of contact is equal to the angle in the alternate segment
  - The tangent at any point on a circle is perpendicular to the radius at that point
  - Triangles formed using the full diameter are right-angled triangles
  - Angles in the same segment are equal
  - The perpendicular from the centre to a chord bisects the chord
- Equations for a circle:
  - $(x - a)^2 + (y - b)^2 = r^2$
  - $x^2 + y^2 + cx + dy + e = 0$
- Equations for a straight line:
  - $y - y_1 = m(x - x_1)$
  - $Ax + by + c = 0$

Series:

- Arithmetic series and Geometric Series
- Summing to a finite and infinite geometric series
- Binomial Expansions
- Factorials

Formulas you **MUST** know:

2D Shapes		3D Shapes		
Area			**Surface Area**	**Volume**
Circle	πr^2	**Cuboid**	Sum of all 6 faces	length $\times$ width $\times$ height
Parallelogram	Base $\times$ Vertical height	**Cylinder**	$2\pi r^2 + 2\pi r l$	$\pi r^2 \times l$
Trapezium	$0.5 \times h \times (a + b)$	**Cone**	$\pi r^2 + \pi r l$	$\pi r^2 \times \frac{h}{3}$
Triangle	$0.5 \times base \times height$	**Sphere**	$4\pi r^2$	$\frac{4}{3}\pi r^3$

Even good students who are studying maths at A level can struggle with certain ECAA maths topics because they're usually glossed over at school. These include:

Quadratic Formula

The solutions for a quadratic equation in the form $ax^2 + bx + c = 0$ are given by: $x = \frac{-b \pm \sqrt{b^2 - 4ac}}{2a}$

Remember that you can also use the discriminant to quickly see if a quadratic equation has any solutions:

$$\text{If } b^2 - 4ac < 0: No \ solutions$$
$$\text{If } b^2 - 4ac = 0: One \ solution$$
$$\text{If } b^2 - 4ac > 2: Two \ solutions$$

Completing the Square

If a quadratic equation cannot be factorised easily and is in the format $ax^2 + bx + c = 0$ then you can rearrange it into the form $a\left(x + \frac{b}{2a}\right)^2 + [c - \frac{b^2}{4a}] = 0$

This looks more complicated than it is – remember that in the ECAA, you're extremely unlikely to get quadratic equations where $a > 1$ and the equation doesn't have any easy factors. This gives you an easier equation: $\left(x + \frac{b}{2}\right)^2 + \left[c - \frac{b^2}{4}\right] = 0$ and is best understood with an example.

Consider: $x^2 + 6x + 10 = 0$

This equation cannot be factorised easily but note that: $x^2 + 6x - 10 = (x + 3)^2 - 19 = 0$

Therefore, $x = -3 \pm \sqrt{19}$. Completing the Square is an important skill – make sure you can do it.

Difference between 2 Squares

If you are asked to simplify expressions and find that there are no common factors but it involves square numbers – you might be able to factorise by using the 'difference between two squares'.

For example, $x^2 - 25$ can also be expressed as $(x + 5)(x - 5)$.

ADVANCED MATHS QUESTIONS

1. How many positive roots does the function $f(x) = x^4 - 8x^3 + 22x^2 - 24x$ have?

A. 0
B. 1
C. 2
D. 3
E.   None of the above

2. Compute the integral $\int_0^1 \frac{x-4}{\sqrt{x}(\sqrt{x}+2)} dx$.

A. -3
B. -1
C. 2
D. 3
E. 1

3. Given that, in the expansion of $(3x + b)^7$, the coefficient of x^4 is the same as the coefficient of x^2 in $(3b + x)^4$, find b.

A. $\frac{2}{105}$
B. $\frac{105}{2}$
C. $\frac{107}{3}$
D. $\frac{3}{107}$
E. $\frac{109}{4}$

4. Consider the tangent to the curve $y = x^2 + bx$ at $x = 2$. For what values of b is the x intercept greater than 4?

A. $-3 < b < 3$
B. $2 < b < 4$
C. $b > 3$
D. $b < -3$
E. $b > -3$

5. Given $f(x) = \left(9x^2 + 12 + \frac{4}{x^2}\right)^{\frac{1}{2}}$ and $\frac{d^n f}{dx^n}(2) = -\frac{3}{4}$ find n.

A. 1
B. 2
C. 3
D. 4
E. 5

6. In which of the following ranges is $(x^2 - 1)(x + 2)(x + 4) > 0$?

A. $-2 < x < 1$
B. $-1 < x < 2$
C. $-2 < x < -1$
D. $x \geq 1$
E. $x < -3$

7. Suppose $5^{4+6+\cdots+2x} = 0.04^{-14}$. Given x is a positive integer, what is x?

A. 5
B. 6
C. 7
D. 8
E. 5.5

8. An arithmetic series is defined by
$$x_1 = 2$$
$$x_{n+1} = x_n + q$$
Given x_{100} is 13, find the sum to infinity of a series with common ratio q, and first term 5.

A. $\frac{78}{5}$
B. $\frac{102}{3}$
C. $\frac{36}{7}$
D. $\frac{52}{9}$
E. $\frac{45}{8}$

9. The roots of $x^2 + 3x + c = 2$ differ by 7. What is c?

A. -10 B. -8 C. 13   D. -4 E. 5

10. Which of the following is a line of symmetry of the graph $y = \dfrac{1}{\sin(4x+\frac{\pi}{3})}$?

A. $x = \dfrac{13\pi}{2}$

B. $x = \dfrac{\pi}{2}$

C. $x = \pi$

D. $x = \dfrac{13\pi}{24}$

E. $y = \dfrac{\pi}{24}$

11. Define a recurrent sequence by $x_{n+1} = \begin{cases} \frac{x_n}{2} \ if \ x_n \ even \\ 3x_n + 1 \ if \ x_n \ odd \end{cases}$

Given $x_1 = 12$, what is x_{100}?

A. 1

B. 4

C. 2

D. 12

E. 0

12. What is the sum of roots of the equation $2^y - 5\sqrt{2}^{y+2} + 24 = 0$?

A. $3 + 4\log_2 5$

B. 4

C. 10

D. $\log_2 24$

E. $6 + 2\log_2 3$

13. For $p > 0$, find the area enclosed by the curves $y = px^2$ and $x = py^2$.

A. $\dfrac{1}{3p}$

B. $3p$

C. $\dfrac{1}{3p^2}$

D. $\dfrac{1}{2}p^2$

E. $3p$

14. What is the complete set of values for which $\frac{x^2+2x}{\sqrt{x^3}}$ is increasing?

A. $x > 3$
B. $x < 2$
C. $2 < x < 4$
D. $x > 2$
E. $0 < x < 2$

15. Compute the shortest distance between the curves below.
$$x^2 + 4x + y^2 + 6y + 10 = 0 \text{ and } x^2 - 4x + y^2 - 8y + 12 = 0$$

A. $\sqrt{65} - \sqrt{2} - \sqrt{3}$
B. $\sqrt{65} - 2\sqrt{2} - 2\sqrt{3}$
C. $\sqrt{65} - 2\sqrt{2} - \sqrt{3}$
D. $\sqrt{65}$
E. $\sqrt{65} - 4\sqrt{2} - 2\sqrt{3}$

16. How many solutions does the equation $\cos 2x \log x = \sin 2x$ have in range $0 < x < 3\pi$

A. 0　　　　　　B. 3　　　　　　C. 5　　　　　　D. 6　　　　　　E. 7

17. The sum to infinity of a geometric progression is 4. The sum to infinity of the squares of each term in the progression is 10. What is the common ratio of the geometric series?

A. $\frac{1}{2}$
B. $\frac{2}{5}$
C. $\frac{3}{7}$
D. $\frac{7}{12}$
E. $\frac{3}{13}$

18. Given that $\frac{dV}{dt} = (1+t)^4$, and $V(1) = 5$, what is $V(2)$?

A. $\frac{174}{5}$
B. $\frac{236}{5}$
C. $\frac{112}{3}$
D. $\frac{89}{4}$

19. The sum of the first n terms of an arithmetic series is S_n. For a particular series, $S_3 = 18$ and the fifth term is k. Which of the following are necessary conditions on k for S_n to be an integer for every value of n?

   I. k has a factor of 6

   II. k has a factor of 18

   III. k is odd

A. None
B. I only
C. II only
D. III only
E. I & II only
F. I & III only
G. II & III only
H. All three

20. When is $\frac{\sin 2x}{1-\cos 2x}(3^x - 2) \leq 0$ in the range $0 < x < \pi$?

A. $\log_3 2 \leq x \leq \frac{\pi}{2}$

B. $\log_3 2 \leq x < \frac{\pi}{2}$

C. $\frac{\pi}{2} < x \leq \log_3 2$

D. $0 < x < \log_3 2$

E. $\frac{\pi}{2} \leq x \leq \log_3 2$

F. $0 < x \leq \log_3 2$

21. What is the difference between the 2 solutions to the equation $25^{x-1} + \frac{96}{25} = 5^x$?

A. $\log_5 \frac{3}{2}$

B. 25

C. 5

D. 1

E. $\log_5 \frac{5}{3}$

22. What is the equation of the line equidistant between the centres of the circles $y^2 + x^2 + 6y - 4x + 12 = 0$ and $y^2 + x^2 - 2y - 80 = 0$?

A. $y = 1 - 2x$

B. $y = \frac{x-3}{2}$

C. $y = \frac{1}{2} - 2x$

D. $y = -x$

E. $y = \frac{x}{2} + 1$

23. A small marble is carried from point A, to point B, and then to point C, which have co-ordinates $(4, 6, 12), (7, 2, 0)$ and $(16, 15, 5)$ respectively. What is the difference between the square of the distance the marble travelled and the square of the distance it is currently from where it started?

A. 170
B. $10(17 + 13\sqrt{11})$
C. 30
D. $10(17 - 13\sqrt{11})$
E. $3\sqrt{61} + 130\sqrt{11}$

24. Find the distance between the stationary points of $y = 5x^3 - 5x + 6 = 0$.

A. $\dfrac{2\sqrt{109}}{3\sqrt{3}}$
B. $\dfrac{2\sqrt{34}}{3\sqrt{3}}$
C. There are 1 or fewer stationary points.
D. $\dfrac{2}{3}$
E. $\sqrt{34}$

25. Consider the sequence defined by
$$x_1 = 1000$$
$$x_{n+1} = \frac{1}{\sqrt{x_n}} \quad n \geq 0$$
What is x_{1000}?

A. $10^{3 \times 2^{1000}}$
B. $10^{-3 \times 2^{-1000}}$
C. $10^{3 \times 2^{999}}$
D. $10^{-3 \times 2^{-999}}$
E. $10^{-3 \times 2^{-1001}}$
F. $10^{3 \times 2^{-999}}$
G. $10^{-3 \times 2^{100}}$

26. $4x^2 - 7x + 1$ is multiplied by $2x - q$ to form $f(x)$. $f(x)$ divided by $(x + 2)$ is -31^2. What is q?

A. 27
B. 35
C. There is no such q.
D. -27
E. -35
F. $\dfrac{21}{2}$

27. What is the value of the integral below?

$$\int_0^2 |x - 1|\left(3\sqrt{x} - x\sqrt{x}\right)dx$$

A. $\frac{48-4\sqrt{2}}{35}$

B. $\frac{4\sqrt{2}}{35}$

C. $\frac{24}{35}$

D. $\frac{48+4\sqrt{2}}{35}$

E. $\frac{24+4\sqrt{2}}{35}$

F. $\frac{24-4\sqrt{2}}{35}$

28. For a function $f(x)$, it is given that $\left(\int_0^2 f(x)dx\right)\left(\int_0^1 f(x)dx + 4\right) = 24$. You are also told that, for this function, $f(x - 1) = f(1 - x)$. Which of the following could the value of $\int_1^2 f(x)dx$ be?

I. -6

II. 8

III. 2

A. None

B. I only

C. II only

D. III only

E. I & II only

F. I & III only

G. II & III only

H. All three

29. Let $f(x)$ be $\left(\frac{x}{2} + 1\right)^3$. What is the value of $f''(2)$?

A. 3

B. 63

C. 27

D. $\frac{63}{2}$

E. -2

30. Let $f(x) = ax^3 + bx^2 + cx - 75$ for some integers a, b, c. $f\left(\frac{3}{4}\right) = f(-5) = 0$ and $f(x) = 0$ for only these values. What is the mean of the numbers a, b, c?

A. 50

B. -35

C. $\frac{115}{3}$

D. 35

E. $-\frac{43}{3}$

F. 12

31. Let $f(x) = ax^5 + \frac{x^4}{2} + cx$. It is given that the gradient of this function at $x = 1$ is $-a^2$. What is the maximum value of $\int_0^2 f(x)dx$?

A. $\frac{67}{36}$

B. $-\frac{67}{18}$

C. $-\frac{67}{36}$

D. $\frac{67}{18}$

32. $1, \frac{2}{3} \, \& \, \frac{4}{9}$ are 3 of the first 7 terms of a geometric series. Which of the following are <u>not</u> possible values of the sum to infinity of the series?

I. $3 + \sqrt{6}$

II. $\frac{9}{2}$

III. $\frac{9+3\sqrt{6}}{2}$

IV. $\frac{27}{4}$

A. I only

B. II only

C. III only

D. IV only

E. I & III only

F. II& III only

G. II & IV only

33. $\frac{dx}{dt} = 6\left(\frac{1}{1-\sin t} - \frac{1}{1+\sin t}\right)$. If $x = 0$ when $t = \frac{\pi}{6}$, find x when $t = \frac{\pi}{3}$. [the integral of $\frac{1}{\cos^2 t}$ is $\tan t$]

A. $4\sqrt{3}$

B. $6\sqrt{3}$

C. $\frac{6}{\sqrt{3}}$

D. $3\sqrt{3}$

E. $\sqrt{3}$

F. $\frac{4}{\sqrt{3}}$

G. $12\sqrt{3}$

34. Consider the parabola $y = (x-3)^2 - 4$ and the line $y = mx + c$. Let R be the size of the interval m which must lie such that the line and parabola do not intersect. What is c in terms of R?

A. $c = 5 - R^2$

B. $c = 5 - \frac{(R+6)^2}{4}$

C. $c = 5 - \frac{R^2}{16}$

D. $c = 20 - \frac{R^2}{4}$

E. $c = 20 - (R+6)^2$

35. Let $f(x) = 3x^5 + 8x^4 + x^3 - 4x - 16 = 0$. You are told that $f(-2) = 0 = f(1)$. How many distinct real roots does $f(x)$ have?

A. 0

B. 1

C. 2

D. 3

E. 4

F. 5

G. 6

36. Let a_n be a geometric series with first term a_0 , common difference d, and the sum of the first n terms be S_n. Which of the following conditions is sufficient for the product of any two terms in the series to always be greater than 0, no matter which two terms are chosen?

I. $S_5 = a_{10}$
II. $S_5 = a_{12}$
III. $a_0 = d$

A. None
B. I only
C. II only
D. III only
E. I & II only
F. I & III only
G. II & III only
H. All three

37. The expansion of $(k + x)^5$ has at least two terms with the same coefficient, as does the expansion of $(1 + 2kx)^2$. How many possible values of k are there?

A. 0
B. 1
C. 2
D. 3
E. 4
F. 5

38. How many solutions are there to $x \times 3^{\tan 2x} = 1$ in the range $0 < x < \pi$?

A. 0
B. 1
C. 2
D. 3
E. 4
F. 5

39. Find the distance between the intersection points of $y = |x - 4|$ and $y = 5 - |x - 1|$.

A. There are no intersections.
B. 4
C. $\sqrt{34}$
D. 5
E. 3
F. $\sqrt{41}$

40. Given that $\int_0^4 (x^3 + ax^2 + bx + 1)dx = 0$, and that $a \leq 0, b \geq 0$, what is the maximum value of $\int_0^3 (x^3 + ax^2 + bx + 1)dx$?

A. -15
B. 15
C. 100
D. -100
E. $\frac{123}{2}$
F. $-\frac{123}{2}$

41. Let $f(x) = \frac{\left(x^2 - \frac{1}{x}\right)^2}{x^{\frac{1}{3}}}$. It is given also that $f'(x) = \frac{x^{\frac{2}{3}}}{3}[ax^p + bx^q + cx^r]$.

What is the value of $abc + pqr$?

A. 388
B. $\frac{520}{3}$
C. 288
D. 316
E. 300
F. -80

42. ABC is a triangle. You are told that the side AB has length 3cm, $\sin B = \frac{1}{\sqrt{2}}$ and $\sin C = \frac{\sqrt{3}}{2}$. How many different triangles can be formed from this information?

A. 0
B. 1
C. 2
D. 3
E. 4
F. 5
G. Infinitely many

43. Which of the following is the largest?

A. $\log_3 8$
B. $(1.4)^2$
C. $\frac{13}{6}$
D. $\sqrt{6}$
E. $\frac{\sqrt{15}}{\sqrt{5}+1}$

44. Let the line l have equation $y = \frac{x}{3} + 3$. Let l_2 be the line perpendicular to l at the point on l where $y = 8$. What is the area between the two lines, the x-axis and the y-axis?

A. $\frac{169}{3}$ B. $\frac{551}{6}$ C. $\frac{559}{6}$ D. $\frac{181}{2}$ E. 70

45. Find the sum of the 2 distinct roots for x in the simultaneous equations:

$$\log_8 x + \log_8 y = \frac{1}{2}$$
$$(\log_8 x)(\log_8 y) = -5$$

A. $2^{\frac{3}{2}}$

B. $2^{\frac{15}{2}} + 2^{-6}$

C. $2^{-7} - 2$

D. $2^{-\frac{7}{2}}$

E. $2^{\frac{3}{2}}$

F. $2^{\frac{5}{2}} + 2^{-2}$

46. A triangle ABC has angle $CAB = 45°$, and angle $ACB = 30°$. It also has side length $AB = 500$mm. What is the area of this triangle?

A.   There are infinitely many possible values

B. $125^2(\sqrt{3} + \sqrt{2})$

C. $250^2(\sqrt{3} + \sqrt{2})$

D. $125^2(\sqrt{3} - 1)$

E. $250^2(\sqrt{3} + 1)$

47. Consider the circle $x^2 + (y - 2)^2 = 4$. A straight line intersects the circle at the lower of the points where $x = \sqrt{3}$ such that the perimeter of the arc of the circle below the line is equal to $\frac{7\pi}{6}$. What is the equation of the line?

A. $y = \left(\sqrt{6} - \sqrt{3} - \sqrt{2} + 2\right)x - \sqrt{18} + 2 - \sqrt{6} + 3\sqrt{3}$

B. $y = \left(\sqrt{6} + \sqrt{3} + \sqrt{2} - 2\right)x - \sqrt{18} + 2 - \sqrt{6} - 3\sqrt{3}$

C. $y = \left(\sqrt{6} - \sqrt{3} - \sqrt{2} - 2\right)x + \sqrt{18} + 2 - \sqrt{6} + 3\sqrt{3}$

D. $y = \left(\sqrt{6} - \sqrt{3} + \sqrt{2} - 2\right)x - \sqrt{18} + 2 - \sqrt{6} + 3\sqrt{3}$

E. $y = \left(\sqrt{6} - \sqrt{3} + \sqrt{2} - 2\right)x - \sqrt{18} - 2 - \sqrt{6} + 3\sqrt{3}$

48. Given that $\frac{dy}{dt} = 2t^{-3} + \frac{3-t^2}{t^{-2}}, t \neq 0.$

And that $y = 2$ when $t = 1$, find y in terms of t.

A. $y = \frac{17}{6} + t^3 - \frac{t^5}{5} + \frac{t^{-4}}{2}$

B. $y = \frac{17}{10} + t^3 - \frac{t^5}{5} - \frac{t^{-4}}{2}$

C. $y = \frac{3}{10} - t^3 - \frac{t^5}{5} - \frac{t^{-4}}{2}$

D. $y = \frac{17}{6} + t^3 - \frac{t^5}{5} - \frac{t^{-4}}{2}$

E. $y = \frac{17}{6} + 2t^3 + \frac{t^5}{5} - \frac{t^{-4}}{2}$

49. The function $f(x) = \frac{\log_7 x}{3}$ is stretched by a factor of 8 parallel to the x-axis.

This stretch is equivalent to a translation in the y-direction by a. What is the value of a?

A. $\frac{\log_7 4}{3}$

B. 2

C. $-\frac{1}{2}$

D. $\log_7 2$

E. 7

F. 49

G. -343

50. What is the shortest distance between these two circles?
$x^2 + y^2 - 14x - 4y + 44 = 0$
$x^2 + y^2 + 6x + 8y = 0$

A. 0

B. $2\sqrt{11} - 8$

C. 44

D. $2\sqrt{26} - 8$

E. $2\sqrt{34} - 8$

F. 64

G. $6\sqrt{7} + 5$

51. What is the coefficient of x^3 in the expansion of $(2 - x)^2(2 + x)^4(x - 2)^2$?

A. 16 B. 8 C. 0 D. -8 E. -16

52. Evaluate the following integral: $\int_3^4 \frac{1}{x^2+x-6} dx$.

A. $0.2\ln(\frac{12}{7})$

B. $0.2\ln(\frac{12}{14})$

C. $-0.2\ln(\frac{12}{14})$

D. $0.2\ln(\frac{6}{7})$

E. $-0.2\ln(\frac{12}{9})$

53. What is the second derivative of $f(x) = e^{-2x} + x^2$?

A. $4e^{-2x} + 2$

B. $4e^{-2x} - 2$

C. $2e^{-2x} + 2$

D. $e^{-2x} + 2$

E. $2e^{-2x} - 2$

54. Find the equation of the tangent to the curve $y = 3x^2$ at point (1,3).

A. $y = 6x + 3$

B. $y = 3x - 3$

C. $y = 6x - 6$

D. $y = 6x - 3$

E. $y = -6x + 3$

55. Differentiate $y = \frac{\sin (2x+5)}{x^2+6x}$ with respect to x.

A. $\frac{2(\cos(2x+5))(x^2+6x)-\sin (2x+5)(2x+6)}{(x^2-6x)^2}$

B. $\frac{2(\cos(2x+5))(x^2+6x)+\sin (2x+5)(2x+6)}{(x^2+6x)^2}$

C. $\frac{2(\cos(2x+5))(x^2+6x)-\sin (2x+5)(2x+6)}{(x^2+6x)^2}$

D. $\frac{2(\sin(2x+5))(x^2+6x)-\sin (2x+5)(2x+6)}{(x^2+6x)^2}$

E. $\frac{2(\cos(2x+5))(x^2+6x)-\cos (2x+5)(2x+6)}{(x^2+6x)^2}$

56. Evaluate the following sum:

$$1 + \frac{1}{2} + \frac{1}{4} + \ldots$$

A. 1.75
B. 2
C. 2.25
D. 2.5
E. 3

57. Find the roots of $x^3 - 7x + 6$ by factorising it.

A. $3, 2$ and -1
B. $3, 2$ and 1
C. $-3, 2$ and 1
D. $3, -2$ and -1
E. $-3, -2$ and -1

58. Find the derivative of $f(x) = 2\cos x + x^2$.

A. $2\sin x + 2x$
B. $-2\sin x + 2x$
C. $-2\sin x - 2x$
D. $-2\cos x + 2x$
E. $2\cos x + 2x$

59. Find the tangent to $y = \sqrt{8x - 4x^2}$ at $x = 2$.

A. $x = 2$
B. $y = 2$
C. $y = 2x$
D. $y = 2x + 2$
E. $y = -2$

60. Let $f(x)$ be a function defined over all real x. You are given that $\int_2^5 2f(2x)dx = 1$, and that $f(x)$ is antisymmetric in the line $\frac{3}{2}$, i.e., $f\left(\frac{3}{2} - x\right) = -f(x)$. Calculate $\int_2^3 f(x) + 1\ dx$.

A. Not enough information
B. 2
C. 4
D. 0
E. $\sqrt{2}$

61. If p is a prime number, which of the following **must** be true?
   I.   p is odd
   II. p is not divisible by 5
   III. p is not divisible by 6

A. I only
B. II only
C. III only
D. I and III only
E. II and III only

62. Let I, II, III, and IV be some statements. I → II → III and IV → Not III and Not I → II, where $a \to b$ means if a is true, then b is true. $not\ a$ is just the opposite to a, so if a is true, not a is false and vice versa. Suppose II is a true statement. What can we say about the rest of the statements?

	I	III	IV
A	true	true	true
B	could be either	true	could be either
C	could be either	true	false
D	false	true	false
E	true	false	false

63. Let $f(x) = ax^7 + bx^6 + cx^5 + dx^4 + ex^3 + fx^2 + gx + h$, with a, b, c, d, e, f, g, h real constants, and $a > 0$. Which of the following is possible?

A. Graph has 1 maxima and 0 minima
B. Graph has 2 maxima and 3 minima
C. Graph has 7 maxima and 7 minima
D. Graph has 1 maxima and 1 minima
E. Graph has 0 maxima and 1 minima

64. What is the coefficient of x^2 in the expansion of $(1 + x)^2 \left(\frac{2}{x^2} - 3x^2\right)^4$?

A. 81
B. 100
C. 121
D. 144
E. 225

~ 80 ~

65. Let I and II be two statements. You are asked to show that I if and only if II. Which of the following does **not** prove the statement?

A. II if I, and I if II
B. Not I if II, and not II if I
C. Not II if not I, and not I if not II
D. Not I if not II, and I if II

66. Which of the following are necessary and sufficient conditions for the equations $y = x - 4$ and $x^2 - 2y^2 = a$ to have solutions?

A. $a < 32$
B. $a \leq 32$
C. $a > 32$
D. $a \geq 32$
E. $a < 16$
F. $a \leq 16$
G. $a > 16$
H. $a \geq 16$

67. Consider the statement: "If n is an integer and n^2 is divisible by 4, then n is divisible by 4". How many counterexamples are there to this in the range $50 \leq n \leq 100$?

A. 24
B. 25
C. 11
D. 12
E. 13

68. It is given that a certain equation $f(x) = 0$ has n roots. Which of the following must be true?
  I. $f(x + 1)$ has n roots
  II. $2f(2x + 2)$ has n roots
  III. $f(x) + 1$ has n roots
  IV. $2^{f(x)} - 1 = 0$ has n roots

A. II and IV
B. I and II
C. All true
D. I, II and IV
E. I and III

69. Calculate the derivative of $(1 + 4x)^3(2x)^{-\frac{1}{2}}$.

A. $\dfrac{(4x+1)^2(15x+1)}{2^{\frac{3}{2}}x^{\frac{3}{2}}}$

B. $\dfrac{(4x+1)^2(15x-1)}{2^{\frac{3}{2}}x^{\frac{3}{2}}}$

C. $\dfrac{(4x+1)^2(20x-1)}{2^{\frac{3}{2}}x^{\frac{3}{2}}}$

D. $\dfrac{(4x+1)^2(20x+1)}{2^{\frac{1}{2}}x^{\frac{3}{2}}}$

E. $\dfrac{(4x+1)^2(20x+1)}{2^{\frac{3}{2}}x^{\frac{1}{2}}}$

70. Let f be a function satisfying the following condition: for all x_1, x_2 and for $0 \leq t \leq 1$,
$$f(tx_1 + (1 - t)x_2 \leq tf(x_1) + (1 - t)f(x_2)$$
Which of the following is a necessary condition for this to hold?

A. $f(x) \geq 0$ for all real x
B. $f(x) \geq 0$ for all real x
C. $f'(x) \geq 0$ for all real x
D. $f'(x) \leq 0$ for all real x
E. $f''(x) \leq 0$ for all real x
F. $f''(x) \geq 0$ for all real x

71. A geometric series has first term $a = \sqrt{32}$ and 6th term $\frac{1}{a^2}$. Find the sum to infinity.

A. $\dfrac{16}{\sqrt{2}+2}$

B. $\dfrac{16}{2\sqrt{2}+1}$

C. $\dfrac{16+32\sqrt{2}}{7}$

D. $\dfrac{16-32\sqrt{2}}{7}$

E. $\dfrac{16+16\sqrt{2}}{7}$

72. A circular room has 2020 light bulbs attached to the edge. Each bulb has a switch, which controls the state of the two adjacent bulbs. Given that all the bulbs start off, how many can be turned on at once?

A. 1010
B. 1515
C. 2020
D. 2019
E. 2018

73. Evaluate the sum below.

$$\left(1 + \frac{1}{3} + \frac{1}{9} + \frac{1}{27} + \cdots\right) + \left(\frac{1}{3} + \frac{1}{9} + \frac{1}{27} + \cdots\right) + \left(\frac{1}{9} + \frac{1}{27} + \cdots\right) + \cdots$$

A. $\frac{3}{2}$

B. $\frac{9}{4}$

C. $\frac{5}{9}$

D. $\frac{12}{9}$

E. The series diverges

74. A student tries to solve the following equation: $\frac{x^2-5x+6}{x^2+x+1} = \frac{x^2-5x+6}{2x^2-3x-2}$ by using the following steps:

I. $\frac{1}{x^2+x+1} = \frac{1}{2x^2-3x-2}$

II. $x^2 + x + 1 = 2x^2 - 3x - 2$

III. $x^2 + 2x - 3 = 0$

IV. $x = -3, 1$

Which of the following best describes the solution?

A. The method is completely correct

B. The method is incorrect and from I to II we have introduced extra solutions

C. The method is incorrect and we are missing 1 solution

D. The solutions given are incorrect

E. The method is incorrect and we are missing 2 solutions

75. Find a necessary and sufficient condition on a, such that $\sqrt{a - \sqrt{a - \sqrt{a - \cdots}}} = \dfrac{1}{a - \dfrac{1}{a - \dfrac{1}{a - \cdots}}}$.

A. True for all real a

B. $a = 0$

C. $a = 1$

D. $a = 2$

E. $a = \sqrt{2}$

76. Let n be a positive integer. Which of the following statements are always true?

I. $n^3 - n$ is divisible by 6

II. $n^3 - n$ is divisible by 4

III. $n^3 - n$ is never prime

A. All of them

B. Only I

C. Only II

D. I and II

E. I and III

77. Let $A = \int_0^1 \sin x \, dx$, $B = \int_0^1 \sin^2 x \, dx$, $C = \int_0^1 \cos x \, dx$, $D = \int_0^1 \cos^2 x \, dx$. Order the integrals.

A. $D < A < C < B$

B. $C < B < A < D$

C. $D < B < C < A$

D. $D < A < B < C$

E. $D < B < A < C$

78. How many solutions in $0 \leq x \leq 2\pi$ are there to the following equation?

$$\tan^2 3x = \frac{1}{\cos 3x}$$

A. 0

B. 1

C. 2

D. 3

E. 4

F. 6

G. 9

H. 12

79. A student tried to solve the following problem:

$$\frac{2^{18x}}{2^{3x^2} 4^6} > 1$$

Here is his solution:

I. $\frac{2^{18x}}{2^{3x^2} 4^6} = 2^{18x-3x^2} 4^{-6} > 1$

II. $8^{6x-3x^2} 4^{-6} > 1$

III. $8^{6x-x^2-3} > 1$

IV. $6x - x^2 - 3 > 0$

V.   Critical values are $x = \frac{6 \pm \sqrt{36-12}}{2} = 3 \pm \sqrt{6}$

VI. So $3 - \sqrt{6} < x < 3 + \sqrt{6}$

Where is the first error?

A. The proof is correct

B. Line I

C. Line II

D. Line IV

E. Line V

F. Line VI

80. Consider the following proof by contradiction that $\sqrt{12}$ is irrational.

I. Suppose $\sqrt{12}$ is irrational. The we can express it in the form $\sqrt{12} = \frac{a}{b}$ for some a and b with no common divisors.

II. $12 = \frac{a^2}{b^2}$

III. $12b^2 = a^2$

IV. 12 divides a^2, which means that 12 must also divide a i.e., $a = 12c$ for some integer c.

V. This means $144c^2 = 12b^2$ i.e., $b^2 = 12c^2$

VI. Using the logic of line IV, $b = 12d$ for some integer d.

VII. But then a and d both have 12 as a divisor, which is a contradiction.

Where is the first error?

A. The proof is correct.
B. Line I
C. Line II
D. Line IV
E. Line V
F. Line VI
G. Line VII

81. A polynomial $f(x)$ has 3 roots at $x = p, q, r$ where $p < q < r$. Which of the following statements are sometimes true, never true, or always true, based on the above information?

I. $f(x + r)$ has fewer positive roots than $f(x)$

II. $f(x) - f(r)$ has no roots

III. $f(x) + 1$ has no roots.

	I	II	III
A	Always	Always	Sometimes
B	Always	Never	Sometimes
C	Always	Sometimes	Never
D	Sometimes	Never	Sometimes
E	Sometimes	Sometimes	Sometimes
F	Never	Always	Never

82. Consider the graph of the curve $y = a(x + b)^2 + c$ where all of $a, b, c > 0$. Now suppose that a decreases and c increases. Which of the following graphs can it not be now?

A. I only
B. II only
C. III only
D. IV only
E. I & II only
F. I & III only
G. II & IV only
H. III & IV only

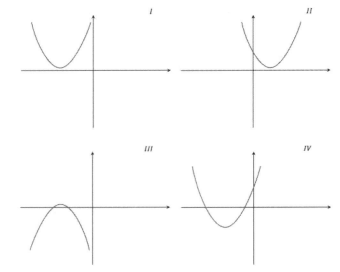

83. Find the coefficient of x^3 in the expansion of $(x^2 - 2)^3 (1 + (3x)^{-1})^4$.

A. $\frac{220}{27}$

B. $\frac{4}{27}$

C. $-\frac{24}{3}$

D. $-\frac{212}{27}$

E. $\frac{100}{27}$

84. Which of the following is a counterexample to the statement below?
If a function has 3 distinct real roots, it is cubic.

A. $\sin x$ in the range $0 < x < 2\pi$
B. $(x - 1)(x - 2)(x - 3)(x - 4)$
C. $\cos x$ in the range $0 < x < 2\pi$
D. $(x - 1)^2 (x - 2)(x - 3)$
E. $(x + 1)(x^2 - x + 5)$
F. $(x - 3)(x + 1)(x - 4)$

85. Consider this student's attempt at finding the solutions to $\sqrt{x+3} = 3x - 1$:

I. $x + 3 = (3x - 1)^2$
II. $x + 3 = 9x^2 - 6x + 1$
III. $0 = 9x^2 - 7x - 2$
IV. $0 = (x - 1)(9x + 2)$
V.   So $x = 1$ and $-\frac{2}{9}$

Is this correct?

A. Both answers are correct.
B. Only one is right and it's due to an error in line I
C. Only one is right and it's due to an error in lines II and III
D. Only one is right and it's due to an error in line IV
E. Neither is right and it's due to an error in line I
F. Neither is right and it's due to an error in lines II and III
G. Neither is right and it's due to an error in line IV

86. Consider the graphs of the two functions $y = mx + 10$ and $y = \log_2 x$. Which of the following correctly identifies the sufficiency and necessity of
I. $m < 0$
II. $m > 10$

in relation to the statement that there are no intersection points of the two graphs?

A. Both necessary and sufficient.
B. Both necessary.
C. Both sufficient.
D. I is sufficient, the other is necessary.
E. Only I is necessary.
F. Only I is sufficient.
G. Neither is necessary or sufficient.

87. Let f be a function such that $f(x) \leq 0$ for all $x \geq 0$. Which one of the following is necessary for
$\int_{-1}^{1} f(x)dx > 0$?

A. $f(x) = -f(-x)$ for all x
B. $f(0) = 0$
C. $f(x) \geq 0$ for all $x < 0$
D. $\int_{-a}^{0} f(x)dx > 0$ for some a
E. $f(x) = f(-x)$ for all x
F. $f(-1) > 0$

88. Let $f(x) = ax^2$ and let $\int_{-b}^{b} f(x)dx = R$. Find the area between the curve $f(x - b) - f(b)$ and the x-axis.

A. $f(b) - R$
B. $f(b) - 2R$
C. $3R + f(b) + b$
D. $f(b) - 2bR$
E. R
F. $2bf(b) - R$

89. A function $f(x)$ has exactly 1 root in the range $0 < x < 2\pi$. Which of the following can not be the function in question?

A. $f(x) = \tan\frac{5x}{7}$
B. $f(x) = \log_{2.9} x$
C. $f(x) = \cos x + 1$
D. $f(x) = \sin x - 1$
E. $f(x) = 3^x$

90. Consider the following proof by induction that $3 \times 7^n + 6$ is divisible by 9 for all non-negative n:

I. Check the base case, $n = 1$; $3 \times 7 + 6 = 27$, which is indeed divisible by 9.
II. First, we suppose $3 \times 7^n + 6$ is divisible by 9 for $n \le k$. i.e., $3 \times 7^k + 6 = 9M$ for some integer M.
III. Then $3 \times 7^{k+1} + 6 = 7 \times \left(3 \times 7^k\right) + 6$
IV. This means $7 \times \left(3 \times 7^k\right) + 6 = 7(9M - 6) + 6$
V. Which means $3 \times 7^{k+1} + 6 = 9(7M - 4)$
VI. So $3 \times 7^{k+1} + 6$ is also divisible by 9, which means $3 \times 7^n + 6$ is divisible by 9 for all non-negative n

Where is the first error?

A. The proof is correct.
B. Line I
C. Line II
D. Line III
E. Line IV
F. Line V
G. Line VI

91. I have a 5 character code for my safe, which is formed by the letters a, b, c, d, e in some order (each occurs only once) and for every wrong attempt, my safe will tell me how many of the characters were in the correct position. Which of the following can never occur?

    I.   I enter $abcde, bcdea, cdeab$ and the safe tells me I got 2 correct on all 3.

    II. I enter $cdaeb, acebd, abecd$ and the safe tells me I got 1, then 2, then 3 correct respectively.

    III. I enter $abcde, bacde$ and the safe tells me I got 3 correct on both.

A. None
B. I only
C. II only
D. III only
E. I & II only
F. I & III only
G. II & III only
H. All three

92. Suppose there is a function $f(x)$, and $\int_0^7 |x - p| f(x) dx = A$, for some $0 \leq p \leq 7$. Which of the following is a valid formula for A? $\left[F_1 = \int (x - p) f(x) dx \right]$?

A. $F_1(7) - F_1(0)$
B. $F_1(7) - pF_1(0)$
C. $F_1(0) - pF_1(7)$
D. $2F_1(0) - F_1(7) + F_1(p)$
E. $F_1(7) + F_1(0) - 2\,F_1(p)$
F. $F_1(p) + F_1(7) - 2F_1(0)$

93. Suppose you have a sphere, S. The cylinder C is such that S fits entirely inside C, and the volume of C is as small as possible. The surface area of C is $B cm^2$.

Which of the following is an expression for the volume of S in terms of B? (The volume of a sphere of radius r is $\frac{4\pi r^3}{3}$)

A. $\dfrac{2B}{9}$

B. $\dfrac{2B}{9\pi}$

C. $\dfrac{B^{\frac{3}{2}}\sqrt{2}}{9\sqrt{3\pi}}$

D. $\dfrac{2B^{\frac{3}{2}}}{27\pi}$

E. B^3

F. $\dfrac{B^3}{2}$

94. I have a bag with many tiles in, each of which has one integer written on it. I pick a tile out of the bag at random. $P(\text{the number is odd}) = \frac{1}{3}$ and $P(\text{the number is prime}) = \frac{1}{5}$.

Consider the following statements:

I. $P(\text{number is even}) - P(\text{the number is 2}) = \frac{4}{5}$

II. $P(\text{the number is not prime and is even}) = \frac{8}{15}$

III. $P(\text{the number is not prime and is odd}) = \frac{2}{15} + P(\text{the number is 2})$

Which of these statements are definitely true?

A. None
B. I only
C. II only
D. III only
E. I & II only
F. I & III only
G. II & III only
H. All three

95. Suppose that the equation $\sqrt{xp} = x + \sqrt{p}$ has exactly 1 solution for x. How many valid values of p are there?

A. Infinitely many (i.e., an interval)
B. 4
C. 3
D. 2
E. 1
F. 0
G. None

96. A woman tosses a fair coin 10 times and records the outcome, with an H for a head, and T for a tail. The sequence she creates is $H\ T\ T\ T\ T\ T\ T\ H\ T\ H\ H$. The probability that this occurred was p. Which of the following are true if she was to repeat what she did?

I. $P(\text{more than 4 heads appearing}) > \frac{1}{2}$

II. $P(\text{7 tails appearing}) < p$

III. $P(\text{same sequence}) = p$

A. None
B. I only
C. II only
D. III only
E. I & II only
F. I & III only
G. II & III only
H. All three

97. Find the sum of the values of a such that the quartic equation

$$x^4 - x^3 - \frac{x^2}{2} = a$$

has an odd number of solutions.

A. $\frac{3}{4}$

B. $-\frac{1}{2}$

C. There are no values of a.

D. $-\frac{139}{256}$

E. $\frac{117}{256}$

F. $-\frac{117}{256}$

98. Differentiate $y = 5x^2 \sin 2x$ with respect to x.

A. $10x(x \cos 2x - \sin 2x)$

B. $10x(x \cos 2x + \sin 2x)$

C. $10x(x^2 \cos 2x + \sin 2x)$

D. $5x(x \cos 2x + \sin 2x)$

E. $10x(x \sin 2x + \cos 2x)$

99. If $x = 1$ is a root of equation $2x^3 + x^2 - 5x = -2$, find the other two roots.

A. $x = 1$ and $x = -2$

B. $x = \frac{1}{2}$ and $x = 2$

C. $x = \frac{1}{2}$ and $x = 1$

D. $x = \frac{1}{2}$ and $x = -2$

E. $x = -\frac{1}{2}$ and $x = -2$

100. Evaluate the following sum: $\sum_{n=0}^{4} 3^{-n}$.

A. $\frac{112}{81}$

B. $\frac{121}{81}$

C. $\frac{121}{80}$

D. $\frac{120}{81}$

E. $\frac{121}{41}$

101. If $\dfrac{\log_2 8^x}{\log_3 9^y} = 12$ and $3x + 5y = 10$, what is $\log_x y$?

A. $\dfrac{80}{29}$

B. $\dfrac{80}{22}$

C. $\dfrac{60}{29}$

D. $\dfrac{40}{29}$

E. $\dfrac{80}{28}$

102. Evaluate the following integral: $\int_0^5 \dfrac{6x}{3x^2+5}\,dx$.

A. $\ln(10)$
B. $\ln(12)$
C. $\ln(16)$
D. $-\ln(16)$
E. $-\ln(20)$

103. What is the function of the following graph?

A. $y = x^2 - 8$
B. $y = 2x^2 + 8$
C. $y = 2x^2 - 8$
D. $y = 2x^2 - 6$
E. $y = x^2 + 8$

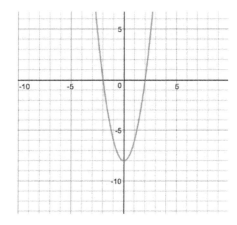

104. What is the coefficient of x^6 in the expansion of $(1 - 2x)^3(2 + x)^4$?

A. $54x^6$
B. $-54x^6$
C. $-52x^6$
D. $-50x^6$
E. $50x^6$

105. What is x in the equation $\log_3 x^2 + \log_4 \frac{1}{64} = 3$?

A. 18
B. 21
C. 27
D. 30
E. 33

106. What is the equation of a line that connects the points $(-3,5)$ and $(2,-6)$?

A. $5y + 11x = 8$
B. $-5y + 11x = -8$
C. $5y - 11x = -8$
D. $5y + 11x = -8$
E. $5y - 11x = 8$

107. Evaluate the sum of the following sequence $1 + 3 + 5 + \cdots.. +99$.

A. 1500
B. 2000
C. 2250
D. 2500
E. 2750

108. How many numbers greater than 3000 may be formed by using some or all of the digits 1,2,3,4, and 5 without repetition?

A. 144
B. 160
C. 176
D. 188
E. 192

109. Evaluate: $(6 \sin x)(3 \sin x) - (9 \cos x)(-2 \cos x)$.

A. 0
B. 0.5
C. 1
D. -1
E. 18
F. -18

110. In the figure to the right, all triangles are equilateral. What is the shaded area of the figure in terms of r?

A. $5r^2(2\sqrt{6} - 3\pi)$
B. $5r^2(5\sqrt{2} - 6\pi)$
C. $5r^2(3\sqrt{3} - \pi)$
D. $5r^2(4\sqrt{3} - 2\pi)$
E. $5r(2\sqrt{6 - 3\pi})$
F. $5r^2(5\sqrt{2} + 6\pi)$

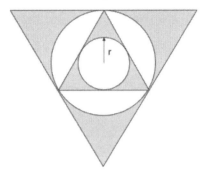

111. Suppose I use a binomial expansion to determine the value of $(3.12)^5$. What is the minimum number of terms that I must obtain in the expansion of $(3.12)^5$ in order to receive a result accurate to 1 decimal place?

A. 4
B. 5
C. 6
D. 7
E. 9
F. 8

112. For all θ what is $(\sin(\theta) + \sin(-\theta))(\cos(\theta) + \cos(-\theta))$ equal to?

A. $2\sin\theta$
B. 0
C. 1
D. $4\sin\theta\cos\theta$
E. -1
F. $2\sin\theta\cos\theta$

113. What is the range of values for which the inequality $|2x - 5| > 3|2x + 1|$ is valid?

A. $-2 < x < 4$
B. $x > -2, x > \frac{1}{4}$
C. $-2 < x < \frac{1}{4}$
D. $x > -2, x > 4$
E. $-2 < x < 4$
F. $x > -2$

114. Which of the following is the equation of the circle whose diameter is the line segment connecting points $(1, -4)$ and $(3,6)$ and is reflected about the line $y = x$?

A. $(x + 4)^2 + (y - 1)^2 = 104$
B. $(x - 1)^2 + (y + 4)^2 = 104$
C. $(x - 1)^2 + (y - 2)^2 = 26$
D. $(x - 2)^2 + (y - 1)^2 = 2$
E. $(x+1)^2 + (y + 2)^2 = 26$
F. $(x + 2)^2 + (y + 1)^2 = 2$

115. A new computer does a calculation in b hours, and an old computer does c calculations in d minutes. If the two computers work together, how many calculations can they perform in m minutes?

A. $60m \left(\frac{a}{b} + \frac{c}{d} \right)$
B. $m \left(\frac{60a}{b} + \frac{c}{d} \right)$
C. $m \left(\frac{a}{b} + \frac{c}{d} \right)$
D. $m \left(\frac{a}{60b} + \frac{c}{d} \right)$
E. $2m \left(\frac{30a}{b} + \frac{c}{d} \right)$
F. $m \left(\frac{a}{60b} + \frac{d}{c} \right)$

116. If -1 is a zero of the function $f(x) = 2x^3 + 3x^2 - 20x - 21$, then what are the other zeroes?

A. 1 and 3
B. -3 and 3
C. $-\frac{7}{2}$ and 1 and 3
D. $-\frac{7}{2}$ and 3
E. -1 and 3
F. 1 and 7

117. The three roots of third order polynomial are $-1, 0$ and 1. Find one of the possible polynomials.

A. $x^3 - x + 1$
B. $x^3 - 2x - 3$
C. $x^3 + x$
D. $x^3 - x$
E. $x^3 - x - 6$

118. Given the two equations $y_1 = (1-x)^6$ and $y_2 = (1+2x)^6$, find the ratio of the coefficients of the 2nd term in the expansion of y_1 and the 3rd term in the expansion of y_2 (The y_1 coefficient should be the numerator, and the y_2 coefficient should be the denominator).

A. $-\dfrac{1}{10}$

B. $\dfrac{1}{9}$

C. $\dfrac{1}{15}$

D. $-\dfrac{1}{7}$

119. What is the sum of the integers from 1 to 300?

A. 9,000

B. 44,850

C. 45,150

D. 45,450

E. 54,450

F. 90,000

120. If $\sin 2\theta = \dfrac{2}{5}$, then what is $\dfrac{1}{\sin\theta \cos\theta}$?

A. $\dfrac{1}{5}$

B. $\dfrac{5}{4}$

C. $\dfrac{5}{2}$

D. 5

E. $\dfrac{3}{2}$

F. 1

121. If $[n]$ represents the greatest integer less than or equal to n, then which of the following is the solution to $-11 + 4[n] = 5$?

A. $n = 4$

B. $4 < n < 5$

C. $-2 \leq n \leq -1$

D. $4 \leq n < 5$

E. $4 < n \leq 5$

F. $4 < n \leq 5$

122. Rearrange the following to make m the subject.

$$T = 4\pi\sqrt{\frac{(M+3m)l}{3(M+2m)g}}$$

A. $m = \dfrac{16\pi^2 lM - 3gMT^2}{48\pi^2 l - 6gT^2}$

B. $m = \dfrac{16\pi^2 lM - 3gMT^2}{6gT^2 - 48\pi^2 l}$

C. $m = \dfrac{3gMT^2 - 16\pi^2 lM}{6gT^2 - 48\pi^2 l}$

D. $m = \dfrac{4\pi^2 lM - 3gMT^2}{6gT^2 - 16\pi^2 l}$

E. $m = \left(\dfrac{16\pi^2 lM - 3gMT^2}{6gT^2 - 48\pi^2 l}\right)^2$

123. Given a curve with the equation $y = 8 - 4x - 2x^2$ and a line $y = k(x+4)$, find the values of k for which the line and the curve are tangent to each other.

A. $-4 < k \leq 4$
B. $k = 4, k = 20$
C. $4 < k < 20$
D. $k = -4, k = 4$

124. Consider the infinite series, $x - \left(\frac{1}{2}\right)x^2 + \left(\frac{1}{4}\right)x^3 - \left(\frac{1}{8}\right)x^4 \ldots$

Given that we know that the fifth term of the series is $\left(\frac{1}{32}\right)$, what is summation of the series given that the series converges as it heads toward infinity?

A. $\dfrac{16^{\frac{1}{5}}}{2 + \frac{(16^{\frac{1}{5}})}{2}}$

B. $\dfrac{1}{1 - (32)^{\frac{1}{4}}}$

C. $\dfrac{8^{\frac{1}{5}}}{1 + 8^{\frac{1}{5}}}$

D. $\dfrac{2}{2 - (16)^{\frac{1}{4}}}$

E. $\dfrac{-2}{2 + (16)^{\frac{1}{4}}}$

F. $\dfrac{1}{64 - 8^{\frac{1}{5}}}$

125. If $\log 23 . \log 34 . \log 45 \ldots \log n(n+1) \leq 10$, what is the largest value of n that satisfies this equation?

A. 1022
B. 824
C. 842
D. 1023
E. 1020
F. 890

126. a, b, c is a geometric progression where a, b, c are real numbers. If $a + b + c = 26$ and $a^2 + b^2 + c^2 = 364$, find b.

A. $3\sqrt{2}$
B. 6
C. $2\sqrt{6}$
D. 9
E. 4
F. $2\sqrt{3}$

127. Given that $a > 0$, find the value of a for which the minimal value of the function $f(x) = (a^2 + 1)x^2 - 2ax + 10$ in the interval $x \in [0; 12]$ is $\frac{451}{50}$.

A. 7
B. 12
C. 5
D. $\frac{50}{125}$
E. 8
F. 10

128. If the probability that it will rain tomorrow is $\frac{2}{3}$ and the probability that it will rain and snow the following day is $\frac{1}{5}$, given that the probability of rain and snow occurring on any given day are independent from one another, what is the probability that it will snow the day after tomorrow?

A. $\frac{10}{3}$
B. $\frac{3}{10}$
C. $\frac{2}{15}$
D. $\frac{15}{2}$
E. $\frac{4}{9}$
F. $\frac{1}{5}$

129. If $\cos 2\theta = \frac{3}{4}$, then what is $\frac{1}{\cos^2\theta - \sin^2\theta}$?

A. $\frac{4}{3}$

B. 4

C. -1

D. $\frac{3}{4}$

E. 2

F. 1

130. Describe the geometrical transformation that maps the graph of $y = 0.2^x$ onto the graph of $y = 5^x$.

A. Reflection in the x-axis

B. Reflection in the y-axis

C. Multiplication by a scale factor of 25

D. Addition of the constant term 4.8

E. Multiplication by scale factor of 5

F. Multiplication by scale factor $\frac{1}{25}$

131. Find the solution to the equation $\log_4(2x + 3) + \log_4(2x + 15) - 1 = \log_4(14x + 5)$.

A. There is no solution

B. $\frac{2}{5}$

C. $\frac{5}{2}$

D. -1

E. 1

F. 0

132. Rearrange the following equation in terms of t: $x = \frac{\sqrt{b^3 - 9st}}{13j} + \int_{-z}^{z} 9a - 7$.

A. $t = \frac{(13jx - \int_{-z}^{z} 9a - 7)^2 - b^3}{9s}$

B. $t = \frac{13jx^2}{b^3 - 9s} - \int_{-z}^{z} 9a - 7$

C. $t = x - \frac{\sqrt{b^3 - 9s}}{13j} - \int_{-z}^{z} 9a - 7$

D. $t = \frac{x^2}{\frac{b^3 - 9s}{13j} + \int_{-z}^{z} 9a - 7}$

E. $t = \frac{[13j(x - \int_{-z}^{z} 9a - 7)]^2 - b^3}{-9s}$

133. Simplify: $m = \sqrt{\dfrac{9xy^3z^5}{3x^9yz^4}} - m$.

A. $m = \sqrt{\dfrac{3y^2z}{x^8}} - m$

B. $m^2 = \dfrac{3y^2z}{x^8} - m$

C. $2m = \sqrt{\dfrac{3y^2z}{x^8}}$

D. $2m^2 = 3x^{-8}y^2z$

E. $4m^2 = 3x^{-8}y^2z$

134. The normal to the curve $y = e^{2x-5}$ at the point $P(2, e^{-1})$ intersects the x-axis at the point A and the y-axis at the point B. Which of the following is an appropriate formula for the area of the triangle that is formed in terms of $e, m,$ and n, where m and n are integers?

A. $\dfrac{(e^2+1)^m}{e^n}$

B. $\dfrac{(e^3+1)^{\frac{1}{n}}}{m}$

C. $\dfrac{e^n}{(e^2+1)^m}$

D. $\dfrac{m^{\frac{1}{n}}}{e^3+1}$

E. $\dfrac{e^{2m}}{e^n+1}$

F. $\dfrac{(e^2-1)^m}{e^{2n}}$

135. Given that $\sec x - \tan x = -5$, find the value of $\cos x$.

A. -0.2

B. 0.2

C. $-\dfrac{13}{5}$

D. $\dfrac{-5}{13}$

E. 0.5

F. -0.5

136. Consider the line with equation $y = 2x + k$ where k is a constant, and the curve $y = x^2 + (3k - 4)x + 13$. Given that the line and the curve do not intersect, what are the possible values of k?

A. $-\frac{1}{3} < k < 3$

B. $-\frac{4}{9} < k < 4$

C. $\frac{1}{2} < k < \frac{5}{3}$

D. $\frac{3}{2} < k \le \frac{8}{3}$

E. $\frac{1}{3} < k < 3$

F. $-3 < k < \frac{1}{3}$

137. A circle with centre $C(5, -3)$ passes through $A(-2, 1)$, and the point T lies on the tangent to the circle such that $AT = 4$. What is the length of the line CT?

A. 9

B. 18

C. $\sqrt{95}$

D. $8\sqrt{2}$

E. $\sqrt{69}$

138. What is the equation of the quadratic function that passes through the x-coordinates of the stationary points of $y = x^2 e^x$?

A. This quadratic function does not exist

B. $x^2 + 2x$

C. x^2

D. $x^2 - 2x$

E. $x^2 + 4x$

F. $2x^2 - 1$

139. Which of the following equations is a correct simplification of the equation $\frac{x^2 - 16}{x^2 - 4x}$?

A. $1 - \frac{4}{x}$

B. $\frac{x+4}{x}$

C. $\frac{x-4}{x}$

D. $\frac{4}{x}$

E. $\frac{x(x-4)}{x}$

F. $\frac{x+4}{4x}$

140. A bag only contains $2n$ blue balls and n red balls. All the balls are identical apart from colour. One ball is randomly selected and not replaced. A second ball is then randomly selected. What is the probability that at least one of the selected balls is red?

A. $\dfrac{4n}{3(3n-1)}$

B. $\dfrac{5n-1}{3(3n-1)}$

C. $\dfrac{5n-5}{3(3n-1)}$

D. $\dfrac{4n-2}{3(3n-1)}$

E. $\dfrac{n-5}{9(n-1)}$

F. $\dfrac{4n-1}{3(3n-1)}$

141. For what values of the non-zero real number a does the equation $ax^2 + (a-2)x = 2$ have real and distinct roots?

A. $a \neq -2$

B. $a > 2$

C. $a > -2$

D. No values of a.

E. $a \neq 0$

F. $a > 5$

142. What is sum of the roots of the equation $2^{2x} - 8 \times 2^x + 15 = 0$?

A. 4

B. 16

C. $\log_{10}\left(\frac{15}{2}\right)$

D. $\dfrac{\log_{10} 15}{\log_{10} 2}$

E. 8

F. $\log_2\left(\frac{2}{3}\right)$

143. Given that $a^{3x}b^x c^{4x} = 2$ where $a > 0$, b > 0, and $c > 0$, then what does x equal?

A. $x = \dfrac{2}{3a+b+4c}$

B. $x = \dfrac{2}{(\log_{10} a^3 bc^4)}$

C. $x = \dfrac{\log_{10} 2}{\log_{10}(a^3 bc^4)}$

D. $x = \log_{10} \dfrac{2}{(ab^2 c^3)}$

E. $x = \dfrac{\log_2 10}{\log_2(a^3 bc^4)}$

F. $x = \log_{10} \dfrac{2}{(a^3 bc^4)}$

144. The curve $y = x^2 + 3$ is reflected about the line $y = x$ and subsequently translated by the vector $\binom{4}{2}$. Which of the following is the x-intercept of the resulting curve?

A. -2

B. 11

C. 7

D. -11

E. 8

F. -8

145. The vertex of an equilateral triangle is covered by a circle whose radius is half the height of the triangle. What percentage of the triangle is covered by the circle?

A. 12%

B. 16%

C. 23%

D. 33%

E. 41%

F. 50%

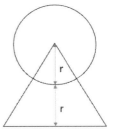

146. Three equal circles fit into a quadrilateral as shown, what is the height of the quadrilateral?

A. $2\sqrt{3}r$

B. $(2 + \sqrt{3})r$

C. $(4 - \sqrt{3})r$

D. $3r$

E. $4r$

F. More information needed

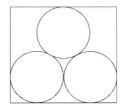

147. Two pyramids have equal volume and height, one with a square of side length a and one with a hexagonal base of side length b. What is the ratio of the side length of the bases?

A. $\sqrt{\frac{3\sqrt{3}}{2}}$

B. $\sqrt{\frac{2\sqrt{3}}{3}}$

C. $\sqrt{\frac{3}{2}}$

D. $\frac{2\sqrt{3}}{3}$

E. $\frac{3\sqrt{3}}{2}$

148. One 9cm cube is cut into 3cm cubes. The total surface area increases by a factor of:

A. $\frac{1}{3}$

B. $\sqrt{3}$

C. 3

D. 9

E. 27

149. A cone has height twice its base width (four times the circle radius). What is the cone angle (half the angle at the vertex)?

A. $30°$

B. $\sin^{-1}\left(\frac{r}{2}\right)$

C. $\sin^{-1}\left(\frac{1}{\sqrt{17}}\right)$

D. $\cos^{-1}(\sqrt{17})$

150. A hemispherical speedometer has a maximum speed of 200 mph. What is the angle travelled by the needle at a speed of 70 mph?

A. $28°$

B. $49°$

C. $63°$

D. $88°$

E. $92°$

151. Two rhombuses, A and B, are similar. The area of A is 10 times that of B. What is the ratio of the smallest angles over the ratio of the shortest sides?

A. 0

B. $\frac{1}{10}$

C. $\frac{1}{\sqrt{10}}$

D. $\sqrt{10}$

E. ∞

152. If $f^{-1}(-x) = \ln(2x^2)$ what is $f(x)$?

A. $\sqrt{\frac{e^y}{2}}$

B. $\sqrt{\frac{e^{-y}}{2}}$

C. $\frac{e^y}{2}$

D. $\frac{-e^y}{2}$

E. $-\sqrt{\frac{e^y}{2}}$

153. Which of the following is largest for $0 < x < 1$?

A. $\log_8(x)$

B. $\log_{10}(x)$

C. e^x

D. x^2

E. $\sin(x)$

154. x is proportional to y cubed, y is proportional to the square root of z. $x \propto y^3, y \propto \sqrt{z}$. If z doubles, x changes by a factor of what?

A. $\sqrt{2}$

B. 2

C. $2\sqrt{2}$

D. $\sqrt[3]{4}$

E. 4

155. The area between two concentric circles (shaded) is three times that of the inner circle. What's the size of the gap?

A. r
B. $\sqrt{2}r$
C. $\sqrt{3}r$
D. $2r$
E. $3r$
F. $4r$

156. Solve $-x^2 \leq 3x - 4$.

A. $x \geq \frac{4}{3}$
B. $1 \leq x \leq 4$
C. $x \leq 2$
D. $x \geq 1$ or $x \geq -4$
E. $-1 \leq x \leq \frac{3}{4}$

157. The volume of a sphere is numerically equal to its projected area. What is its radius?

A. $\frac{1}{2}$
B. $\frac{2}{3}$
C. $\frac{3}{4}$
D. $\frac{4}{3}$
E. $\frac{3}{2}$

158. What is the range where $x^2 < \frac{1}{x}$?

A. $x < 0$
B. $0 < x < 1$
C. $x > 0$
D. $x \geq 1$
E. None

159. Simplify and solve: $(e - a)(e + b)(e - c)(e + d) \ldots (e - z)$?

A. 0
B. e^{26}
C. $e^{26}(a - b + c - d \ldots + z)$
D. $e^{26}(a + b - c + d \ldots - z)$
E. $e^{26}(abcd \ldots z)$
F. None of the above.

160. Find the value of k such that the vectors $a = -i + 6j$ and $b = 2i + kj$ are perpendicular.

A. -2

B. $-\frac{1}{3}$

C. $\frac{1}{3}$

D. 2

161. What is the perpendicular distance between point p with position vector $4i + 5j$ and the line L given by vector equation $r = -3i + j + \lambda(i + 2j)$?

A. $2\sqrt{7}$

B. $5\sqrt{2}$

C. $2\sqrt{5}$

D. $7\sqrt{2}$

162. Find k such that point $\begin{pmatrix} 2 \\ k \\ -7 \end{pmatrix}$ lies within the plane $r = \begin{pmatrix} 2 \\ 3 \\ -1 \end{pmatrix} + \lambda \begin{pmatrix} 4 \\ 1 \\ 0 \end{pmatrix} + \mu \begin{pmatrix} 2 \\ 1 \\ 3 \end{pmatrix}$?

A. -2

B. -1

C. 0

D. 1

E. 2

163. What is the largest solution to $\sin(-2\theta) = 0.5$ for $\frac{\pi}{2} \le x \le 2\pi$?

A. $\frac{5\pi}{3}$

B. $\frac{4\pi}{3}$

C. $\frac{5\pi}{6}$

D. $\frac{7\pi}{6}$

E. $\frac{11\pi}{6}$

164. What is $\cos^4(x) - \sin^4(x)$ equal to?

A. $\cos(2x)$

B. $2\cos(x)$

C. $\sin(2x)$

D. $\sin(x)\cos(x)$

E. $\tan(x)$

165. How many real roots does $y = 2x^5 - 3x^4 + x^3 - 4x^2 - 6x + 4$ have?

A. 1
B. 2
C. 3
D. 4
E. 5

166. What is the sum of 8 terms, $\sum_1^8 u_n$, of an arithmetic progression with $u_1 = 2$ and $d = 3$.

A. 15
B. 82
C. 100
D. 184
E. 282

167. What is the coefficient of the x^2 term in the binomial expansion of $(2 - x)^5$?

A. -80
B. -48
C. 40
D. 48
E. 80

168. Differentiate and simplify $y = x(x + 3)^4$.

A. $(x + 3)^3$
B. $(x + 3)^4$
C. $x(x + 3)^3$
D. $(5x + 3)(x + 3)^3$
E. $5x^3(x + 3)$

169. Evaluate $\int_1^2 \frac{2}{x^2} dx$.

A. -1
B. $\frac{1}{3}$
C. 1
D. $\frac{21}{4}$
E. 2

170. Express $\frac{5i}{1+2i}$ in the form $a + bi$.

A. $1 + 2i$
B. $4i$
C. $1 - 2i$
D. $2 + i$
E. $5 - i$

171. Simplify $7\log_a(2) - 3\log_a(12) + 5\log_a(3)$.

A. $\log_{2a}(18)$
B. $\log_a(18)$
C. $\log_a(7)$
D. $9\log_a(17)$
E. $-\log_a(7)$

172. What is the equation of the asymptote of the function $y = \frac{2x^2-x+3}{x^2+x-2}$.

A. $x = 0$
B. $x = 2$
C. $y = 0.5$
D. $y = 0$
E. $y = 2$

173. Find the intersection(s) of the functions $y = e^x - 3$ and $y = 1 - 3e^{-x}$.

A. 0 and $\ln(3)$
B. 1
C. $\ln(4)$ and 1
D. $\ln(3)$

174. Find the radius of the circle $x^2 + y^2 - 6x + 8y - 12 = 0$.

A. 3
B. $\sqrt{13}$
C. 5
D. $\sqrt{37}$
E. 12

175. What value of a minimises $\int_0^a 2\sin(-x)\,dx$?

A. 0.5π
B. π
C. 2π
D. 3π
E. 4

176. When $\frac{2x+3}{(x-2)(x-3)^2}$ is expressed as partial fractions, what is the numerator in the $\frac{A}{(x-2)}$ term?

A. -7
B. -1
C. 3
D. 6
E. 7

END OF SECTION

SECTION 2: WRITING TASK

THE BASICS

In section 2, you have to write an essay based upon a passage. **There is no choice of essay title** meaning that you have to do the question that comes up. Whilst different questions will inevitably demand differing levels of comprehension and knowledge, it is important to realise that one of the major skills being tested is actually your ability to construct a logical and coherent argument- and to convey it to the lay reader.

Section 2 of the ECAA is frequently neglected by lots of students, who choose to spend their time on section 1 instead. However, it is possible to rapidly improve in it and given that it may come up at your interview, well worth the time investment!

The aim of section 2 is not to write as much as you can. Rather, the examiner is looking for you to make interesting and well supported points, and tie everything neatly together for a strong conclusion. Make sure you're writing critically and concisely; not rambling on. **Irrelevant material can actually lower your score.**

ESSAY STRUCTURE

Basic Structure
ECAA Essays should follow the standard format of Introduction → Main Body → Conclusion.

The introduction should be the smallest portion of the essay (no more than one small paragraph) and be used to provide a smooth segue into the rather more demanding "argue for/against" part of the question. This main body requires a firm grasp of the concept being discussed and the ability to strengthen and support the argument with a wide variety of examples from multiple fields. This section should give a balanced approach to the question, exploring **at least two distinct ideas**. Supporting evidence should be provided throughout the essay, with examples referred to when possible.

The concluding final part effectively is a chance for you to shine. e brave and make an **innovative yet firmly grounded conclusion** for an exquisite mark. The conclusion should bring together all sides of the argument, in order to reach a clear and concise answer to the question. There should be an obvious logical structure to the essay, which reflects careful planning and preparation.

Paragraphs
Paragraphs are an important formatting tool which show that you have thought through your arguments and are able to structure your ideas clearly. A new paragraph should be used every time a new idea is introduced. There is no single correct way to arrange paragraphs, but it's important that each paragraph flows smoothly from the last. A slick, interconnected essay shows that you have the ability to communicate and organise your ideas effectively. Remember- the emphasis should remain on quality and not quantity. An essay with fewer paragraphs, but with well-developed ideas, is much more effective than a number of short, unsubstantial paragraphs that fail to fully grasp the question at hand.

PLANNING

Why should I plan my essay?
The vast **majority of problems are caused by a lack of planning** - usually because students just want to get writing as they are worried about finishing on time. Forty minutes is long enough to be able to plan your essay well and *still* have time to write it so don't feel pressured to immediately start writing.

There are multiple reasons you should plan your essay for the first 5-10 minutes of section 2:
- It allows you to get all your thoughts ready before you put pen to paper.
- You'll write faster once you have a plan.
- You run the risk of missing the point of the essay or only answering part of it if you don't plan adequately.

How much time should I plan for?
There is no set period of time that should be dedicated to planning, and everyone will dedicate a different length of time to the planning process. You should spend as long planning your essay as you require, but it is essential that you leave enough time to write the essay. As a rough guide, it is **worth spending about 5-10 minutes to plan** and the remaining time on writing the essay. However, this is not a strict rule, and you are advised to tailor your time management to suit your individual style.

How should I go about the planning process?
There are a variety of methods that can be employed in order to plan essays (e.g., bullet-points, mind-maps etc). If you don't already know what works best, it's a good idea to experiment with different methods.

Generally, the first step is to gather ideas relevant to the question, which will form the basic arguments around which the essay is to be built. You can then begin to structure your essay, including the way that points will be linked. At this stage it is worth considering the balance of your argument, and confirming that you have considered arguments from both sides of the debate. Once this general structure has been established, it is useful to consider any examples or real-world information that may help to support your arguments. Finally, you can begin to assess the plan as a whole, and establish what your conclusion will be based on your arguments.

Introduction

Why are introductions important?
An introduction provides tutors with their first opportunity to examine your work. The introduction is where first impressions are formed, and these can be extremely important in producing a convincing argument. A well-constructed introduction shows that you have really thought about the question, and can indicate the logical flow of arguments that is to come.

What should an introduction do?
A good introduction should **briefly explain the statement or quote** and give any relevant background information in a concise manner. However, don't fall into the trap of just repeating the statement in a different way. The introduction is the first opportunity to suggest an answer to the question posed- the main body is effectively your justification for this answer.

Main Body

How do I go about making a convincing point?

Each idea that you propose should be supported and justified, in order to build a convincing overall argument. A point can be solidified through a basic Point → Evidence → Evaluation process. By following this process, you can be assured each sentence within a paragraph builds upon the last, and that all the ideas presented are well solidified.

How do I achieve a logical flow between ideas?

One of the most effective ways of displaying a good understanding of the question is to keep a logical flow throughout your essay. This means linking points effectively between paragraphs, and creating a congruent train of thought for the examiner as the argument develops. A good way to generate this flow of ideas is to provide ongoing comparisons of arguments, and discussing whether points support or dispute one another.

Should I use examples?

In short – yes! Examples can help boost the validity of arguments, and can help display high quality writing skills. Examples can add a lot of weight to your argument and make an essay much more relevant to the reader. When using examples, you should ensure that they are relevant to the point being made, as they will not help to support an argument if they are not.

Some questions will provide more opportunities to include examples than others so don't worry if you aren't able to use as many examples as you would have liked. There is no set rule about how many examples should be included!

> *Top tip!* Remember that there is no single correct answer to these questions and you're not expected to be able to fit everything onto one page. Instead, it's better to pick a few key points to focus on.

Conclusion

The conclusion provides an opportunity to emphasise the **overall sentiment of your essay** which readers can then take away. It should summarise what has been discussed during the main body and give a definitive answer to the question.

Some students use the conclusion to **introduce a new idea that hasn't been discussed**. This can be an interesting addition to an essay, and can help make you stand out. However, it is by no means, a necessity. In fact, a well-organised, 'standard' conclusion is likely to be more effective than an adventurous but poorly executed one.

Common Mistakes

Ignoring the other side of the argument

You need to ensure that you show an appreciation for the fact that there are often two sides to the argument. Where appropriate, you should outline both points of view and how they pertain to the essay's main principles and then come to a reasoned judgement.

A good way to do this is to propose an argument that might be used against you, and then to argue why it doesn't hold true or seem relevant. You may use the format: *"some may say that…but this doesn't seem to be important because…"* in order to dispel opposition arguments, whilst still displaying that you have considered them. For example, *"some may say that fox hunting shouldn't be banned because it is a tradition. However, witch hunting was also once a tradition – we must move on with the times"*.

Missing Topic Sentences

A reader who is pressed for time should be able to read your introduction, the first line of every paragraph and your conclusion and be able to follow your argument. The filling of a paragraph will elaborate your point with examples. But the first sentence of the paragraph should provide the key point.

- *Use topic sentences as punchy summaries for the theme of each paragraph*
- *Include a clear summary of the structure of your essay in your introduction*
- *Summarize briefly the theme of your points in your conclusion*
- *Ensure your conclusion also tells the reader your final decision*

Undefined Terms

Debates can be won or lost on the basis of the interpretation of a key term; ensure your interpretation of the key words is clearly explained. For example: "Does science or art shape our world?" Here, your interpretation of what it means to *shape* something is absolutely crucial to lay out before you start writing, so that your reader knows the scope of your argument. If *shape* to you means invent something new (like a potter shaping a pot out of a lump of clay), state this. But if you interpret *shape* to mean a gentle guide or influence on something, state that. You can then be more focused and precise in your discussion. Likewise, for this title ensure you are clear about the scope of what science and art are.

- *Define the key terms within the particular context of the question*
- *Be clear about your understanding of the scope*

No Sign-Posting

There is a delight to enjoying a long journey if you know (1) where you are going, (2) what you will see on the way and (3) how long it will take to get there. For the reader of your essay, the same logic applies. State briefly but clearly in the final sentence of your introduction the topics you will cover (preferably in the order you will cover them!). You don't need to give the entire game away (don't necessarily tell your reader precisely what your 'wow-factor' will be) but you can give them a solid hint as to your final destination. For example, "Having discussed these arguments in favour and against fox hunting, we conclude with a consideration of the wider issue of the role of governmental institutions in condoning and condemning the traditional pursuits of citizens." It is sometimes tempting to try to surprise your reader with an unexpected twist but this is not best practice for an academic essay.

- *Don't surprise your reader with unexpected twists in the main essay*
- *Do be clear in your introduction about the number of points you will make*
- *Do include your points in the order they will appear*

Long Introductions

Some students can start rambling and make introductions too long and unfocussed. Although background information about the topic can be useful, it is normally not necessary. Instead, the **emphasis should be placed on responding to the question**. Some students also just **rephrase the question** rather than actually explaining it. The examiner knows what the question is, and repeating it in the introduction is simply a waste of space in an essay where you are limited to just one A4 side.

Not including a Conclusion

An essay that lacks a conclusion is incomplete and can signal that the answer has not been considered carefully or that your organisation skills are lacking. **The conclusion should be a distinct paragraph** in its own right and not just a couple of rushed lines at the end of the essay.

Sitting on the Fence

Students sometimes don't reach a clear conclusion. You need to **ensure that you give a decisive answer to the question** and clearly explain how you've reached this judgement. Essays that do not come to a clear conclusion generally have a smaller impact and score lower.

Conclusions with no 'Wow-Factor'

Try to 'zoom out' in your conclusion, rather than merely summarising the points you have made and deciding that one set outweighs the other. Put the question back in a wider context, so that your decision has a wow-factor for why it really matters. For instance, if you have answered the question, "Is world peace achievable?" and you think it isn't, say why this matters. For example: "In an age of nuclear capability, attempts to achieve the impossible is a waste of scarce resources, so we'd be better off focusing policy and diplomacy on building safety nets to prevent escalations of inevitable conflicts into another world war."

- *Don't only repeat your arguments again in your conclusion*
- *Don't sit on the fence in your conclusion*
- *Do use the conclusion to zoom out for the final punchline: why does this matter?*

Missing the Point

Ensure you have identified what you think the 'Turning Point' of the question is, before you start writing. Within the title, which may be long and literary, identify the single core issue for you that you will discuss. For example, with the question, "Has the "digital age" destroyed the human right to anonymity?", restate it as a simple statement: the key question is whether previous to the introduction of digital technology we had a human right to anonymity which has now disappeared. You can then anchor your argument clearly on whether such a right had always existed before (perhaps so, perhaps not) and whether it has now disappeared (if it ever existed). By restating the key question, you will auto-generate a clear structure for yourself to follow.

- *Work out the hinge of the question before you start writing and state it clearly*

WORKED ESSAY QUESTIONS

Passage 1

In 1972, the teenage king of Bhutan, Jigme Singye Wangchuck, declared that "gross national happiness is more important than gross domestic product". The sound bite has been echoed approvingly down the years, although the king may just have been making excuses. Bhutanese GDP per person was then the grinding poverty of about a dollar a day. If I were king of such a country, I'd be tempted to change the subject, too.

Clearly he had a point. Most of us would rather be poor and happy than rich and depressed. If so, gross national happiness seems a fine goal. But it is one thing for a monarch to announce that happiness is important. It's quite another to make people happy. Shangri-La does not move from fiction to reality just because we desire it.

Bhutan has not always lived up to its own hype. Same-sex intercourse is illegal, which suggests a country with a less-than-expansive view of whose happiness matters. Three decades ago, around 100,000 of the Nepali-speaking Lhotshampa minority fled Bhutan to escape military persecution during a campaign of ethnic cleansing on a colossal scale. One-sixth of the entire population of Bhutan ended up in refugee camps in Nepal.

Even setting aside this enormity, it's hard to see that Bhutan paid much more than lip service to gross national happiness. They hosted conferences, but according to a recent IMF working paper, nobody in the government collected systematic indicators on happiness until 2005. The World Happiness Report ranks Bhutan at 97th out of 156 countries, down from 84th a few years ago. Happiness is easy to venerate, but hard to generate, and even harder to measure.

Consider some of the issues that are notoriously bypassed by GDP, the most common measure of economic activity: digital services are hard to value, while by design GDP omits any consideration of inequality or environmental damage. Unpaid work — of which men do a great deal, and women a great deal more — is also left out.

But if our aim is (for example) to reduce carbon emissions, we don't achieve it by moaning about GDP. We achieve it with specific policies such as carbon taxes and investments in public transport and a renewable-friendly electric grid. Neither gender equality nor respect for unpaid work would be automatically improved by any change in the way national income accounts are computed.

The specifics matter when it comes to happiness, too. Broad research into the causes of national happiness has tended to produce banal conclusions: we tend to compare ourselves to others, unemployment makes us miserable, and we hate being ill. There is nothing here to suggest that we need to overhaul commonplace policies such as redistributive taxation, the avoidance of recessions, and support for public health.

Just as with GDP itself, it is only when we move to the specifics that gross national happiness becomes useful. Richard Layard, one of the leading happiness researchers, argues that mental illness is a leading cause of misery, and that it can be treated very cost-effectively. That seems useful enough to me, but that doesn't seem to require economists' focus to realise.

QUESTION
"Economists should be more concerned with happiness and wellbeing than GDP."
Discuss with reference to the passage above.

Example Plan

Introduction: Set the scene…
- Define "concerned with". This could mean "focus on…" or "worried about". Here I take it here to mean a that latter because it allows for a more expansive essay, however either would be appropriate given context.
- The key question to be answered is therefore: Should economic analysis and policies be focussed on improving a nation's happiness, instead of conventional measures of wealth and prosperity?

Paragraph 1: Just because it's better doesn't make it the focus…
- Traditionally economic analysis and economic policies have been focussed on promoting economic growth conventionally measured through GDP per capita. The article makes the assertion that "many of us would rather be poor and happy, than rich and miserable".
- On this logic, economists and the policies they devise to help governments, should be focussed on generating happiness for people rather than wealth.
- Yet this assumes that economists and their policies should be focussed on outcomes that are most desirable, without paying attention to pragmatics.

Paragraph 2: Challenge 1 – It isn't pragmatic to be concerned with happiness…
- One reason for economists remaining focussed on GDP is that it isn't pragmatic to be focussed on the alternative; namely happiness and wellbeing.
- Happiness is notoriously hard to measure. As the article explains generic measures of happiness are subject to the same criticisms as GDP (see paragraph 7 in the article).
- Equally it is not clear that happiness is the same for every person. Whilst wealth is somewhat consistent across individuals e.g., more money and better-quality stuff = more wealth; it is not clear that what makes me happy makes any other individual happy. In a world where policy is general and impacts all, economists cannot aim to please everyone.

Paragraph 3: It isn't right to be concerned with happiness...

- This all assumes thus far that happiness is what economists **should** be concerned about if only it were possible to measure and practical to increase.
- However, GDP has a lot going for it, indeed it has remained the headline measure for the IMF even for Bhutan for much of the last few decades (paragraph 4).
- The criticism of GDP in paragraph 5, makes a compelling case against its general nature, but whilst it advocates for measuring specifics, it does not say that national income (GDP) is the wrong measure entirely.
- Indeed, measuring wealth/national income is crucially important – without it public services cannot be provided, a country struggles to trade for things it needs and its people have limited access to resources, capital or goods that are required for living a reasonable quality of life.
- There is therefore a compelling argument for national income/GDP to remain the concern of economists for both analysis and policy purposes.

Conclusion

- Summarize the points:
  - The article seems to suggest at points that happiness should be the concern of economists, above GDP and that it should be considered with specificity to be useful to economists.
- Having decided in this plan to argue against the statement summarise your three points:
  - Take the assertion that happiness is more important than GDP to be right however this isn't enough to suggest that it should be the primary concern of economists.
  - It isn't pragmatic to be concerned with happiness and therefore it shouldn't be the primary concern
  - It isn't even right to be concerned with happiness anyway.
- Zoom out and say why the question really matters and conclude.

Passage 2

The annual labour of every nation is the fund which originally supplies it with all the necessaries and conveniences of life which it annually consumes, and which consist always either in the immediate produce of that labour, or in what is purchased with that produce from other nations.

According therefore as this produce, or what is purchased with it, bears a greater or smaller proportion to the number of those who are to consume it, the nation will be better or worse supplied with all the necessaries and conveniences for which it has occasion.

But this proportion must in every nation be regulated by two different circumstances; first, by the skill, dexterity, and judgment with which its labour is generally applied; and, secondly, by the proportion between the number of those who are employed in useful labour, and that of those who are not so employed. Whatever be the soil, climate, or extent of territory of any nation, the abundance or scantiness of its annual supply must, in that particular situation, depend upon those two circumstances.

The abundance or scantiness of this supply, too, seems to depend more upon the former of those two circumstances than upon the latter. Among the savage nations of hunters and fishers, every individual who is able to work, is more or less employed in useful labour, and endeavours to provide, as well as he can, the necessaries and conveniences of life, for himself, or such of his family or tribe as are either too old, or too young, or too infirm to go a hunting and fishing. Such nations, however, are so miserably poor that, from mere want, they are frequently reduced, or, at least, think themselves reduced, to the necessity sometimes of directly destroying, and sometimes of abandoning their infants, their old people, and those afflicted with lingering diseases, to perish with hunger, or to be devoured by wild beasts. Among civilised and thriving nations, on the contrary, though a great number of people do not labour at all, many of whom consume the produce of ten times, frequently of a hundred times more labour than the greater part of those who work; yet the produce of the whole labour of the society is so great that all are often abundantly supplied, and a workman, even of the lowest and poorest order, if he is frugal and industrious, may enjoy a greater share of the necessaries and conveniences of life than it is possible for any savage to acquire

(Adam Smith, Wealth of Nations)

QUESTION
"What is Adam Smith argument in the passage. Do you agree or disagree? (Use examples from modern economics)

Discuss with reference to the passage above.

Example Plan

Introduction: What is Adam Smith's Argument in the passage?

- Smith's argument can essentially be deconstructed as follows:
  - Refer first to Para 3 where he explains that the proportion that is produced in a country versus the population (GDP per capita) will be determined by the application of labour (skill/productivity) and the number of people employed. The influence of soil, climate, geography on the economic wealth of that country are all mediated by labour force participation and skill.
  - Smith then goes on to claim in paragraph 4 that wealth in fact whilst dependent on both factors, depends on the former of the two more than the latter; that production is about skill not number of workers. He claims nations that are poor are often at full employment but do not work with skill. In a wealthy society however, it is often the case that individuals are not all employed, but the production of a few well employed is so great to as provide for all.

Paragraph 1: Adam Smith's logic does seem to apply to modern countries?

- Smith is arguing that the reason countries have become wealthy is because they apply labour with more precision, and have more skilled labour.
- Take the cadre of modern day developed economies: they are not the most populous countries in the world e.g., UK, Japan, European countries are all some of the most developed. They do however all have developed industries (service orientated or high-skilled manufacturing economies with highly skilled labour forces). Additionally, they do also have higher rates of unemployment.
- This all seems to validate Smith's argument that it matters not the rate of employment but rather the skill of the employed that drive economic prosperity.
- Expand with examples of your own e.g., UK development in 80s and 90s, rise of Japan and the Far-East as skilled labour economies for hi-tech manufacturing (Sony, Samsung etc...)

Paragraph 2: Employing lots of people hasn't seemed to drive wealth.

- Adam Smith make's a coherent argument for population size and even employment rates not being a significant contributing factor to the wealth of a nation. In fact, he suggests that you have historically seen many societies where all employable individual's (health and age dependent) work but are savage and primitive.
- Whilst extreme, there is validation for Adam Smith's logic in modern day examples. Possible examples include Asian economies where numerous individuals (young, old, infirm and those who can work) are employed in low wage jobs such as sweat shops etc... other examples could be rural economies in Africa.
- The economies whilst at full employment do not reap the rewards of their labour, the lack of high skilled individuals to develop high value products means that the majority of the valuable assets are owned or traded overseas.

Paragraph 3: However, Adam Smith ignores key factors that influence growth in a globalised world.

* Some could argue that Adam Smith's argument no longer applies in today's globalised world.
* Today when economies are integrated it could be no longer argued that wealth need be driven by internal processes, instead the ways in which a country is linked with, and to whom, can be said to drive growth and wealth.
* Take for example some of the countries in Africa where it is shown that post-colonial connections to their former colonial power, are correlated with wealth because of trade links. This has nothing to do with labour etc...

Conclusion

* Summarize the points:
  o Adam Smith's argument does seem to reflect the economic facts we see in the modern world.
    ▪ This applies in terms of the precise application of skilled labour
    ▪ It also appears to apply in the idea that large populations and close to full employment does not drive economic wealth.
* Zoom out and say why the question really matters (give your essay the 'wow-factor'):
  o It is important to understand that to drive economic growth economic policy should focus on training and skills development, rather than getting everyone to full employment. However, it should be noted that this may rely on strong redistribution as wealth can become overly concentrated.

Passage 3 – Animal Spirits

Even apart from the instability due to speculation, there is the instability due to the characteristic of human nature that a large proportion of our positive activities depend on spontaneous optimism rather than on a mathematical expectation, whether moral or hedonistic or economic. Most, probably, of our decisions to do something positive, the full consequences of which will be drawn out over many days to come, can only be taken as a result of animal spirits—of a spontaneous urge to action rather than inaction, and not as the outcome of a weighted average of quantitative benefits multiplied by quantitative probabilities. Enterprise only pretends to itself to be mainly actuated by the statements in its own prospectus, however candid and sincere. Only a little more than an expedition to the South Pole, is it based on an exact calculation of benefits to come. Thus if the animal spirits are dimmed and the spontaneous optimism falters, leaving us to depend on nothing but a mathematical expectation, enterprise will fade and die; —though fears of loss may have a basis no more reasonable than hopes of profit had before.

It is safe to say that enterprise which depends on hopes stretching into the future benefits the community as a whole. But individual initiative will only be adequate when reasonable calculation is supplemented and supported by animal spirits, so that the thought of ultimate loss which often overtakes pioneers, as experience undoubtedly tells us and them, is put aside as a healthy man puts aside the expectation of death.

This means, unfortunately, not only that slumps and depressions are exaggerated in degree, but that economic prosperity is excessively dependent on a political and social atmosphere which is congenial to the average business man.

(John Maynard Keynes)

QUESTION
What does Keynes mean by "Animal Spirits"? What are the implications, if true, for current economic policy? (Discuss with examples).

Example Plan

Introduction:

- Animal Spirits according to Keynes are the "spontaneous urge to action rather than inaction, and not as the outcome of a weighted average of quantitative benefits multiplied by quantitative probabilities".
- By this Keynes means that despite the economic assumption of rationality, a great deal of decision making is dependent upon unexplained or spontaneous feelings by humans; those animal spirits that exist within us all.
- Keynes sees animal spirits as that part of us all that emotionally drives our decision making either by instilling confidence or fear and so, "economic prosperity is excessively dependent the political and social atmosphere".

Paragraph 1: Implication for economic policy 1 – Policy based on assumptions of rationality can sometimes not have the desired impact

- One of the major implications for economic policy of animal spirits is that when economic policy is implemented then the consequences are often unpredictable.
- For example: at this point you could use any example but below is an example
  - Expansionary Fiscal policy: e.g., monetary spending or tax cuts/breaks. The intention of this policy is to increase disposable income with the intention of increasing consumption and investment, yielding economic growth. However, animal spirits suggest that whilst theoretically, a rational individual would act in accordance with a rational analysis of the benefits from spending increases, in fact their propensity to spend is highly dependent on animal spirits in the form of confidence, trust and other emotions that could induce spending decisions.
- This would then lead into the next implication – that governments should try and influence animal spirits.

Paragraph 2: Implication for policy 2 – Policy should sometimes aim to impact animal spirits

- To ensure the effectiveness of economic policies enacted by governments, they should sometimes try to impact animal spirits, or at least not neglect them.
- Why? The government cannot neglect animal spirits because they are so influential. Therefore, in making decisions around policy the government should consider the impact they can have on these sentiments e.g., confidence, trust etc...
- Examples for this could include scheduling of events such as forecasts and economic announcements, central bank messaging, statements to the media, geo-political events and their handling, elections, wars and other national social events.

Paragraph 3: Implication for policy 3 – Recessions can be unpredictable

- Another major implication stemming from the concept of animal spirits, is its consequences for the unpredictable nature of certain events.
- For example, stories of corruption and broken trust can reduce confidence, and that can greatly contribute to economic depressions and confidence being undermined can lead to crisis. Possible examples include:
  - Stories – humans get behind stories and can be positive. E.g., is story of the internet and a new era of tech fuelled one of history's biggest stock market bubbles in the early 2000s. Similarly, during the depression in the US in the 1890s the run on the banks was caused by stories spread of corruption and fragility in the financial system, when in fact many were untrue.
  - In the 1980s crisis ensued when moral hazard undermined confidence; savings and loan entrepreneurs made risky investments knowing that the government would rescue them – similar example in 2008 Sub-Prime Mortgage crisis. Erosion of confidence from this in some cases sparked and certainly deepened the recessions.
- This is worrying for policy makers because it seems to imply that there are some factors that are simply out of their control. (At this point you could introduce an argument in defence of policy makers which suggests that since they cannot control animal spirits perhaps, they need to be wholly reactive etc…).

Conclusion:

- Summarize the points:
  - Animal Spirits can distort the theoretically predicted impact of economic policies which are based on the assumptions of rationality
  - A second implication for policy makers is that they should sometime not only account for, but aim to influence animal spirits using communications or timings of events.
  - A third implication of animal spirits is that they render economic events such as recessions somewhat unpredictable.
- Likely conclusion is that clearly animal spirits hold great implications of economic policy makers in a variety of ways; including potentially very negative and therefore cannot be ignored and must be accounted for as much as possible.

Passage 4

Most institutions in the country are businesses – shops, factories, energy companies, airlines, and train companies, to name a few types. They are the bedrock of society, employ most people in it and it is, thus, crucial that we examine their values.

The overriding objective of businesses is to make the most profit (i.e., maximise on revenue and minimise on costs). The notion was first popularly expounded by Adam Smith in his book, 'The Wealth of Nations' in 1776. Furthermore, his view was that if an individual considers merely their own interests to create and sell goods or services for the most profit, the invisible hand of the market will lead that activity to maximise the welfare of society. For example, in order to maximise profits, sellers will only produce and sell goods that society wants. If they try to sell things people don't want, no one would buy it. This is how the free market works. Indeed, the focus on profit is the basis on which companies operate and encourages them to innovate and produce goods that consumers want, such as iPhones and computers. So there are clear benefits to the profit maximisation theory.

This is a more effective society than, for example, a communist society where the government decides what to produce – as the government has no accurate way of deciding what consumers need and want. Arguably, the poverty that communist regimes such as the Soviet Union created have instilled this notion further.

However, were companies left to their own devices to engage in profit maximisation, what would stop them from exploiting workers? What would stop them from dumping toxic chemicals into public rivers? Engaging in such practices would reduce their costs of production, which would increase their profits. However, this would be very damaging to the environment. Accordingly, other objectives should be relevant. Businesses can also do other bad things to make a profit as well. For example, selling products to people who don't want or need them.

Corporate social responsibility entails other possible objectives for businesses, such as a consideration of the interests of stakeholders. A stakeholder is, in essence, anyone who is significantly affected by a company decision, such as employees or the local community. One business decision can have huge impacts on stakeholders. For example, a decision to transfer a call centre from the UK to India would likely increase profits, as wage costs for Indian workers can be much lower than that of British workers. This increase in profits would benefit the shareholders, however, it negatively harms other stakeholders. It would make many employees redundant. Here, there is arguably a direct conflict between profit maximisation and employees' interest. Nonetheless, moving call centres abroad does not always work. Given the different cultures and accents, companies have received complaints from frustrated customers. This, in fact, led BT to bring back a number of call centres to the UK.

However, the objective of profit maximisation has not always led to maximum welfare for society. Arguably, as banks sought to maximise their profits, they lent money to individuals who could not afford to pay it back. Eventually, many borrowers stopped meeting their repayments and lost banks enormous amounts. This led to a need for banks to be bailed out by the government and Lehman Brothers; one of the largest US banks that collapsed. Arguably, though, this was more due to idiocy rather than profit maximisation alone – in the end, the banks lost billions.

QUESTION
"Enforcing Corporate Social Responsibility interferes with the market's ability to give people what they want." Discuss with reference to the passage above.

Example Plan

Introduction:

- Define terms: Corporate Social Responsibility (CSR) is defined in the passage. The market: goods and services offered for sale by businesses and bought by consumers. People: both the consumers in the market and those not participating in the market.
- Key question: If business is driven by profit maximisation, does the market truly give people what they want?

Paragraph 1:

- Adam Smith's invisible hand tells us that the market will allocate resources to maximise the welfare of society. If goods were produced and not demanded, this would waste resources. This cannot happen as the resources used to make these goods would be allocated to make other, demanded, goods.
- *Passage Example:* "Sellers will only produce and sell goods that society wants." The businesses may be maximising profits, but they can only do so within the constraints of selling items that are wanted by the people. Thus, what is on offer in a market is determined by the people's wants.

Paragraph 2:

- We need CSR to prevent the profit maximisation affecting stakeholders who are not necessarily the direct consumer. Their loss may outweigh the gains of those engaged in the transaction and so we have a net loss,
- *Passage Example*: "Corporate social responsibility entails other possible objectives for businesses, such as consideration of the interests of stakeholders."

Paragraph 3:

- The problem here is not the functioning of the market, but instead all the people not fully understanding the impact of their consumption: with full information, people's wants will be satisfied by the market,
- *Passage Example:* "Dumping toxic chemicals into public rivers... would be very damaging to the environment." If the pollution is common knowledge, and if the majority of people think it is bad, they will buy goods from an alternative green business, and the polluting company will go out of business.
- *Passage Example:* "A decision to transfer a call centre from the UK to India … would make many employees redundant." If this is common knowledge the majority will switch their consumption to another business; indeed, we see BT had to relocate back to the UK to re-cooperate customers.

Paragraph 4:

- It may not be possible to fully inform customers, in which case: external referees are needed to identify the good which is preferred for people and ensure they get the right one in the market (i.e., we need external regulation).
- *Passage Example*: "Many borrowers stopped meeting their repayments…" Borrowers bought loans that were not fully understood by the players in the market and were too risky.

Conclusion

- Summarize the points:
    - Allocation is determined by people's demand: any interferences undermine people's wants.
    - Allocations may affect other stakeholders resulting in net-loss of welfare.
    - If all stakeholders (consumers, businesses and externally affected people) understand all the repercussions of production, wants will be satisfied directly in the market.
    - Full information for everyone is not feasible in some contexts.
- Now decide for yourself one way or another...
- Zoom out and say why the question really matters (just pick one to give your essay the 'wow-factor'):
    - Government Intervention is needed to ensure market interactions are net-beneficial to society, not just to the active buyers and sellers. CSR gives a voice to the wants of the silent victims of markets.

Passage 5

"What are the rules which men naturally observe in exchanging them [goods] for money or for one another, I shall now proceed to examine. These rules determine what may be called the relative or exchangeable value of goods. The word 'Value', it is to be observed, has two different meanings, and sometimes expresses the utility of some particular object, and sometimes the power of purchasing other goods which the possession of that object conveys. The one may be called "value in use;" the other, "value in exchange." The things which have the greatest value in use have frequently little or no value in exchange; on the contrary, those which have the greatest value in exchange have frequently little or no value in use. Nothing is more useful than water: but it will purchase scarcely anything; scarcely anything can be had in exchange for it. A diamond, on the contrary, has scarcely any use-value; but a very great quantity of other goods may frequently be had in exchange for it."

(Adam Smith, Wealth of Nations)

This passage articulates a paradox in economics knows as the Paradox of Value or Diamond-Water Paradox. Smith noted that, even though life cannot exist without water and can easily exist without diamonds, diamonds are, pound for pound, vastly more valuable than water.

In a further passage Smith explains: "The real price of everything, what everything really costs to the man who wants to acquire it, is the toil and trouble of acquiring it."
(Adam Smith, Wealth of Nations)

Thus, Smith's explanation was the labour theory of value. This theory stated that the price of a good reflected the amount of labour and resources required to bring it to market. Smith believed diamonds were more expensive than water because they were more difficult to bring to market. Price on this view was related to a factor of production (namely, labour) and not to the point of view of the consumer (in which case there would be a relationship between price and utility.

QUESTION
How convincing is Smith's explanation of Labour Theory of Value as a resolution of the 'Diamond-Water Paradox'? What other explanations are there, and are they more convincing?

Example Plan

Introduction:

- Introduce and summarize Smith's problem: simply that despite their differing values to humans, with water being integral to life and diamonds a superficial luxury diamonds hold far more value.
- Smith explains this by suggesting that the value of a good is related to the labour involved in its production.
- State the structure of the essay and your likely conclusion since this is an argumentative piece.

Paragraph 1: The Labour Theory of Value

- Start by assessing the Labour Theory of Value as a convincing argument for resolving the Diamond-Water Paradox.
- On the one hand this seems logical because products which take a lot of skill to produce, or a lot of time will often cost more. E.g., for something with high production costs (directly related to the labour) such as an iPhone which must be designed, produced and shipped.
- However, labour theory of value struggles when trying to explain the price attached to good which have little or no production process or value. For example, consider a perfectly formed gemstone found on a path, which would not have a lower market price than one which is produced artificially through significant labour or even one which has been mined and cut and polished through hard work.

Paragraph 2: Subjective Value – the opposite of Labour Theory seems more likely

- Another argument against the validity of the Labour theory of value is that it is not the case that costs and labour drive price, in fact price drives labour and cost.
- Consider goods that have high value such as fine wine, which is not valuable because it derives from expensive land and is produced by highly paid workers who exert effort. In fact, the price seems more likely to be the driver of the costs, because the product is valuable, the means of production are valuable.
- This suggests that the value of a product lies in the value people attach to it; so, for a solution to this paradox we must look to why people value diamonds more than water.

Paragraph 3: Alternative 1 – Scarcity: Supply and Demand

- One clear alternative way of solving the argument lies in the relative rarity of the products.
- Diamonds are rarer and therefore utility from a single diamond, is more valuable demand outstrips supply by a greater amount, than with water which is in abundant supply, thereby driving the price up.
- This is simple demand and supply, but can be countered by the following logic: Whilst it is true that supply of diamonds is much lower, it is not clear why demand would be the same. Indeed, it seems likely that demand for water is much higher since, water is more essential for life and has more uses.

Paragraph 4: Alternative 2 – Scarcity: marginal Utility

- The alternative means of solving this paradox lie in the theory of marginal utility; which suggests that the price of a good is derived from its most important use – namely that the price is determined by the usefulness of each unit of a good not the total utility of a good.

- Since diamonds are rarer, it is likely that they are put to their most important use thereby holding greater value. Since water is so abundant, each additional unit of water that becomes available can be applied to less urgent uses as more urgent uses for water are satisfied.

- Under this logic, any unit of water becomes less valuable because it is put to less and less valuable use. Conversely each unit of diamond is more valuable because it is in less supply so put to more use. One additional diamond is worth more than one additional glass of water for example.

- A further example for this logic comes from considering a man in a desert who would have greater marginal use for water than for diamonds, so water would hold more value for him, due to scarcity.

Conclusion

- Summarize the points:
  - Adam Smith solves the paradox with the labour theory of value
  - There is an opposite argument: subjective theory of value which yields two alternatives
  - Supply and Demand simply drives the higher price
  - The answer lies in the different marginal utilities of the goods due to their scarcity

- Give your answer as to which is more convincing backing it up with either logical reasoning or persuasive examples.

- Zoom out and say why this is important – fundamentally important question about value of goods and services. Important to consider how prices of these essential, yet currently abundant goods, may change as they become scarcer e.g., fossil fuels, clean water etc...

Final Advice

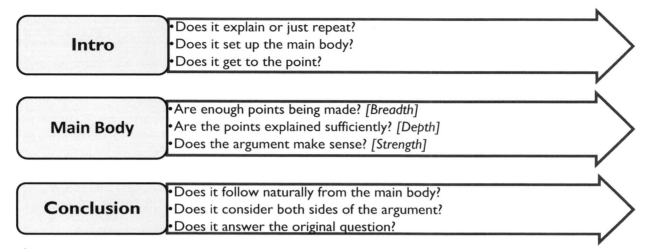

Intro
- Does it explain or just repeat?
- Does it set up the main body?
- Does it get to the point?

Main Body
- Are enough points being made? *[Breadth]*
- Are the points explained sufficiently? *[Depth]*
- Does the argument make sense? *[Strength]*

Conclusion
- Does it follow naturally from the main body?
- Does it consider both sides of the argument?
- Does it answer the original question?

✓ Always answer the question clearly – this is the key thing that examiners look for in an essay.

✓ Analyse each argument made, justifying or dismissing with logical reasoning.

✓ Keep an eye on the time/space available – an incomplete essay may be taken as a sign of a candidate with poor organisational skills.

✓ Ensure each paragraph has a new theme that is clearly differentiated from the previous one (don't just use a new paragraph to break your text up)

✓ Leave yourself time to write a conclusion – however short – that tells your reader which side of the fence you're on

✓ Do plan your essay before you start writing even the introduction; don't be tempted to dive straight in

✓ Use pre-existing knowledge when possible – examples and real-world data can be a great way to strengthen an argument- but don't make up statistics!

✓ Present ideas in a neat, logical fashion (easier for an examiner to absorb).

✓ Complete some practice questions in advance, in order to best establish your personal approach to the paper (particularly timings, how you plan etc.).

✗ Attempt to answer a question that you don't fully understand, or ignore part of a question.

✗ Rush or attempt to use too many arguments – it is much better to have fewer, more substantial points.

✗ Attempt to be too clever, or present false knowledge to support an argument – a tutor may call out incorrect facts etc.

✗ Panic if you don't know the answer the examiner wants – there is no right answer, the essay is not a test of knowledge but a chance to display reasoning skill. Start by defining the words in the question to get your mind thinking about ways to approach it

✗ Leave an essay unfinished – if time/space is short, wrap up the essay early in order to provide a conclusive response to the question. If you've only got a couple of minutes left, summarize your remaining points in a short bullet point each; these bullets contain just the topic sentence and (optionally) a quote from the passage to illustrate your point

ANSWERS

SECTION 1A

Q	A	Q	A	Q	A	Q	A
1	B	40	C	79	B	117	B
2	C	41	B	80	D	118	A
3	C	42	D	81	B	119	D
4	C	43	C	82	A	120	C
5	E	44	A	83	C	121	D
6	A	45	C	84	E	122	B
7	C	46	C	85	A	123	D
8	E	47	C	86	C	124	D
9	E	48	B	87	C	125	D
10	C	49	D	88	B	126	C
11	E	50	E	89	C	127	B
12	E	51	D	90	C	128	B
13	E	52	D	91	A	129	C
14	B	53	B	92	E	130	C
15	C	54	E	93	C	131	E
16	B	55	E	94	B	132	B
17	B	56	B	95	C	133	B
18	C	57	C	96	B	134	A
19	D	58	A	97	B	135	D
20	C	59	C	98	C	136	C
21	B	60	B	99	C		
22	A	61	B	100	B		
23	F	62	B	101	B		
24	D	63	C	102	F		
25	A	64	C	103	D		
26	B	65	A	104	D		
27	A	66	C	105	E		
28	F	67	D	106	B		
29	D	68	C	107	C		
30	A	69	D	108	E		
31	D	70	A	109	C		
32	D	71	C	110	D		
33	F	72	B	111	B		
34	B	73	B	112	C		
35	C	74	A	113	B		
36	B	75	C	114	A		
37	C	76	B	115	C		
38	A	77	B	116	C		
39	A	78	A				

SECTION 1B

Q	A	Q	A	Q	A	Q	A	Q	A
1	B	40	A	79	D	118	A	157	C
2	A	41	D	80	D	119	C	158	B
3	A	42	D	81	D	120	D	159	A
4	D	43	D	82	G	121	D	160	C
5	C	44	C	83	D	122	B	161	C
6	C	45	B	84	D	123	B	162	E
7	A	46	E	85	B	124	A	163	E
8	E	47	D	86	F	125	D	164	A
9	B	48	B	87	D	126	B	165	C
10	D	49	D	88	F	127	A	166	C
11	A	50	E	89	E	128	B	167	E
12	E	51	C	90	B	129	A	168	D
13	C	52	A	91	F	130	B	169	A
14	D	53	A	92	E	131	C	170	D
15	C	54	D	93	C	132	E	171	B
16	C	55	C	94	D	133	E	172	E
17	E	56	B	95	D	134	A	173	A
18	B	57	C	95	F	135	D	174	D
19	B	58	B	97	D	136	B	175	C
20	A	59	A	98	B	137	A	176	E
21	A	60	B	99	D	138	B		
22	B	61	C	100	B	139	B		
23	B	62	C	101	A	140	B		
24	A	63	D	102	C	141	A		
25	D	64	D	103	C	142	D		
26	A	65	B	104	C	143	C		
27	A	66	D	105	C	144	B		
28	B	67	E	106	D	145	C		
29	A	68	D	107	D	146	B		
30	C	69	C	108	E	147	A		
31	D	70	F	109	E	148	C		
32	C	71	C	110	C	149	E		
33	A	72	C	111	A	150	C		
34	C	73	B	112	B	151	C		
35	C	74	E	113	C	152	E		
36	G	75	D	114	C	153	C		
37	D	76	E	115	D	154	C		
38	D	77	E	116	D	155	A		
39	C	78	F	117	D	156	D		

Worked Answers: Basic Maths

1.   B

Each three-block combination is mutually exclusive, so the probabilities are added. Each block pick is independent of all other picks, so the probabilities are multiplied. There are three possible combinations:

$P(2\ red\ blocks\ and\ 1\ yellow\ block) = P(red\ then\ red\ then\ yellow) + P(red\ then\ yellow\ then\ red) + P(yellow\ then\ red\ then\ red)$

$(\frac{12}{20} \times \frac{11}{19} \times \frac{8}{18}) + (\frac{12}{20} \times \frac{8}{19} \times \frac{11}{18}) + (\frac{8}{20} \times \frac{12}{19} \times \frac{11}{18}) = \frac{3 \times 12 \times 11 \times 8}{20 \times 19 \times 18} = \frac{44}{95}$

2.   C

First get rid of the brackets: $3(3x + 5) + 5(2x - 2)$

Thus: $9x + 15 + 10x - 10 = 270$

$9x + 10x = 270 - 15 + 10$

$19x = 265$

$x = 13.95$

3.   C

This is a rare case where you need to factorise a complex polynomial: $3x^2 + 11x - 20 = 0$

$(3x\pm\ ?)(x\pm\ ?) = 0$, possible pairs: $2 \times 10, 10 \times 22, 4 \times 5, 5 \times 4$

$(3x - 4)(x + 5) = 0$

$3x - 4 = 0$, so $x = \frac{4}{3}$

$x + 5 = 0$ so $x = -5$

4.   C

Multiply the numerators through by the corresponding fraction's denominator in order to place the fractions in like terms and solve.

$\frac{5(x-4)}{(x+2)(x-4)} + \frac{3\ (x+2)}{(x+2)(x-4)}$

$= \frac{5x-20+\ 3x+6}{(x+2)(x-4)}$

$= \frac{8x-14}{(x+2)(x-4)}$

5.   E

$p = k\sqrt[3]{q}$

$p = 12$ when $q = 27$ gives $12 = k\sqrt[3]{27}$, so $12 = 3k$ and $k = 4$

so $p = 4\sqrt[3]{q}$

Now $p = 24$:

$24 = 4\sqrt[3]{q}$, so $6 = \sqrt[3]{q}$ and $q = 6^3 = 216$

6. A

$8 \times 9 = 72$

$8 = (4 \times 2) = 2 \times 2 \times 2$

$9 = 3 \times 3$

$(2 \times 2 \times 2 \times 3 \times 3)^2 = 2 \times 2 \times 2 \times 2 \times 2 \times 2 \times 3 \times 3 \times 3 \times 3 = 2^6 \times 3^4$

7. C

Note that $1.151 \times 2 = 2.302$

Let 1.151 be x

Thus: $\frac{2x \times 10^5 + 2x \times 10^2}{x \times 10^{10}} = 2 \times 10^{-5} + 2 \times 10^{-8}$

$= 0.00002 + 0.00000002 = 0.00002002$

8. E

$y^2 + ay + b$

$(y + 2)^2 - 5 = y^2 + 4y + 4 - 5$

$y^2 + 4y - 1$

So $a = 4$ and $b = -1$

9. E

Take $5(m + 4n)$ as a common factor to give: $\frac{4(m+4n)}{5(m+4n)} + \frac{5(m-2n)}{5(m+4n)}$

Simplify to give: $\frac{4m+16n+5m-10n}{5(m+4n)} = \frac{9m+6n}{5(m+4n)} = \frac{3(3m+2n)}{5(m+4n)}$

10. C

$A = \frac{k}{\sqrt{B}}$.

Substitute the values in to give: $4 = \frac{k}{\sqrt{25}}$.

Thus, $k = 20$.

Therefore, $A = \frac{20}{\sqrt{B}}$.

When $B = 16$, $A = \frac{20}{\sqrt{16}} = \frac{20}{4} = 5$

11. E

Angles SVU and STU are opposites and add up to $180°$, so STU $= 91°$

The angle of the centre of a circle is twice the angle at the circumference so

SOU $= 2 \times 91° = 182°$

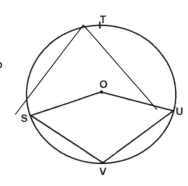

12. E

The surface area of an open cylinder $A = 2\pi rh$. Cylinder B is an enlargement of A, so the increases in radius (r) and height (h) will be proportional: $\frac{r_A}{r_B} = \frac{h_A}{h_B}$. Let us call the proportion coefficient n, where n $= \frac{r_A}{r_B} = \frac{h_A}{h_B}$.

So $\frac{Area\ A}{Area\ B} = \frac{2\pi r_A h_A}{2\pi r_B h_B} = n \times n = n^2$. $\frac{Area\ A}{Area\ B} = \frac{32\pi}{8\pi} = 4$, so, n = 2.

The proportion coefficient $n = 2$ also applies to their volumes, where the third dimension (also radius, i.e., the r^2 in $V = \pi r^2 h$) is equally subject to this constant of proportionality. The cylinder's volumes are related by $n^3 = 8$. If the smaller cylinder has volume 2π cm³, then the larger will have volume $2\pi \times n^3 = 2\pi \times 8 = 16\pi$ cm³.

13. E

$$= \frac{8}{x(3-x)} - \frac{6(3-x)}{x(3-x)}$$
$$= \frac{8 - 18 + 6x}{x(3-x)}$$
$$= \frac{6x - 10}{x(3-x)}$$

14. B

For the black ball to be drawn in the last round, white balls must be drawn every round. Thus, the probability is given by $P = \frac{9}{10} \times \frac{8}{9} \times \frac{7}{8} \times \frac{6}{7} \times \frac{5}{6} \times \frac{4}{5} \times \frac{3}{4} \times \frac{2}{3} \times \frac{1}{2}$

$$= \frac{9 \times 8 \times 7 \times 6 \times 5 \times 4 \times 3 \times 2 \times 1}{10 \times 9 \times 8 \times 7 \times 6 \times 5 \times 4 \times 3 \times 2 \times 1} = \frac{1}{10}$$

15. C

The probability of getting a king the first time is $\frac{4}{52} = \frac{1}{13}$, and the probability of getting a king the second time is $\frac{3}{51}$. These are independent events, so, the probability of drawing two kings is $\frac{1}{13} \times \frac{3}{51} = \frac{3}{663} = \frac{1}{221}$

16. B

The probabilities of all outcomes must sum to one, so if the probability of rolling a 1 is x, then: $x + x + x + x + 2x = 1$. Therefore, $x = \frac{1}{7}$.

The probability of obtaining two sixes $P_{12} = \frac{2}{7} \times \frac{2}{7} = \frac{4}{49}$

17. B

There are plenty of ways of counting, however the easiest is as follows: 0 is divisible by both 2 and 3. Half of the numbers from 1 to 36 are even (i.e., 18 of them). $3, 9, 15, 21, 27, 33$ are the only numbers divisible by 3 that we've missed. There are 25 outcomes divisible by 2 or 3, out of 37.

In this instance because the range of numbers is quite small it's feasible to simply list numbers divisible by three as the final step. In situations in which the range is large you may want calculate it more systematically. This can be done as follows:

Calculate how many figures between 36 and 1 are divisible by 2, so: $\frac{36}{2} = 18$

Calculate how many figures between 36 and 1 are divisible by 3, so: $\frac{36}{3} = 12$

Find how many numbers are divisible by both 2 and 3 $\frac{36}{3 \times 2} = 6$

Sum to the total figures divisible by 3, total figures divisible by 2, subtract the total numbers divisible by 2 and 3 (you do not want to double count these numbers). Finally, 1 to account for 0 which is also divisible by 2 and 3.

So $12 + 18 - 6 + 1 = 25$. So, the final answer is $\frac{25}{37}$.

18. C

List the six ways of achieving this outcome: HHTT, HTHT, HTTH, TTHH, THTH and THHT. There are 2^4 possible outcomes for 4 consecutive coin flips, so the probability of two heads and two tails is: $6 \times \frac{1}{2^4} = \frac{6}{16} = \frac{3}{8}$.

As in the prior question because of the limited number of possible combinations listing combinations may be the most time efficient strategy. However, in instances where the number of possible combinations is much larger you may simply want to calculate it using a combinations formula. In this case, we can write the formula as $\frac{n!}{h!t!}$ where n is the number of coin flips and h and t represent the number of heads and tails. In this case $\frac{4!}{2!2!} = \frac{4 \times 3 \times 2 \times 1}{4}$ which would give you 6 (from there you can proceed as above).

19. D

Count the number of ways to get a $5, 6$ or 7 (draw the square if helpful). The ways to get a 5 are: $1, 4; 2, 3; 3, 2; 4, 1$. The ways to get a 6 are: $1, 5; 2, 4; 3, 3; 4, 2; 5, 1$. The ways to get a 7 are: $1, 6; 2, 5; 3, 4; 4, 3; 5, 2; 6, 1$. That is 15 out of 36 possible outcomes. Which simplifies down to 5 out of 12.

	1	2	3	4	5	6
1	2	3	4	5	6	7
2	3	4	5	6	7	8
3	4	5	6	7	8	9
4	5	6	7	8	9	10
5	6	7	8	9	10	11
6	7	8	9	10	11	12

20. C

There are $x + y + z$ balls in the bag, and the probability of picking a red ball is $\frac{x}{(x+y+z)}$ and the probability of picking a green ball is $\frac{z}{(x+y+z)}$. These are independent events, so the probabilities are multiplied giving $\frac{xz}{(x+y+z)^2}$ and the probability of picking green then red is the same. These outcomes are mutually exclusive, so are added giving $\frac{2xz}{(x+y+z)^2}$.

21. B

There are two ways of doing it, pulling out a red ball then a blue ball, or pulling out a blue ball and then a red ball. Let us work out the probability of the first by multiplying probabilities of pulling out red $\frac{x}{(x+y+z)}$ by the probability of then pulling out blue $\frac{y}{x+y+z-1}$, and the probability of the second option will be the same. These are mutually exclusive options, so the probabilities may be summed giving $\frac{2xy}{(x+y+z)(x+y+z-1)}$.

22. A

[x: Player 1 wins point, y: Player 2 wins point]
Player 1 wins in five rounds if we get: $yxxxx, xyxxx, xxyxx, xxxyx$.
(Note the case of $xxxxy$ would lead to player 1 winning in 4 rounds, which the question forbids.)
Each of these have a probability of $p^4(1-p)$ Thus, the solution is $4p^4(1-p)$.

Due to the limited number of rounds, we can simply list the possible acceptable rounds, as a above. However, we can also calculate it systematically using a combinations formula $\frac{n!}{y!x!}$ where n is the total number of games. In this instance we $\frac{5!}{4!1!} = \frac{5 \times 4!}{4!}$ which would give us 5. Because $xxxxy$ is not an acceptable combination we would want to subtract 1 leaving us with 4 possible combinations.

23. F

$4x + 7 + 18x + 20 = 14$
$22x + 27 = 14$
Thus, $22x = -13$
Giving $x = -\frac{13}{22}$

24. D

$r^3 = \frac{3V}{4\pi}$

Thus, $r = \left(\frac{3V}{4\pi}\right)^{\frac{1}{3}}$

Now substitute r into the S formula so that, $S = 4\pi \left[\left(\frac{3V}{4\pi}\right)^{\frac{1}{3}}\right]^2 = 4\pi \left(\frac{3V}{4\pi}\right)^{\frac{2}{3}}$

$= \frac{4\pi(3V)^{\frac{2}{3}}}{(4\pi)^{\frac{2}{3}}} = (3V)^{\frac{2}{3}} \times \frac{(4\pi)^1}{(4\pi)^{\frac{2}{3}}}$

$= (3V)^{\frac{2}{3}} (4\pi)^{1-\frac{2}{3}} = (4\pi)^{\frac{1}{3}}(3V)^{\frac{2}{3}}$

25. A

Let each unit length be x.

Thus, $S = 6x^2$. Therefore, $x = \left(\frac{S}{6}\right)^{\frac{1}{2}}$

$V = x^3$. Thus, $V = [\left(\frac{S}{6}\right)^{\frac{1}{2}}]^3$ so $V = \left(\frac{S}{6}\right)^{\frac{3}{2}}$

26. B

Multiplying the second equation by 2 we get $4x + 16y = 24$. We can rearrange this and substitute it into the first equation so $24 - 16y + 3y = 7$ which we can then simplify to $y = \frac{17}{13}$. Then solving for x we get $x = \frac{10}{13}$. You could also try substituting possible solutions one by one, although given that the equations are both linear and contain easy numbers, it is quicker to solve them algebraically.

27. A

Multiply by the denominator to give:	$(7x + 10) = (3y^2 + 2)(9x + 5)$
Partially expand brackets on right side:	$(7x + 10) = 9x(3y^2 + 2) + 5(3y^2 + 2)$
Take x terms across to left side:	$7x - 9x(3y^2 + 2) = 5(3y^2 + 2) - 10$
Take x outside the brackets:	$x[7 - 9(3y^2 + 2)] = 5(3y^2 + 2) - 10$
Thus:	$x = \frac{5(3y^2 + 2) - 10}{7 - 9(3y^2 + 2)}$
Simplify to give:	$x = \frac{15y^2}{7 - 9(3y^2 + 2)}$

28. F

$$3x \left(\frac{3x^7}{x^{\frac{1}{3}}} \right)^3 = 3x \left(\frac{3^3 x^{21}}{x^{\frac{3}{3}}} \right)$$

$$= 3x \frac{27x^{21}}{x} = 81x^{21}$$

29. D

$$2x[2^{\frac{7}{14}} x^{\frac{7}{14}}] = 2x[2^{\frac{1}{2}} x^{\frac{1}{2}}]$$
$$= 2x(\sqrt{2} \sqrt{x}) = 2 \left[\sqrt{x}\sqrt{x} \right][\sqrt{2} \sqrt{x}]$$
$$= 2\sqrt{2x^3}$$

30. A

$A = \pi r^2$, therefore $10\pi = \pi r^2$
Thus, $r = \sqrt{10}$
Therefore, the circumference is $2\pi\sqrt{10}$.

31. D

$3.4 = (3 \times 4) + (3 + 4) = 19$
$19.5 = (19 \times 5) + (19 + 5) = 119$

32. D

$$2.3 = \frac{2^3}{2} = 4$$
$$4.2 = \frac{4^2}{4} = 4$$

33. F

This is a tricky question that requires you to know how to 'complete the square'.

$(x + 1.5)(x + 1.5) = x^2 + 3x + 2.25$

$(x + 1.5)^2 - 7.25 = x^2 + 3x - 5 = 0$

Therefore, $(x + 1.5)^2 = 7.25 = \frac{29}{4}$

Thus, $x + 1.5 = \sqrt{\frac{29}{4}}$

Thus $x = -\frac{3}{2} \pm \sqrt{\frac{29}{4}} = -\frac{3}{2} \pm \frac{\sqrt{29}}{2}$

34. B

Whilst you definitely need to solve this graphically, it is necessary to complete the square for the first equation to allow you to draw it more easily:

$(x + 2)^2 = x^2 + 4x + 4$

Thus, $y = (x + 2)^2 + 10 = x^2 + 4x + 14$

This is now an easy curve to draw ($y = x^2$ that has moved 2 units left and 10 units up). The turning point of this quadratic is to the left and well above anything in x^3, so the only solution is the first intersection of the two curves in the upper right quadrant around $(3.4, 39)$.

35. C

The easiest way to solve this is to sketch them (don't waste time solving them algebraically). As soon as you've done this, it'll be very obvious that $y = 2$ and $y = 1{-}x^2$ don't intersect, since the latter has its turning point at $(0, 1)$ and zero points at $x = -1$ and 1. $y = x$ and $y = x^2$ intersect at the origin and $(1, 1)$, and $y = 2$ runs through both.

36. B

Notice that you're not required to get the actual values – just the number's magnitude. Thus, 897,653 can be approximated to 900,000 and 0.009764 to 0.01. Therefore, $900{,}000 \times 0.01 = 9{,}000$ which is closest to 8,764.68 (answer B).

37. C

Multiply initial equation by the product of the denominators of both fractions (i.e., 70):

$7(7x + 3) + 10(3x + 1) = 14 \times 70$

Simplify: $49x + 21 + 30x + 10 = 980$

$79x + 31 = 980$

$x = \frac{949}{79}$

38. A

Split the equilateral triangle into 2 right-angled triangles and apply Pythagoras' theorem to find height of equilateral triangle.

$x^2 = \left(\frac{x}{2}\right)^2 + h^2$. Thus $h^2 = \frac{3}{4}x^2$

$h = \sqrt{\frac{3x^2}{4}} = \frac{\sqrt{3x^2}}{2}$

The area of a triangle $= \frac{1}{2} \times base \times height = \frac{1}{2}x\frac{\sqrt{3x^2}}{2}$

Simplifying gives: $x\frac{\sqrt{3x^2}}{4} = x\frac{\sqrt{3}\sqrt{x^2}}{4} = \frac{x^2\sqrt{3}}{4}$

39. A

This is a question testing your ability to spot 'the difference between two squares'.

Factorise to give: $3 - \frac{7x(5x-1)\,(5x+1)}{(7x)^2(5x+1)}$

Cancel out: $3 - \frac{5x-1}{7x}$

40. C

The easiest way to do this is to 'complete the square':

$(x-5)^2 = x^2 - 10x + 25$

Thus, $(x-5)^2 - 125 = x^2 - 10x - 100 = 0$

Therefore, $(x-5)^2 = 125$

$x - 5 = \pm\sqrt{125} = \pm\sqrt{25}\sqrt{5} = \pm 5\sqrt{5}$

$x = 5 \pm 5\sqrt{5}$

41. B

Factorise by completing the square:

$x^2 - 4x + 7 = (x-2)^2 + 3$

Simplify: $(x-2)^2 = y^3 + 2 - 3$

$x - 2 = \pm\sqrt{y^3 - 1}$

$x = 2 \pm \sqrt{y^3 - 1}$

42. D

Square both sides to give: $(3x+2)^2 = 7x^2 + 2x + y$

Thus: $y = (3x+2)^2 - 7x^2 - 2x = (9x^2 + 12x + 4) - 7x^2 - 2x$

$y = 2x^2 + 10x + 4$

43. C

This is a fourth order polynomial, which you are unlikely to be expected to be able factorise immediately. This is where looking at the options makes your life a lot easier. First notice that all the possible answers have the same basic structure $y = \pm 1 + (...)^{\frac{1}{4}}$. As a result, in all of the possible answers you can start with the same two steps, rearranging the equation and opening up the brackets on the right side.

In doing this the left side becomes $(y \pm 1)^4$, i.e., the answers are hinting that $(y \pm 1)^4$ is the solution to the fourth order polynomial.

Since there are negative terms in the equations (e.g., $-4y^3$) there must be a negative number to create a negative product.

So, of $(y-1)^4$ or $(y+1)^4$ the solution has to be $(y-1)^4$

Now expand the brackets to get $y^4 - 4y^3 + 6y^2 - 4y + 1$ which is 1 off our original equation

Therefore, $(y-1)^4 + 1 = x^5 + 7$

Thus, $y - 1 = (x^5 + 6)^{\frac{1}{4}}$

$y = 1 + (x^5 + 6)^{\frac{1}{4}}$

44. A

Let the width of the television be $4x$ and the height of the television be $3x$.

Then by Pythagoras: $(4x)^2 + (3x)^2 = 50^2$

Simplify: $25x^2 = 2500$

Thus: $x = 10$. Therefore: the screen is 30 inches by 40 inches, i.e., the area is 1,200 inches².

45. C

Square both sides to give: $1 + \frac{3}{x^2} = (y^5 + 1)^2$

Multiply out: $\frac{3}{x^2} = (y^{10} + 2y^5 + 1) - 1$

Thus: $x^2 = \frac{3}{y^{10} + 2y^5}$

Therefore: $x = \sqrt{\dfrac{3}{y^{10} + 2y^5}}$

46. C

The easiest way is to double the first equation and triple the second to get:

$6x - 10y = 20$ and $6x + 6y = 39$

Subtract the first from the second to give: $16y = 19$

Therefore, $y = \frac{19}{16}$.

Substitute back into the first equation to give $x = \frac{85}{16}$.

47. C

This is fairly straightforward; the first inequality is the easier one to work with: B and D and E violate it, so we just need to check A and C in the second inequality.

C: $1^3 - 2^2 < 3$ but A: $2^3 - 1^2 > 3$

48. B

Whilst this can be done graphically, it's quicker to do algebraically (because the second equation is not as easy to sketch). Intersections occur where the curves have the same coordinates.

Thus: $x + 4 = 4x^2 + 5x + 5$

Simplify: $4x^2 + 4x + 1 = 0$

Factorise: $(2x + 1)(2x + 1) = 0$

Thus, the two graphs only intersect once at $x = -\frac{1}{2}$

49. D

It's better to do this algebraically as the equations are easy to work with and you would need to sketch very accurately to get the answer. Intersections occur where the curves have the same coordinates. Thus: $x^3 = x$

$x^3 - x = 0$

Thus: $x(x^2 - 1) = 0$

Spot the 'difference between two squares': $x(x + 1)(x - 1) = 0$

Thus, there are **3** intersections: at $x = 0, 1$ and -1

50. E

Note that the line is the hypotenuse of a right-angled triangle with one side unit length and one side of length $\frac{1}{2}$.

By Pythagoras, $\left(\frac{1}{2}\right)^2 + 1^2 = x^2$

Thus, $x^2 = \frac{1}{4} + 1 = \frac{5}{4}$

$x = \sqrt{\frac{5}{4}} = \frac{\sqrt{5}}{\sqrt{4}} = \frac{\sqrt{5}}{2}$

51. D

The general principle at hand is to rearrange the equations progressively substituting them into each other to eliminate terms. Below is an example of how we could do this.

First multiply $x + y - z = -1$ (equation 1) by 3 $\quad\quad$ $3x + 3y - 3z = -3$

Add new equation 1 to equation 2 to get rid of z $\quad\quad$ $2x - 2y + 3z + (3x + 3y - 3z) = 8 + (-3)$

We can simplify this and call it equation 4 $\quad\quad$ $5x + y = 5$

Now create a second equation with only two unknowns

As before, start by multiplying equation 1 this time by 2 $\quad$ $2x + 2y - 2z = -2$

Add new equation 1 to equation 3 to get rid of z $\quad\quad$ $2x - y + 2z + (2x + 2y - 2z) = 9 + (-2)$

We can simplify this and call it equation 5 $\quad\quad$ $4x + y = 7$

Now we have two equations with two only unknowns so we can substitute to get the value of x and y

Rearrange equation 4 and substitute it into equation 5 $\quad$ $4x + (5 - 5x) = 7$

Simplify to obtain x $\quad\quad$ $x = -2$

Substitute the value of x into equation 4 or 5 to get y $\quad$ $4 \times -2 + y = 7$

Simplify to obtain y $\quad\quad$ $y = 15$

Substitute x and y back in to calculate z: $\quad\quad$ $(-2) + (15) - z = -1$

Simplify to obtain z $\quad\quad$ $z = 14$

52. D

This is one of the easier questions. Take $3a$ as a factor to give:
$$3a(a^2 - 10a + 25) = 3a(a - 5)(a - 5) = 3a(a - 5)^2$$

53. B

Note that 12 is the lowest common multiple of 3 and 4. Thus:

Multiply the first equation by -3 $\quad\quad$ $-3(4x + 3y) = -3(48)$

Multiply the second equation by 4 $\quad\quad$ $4(3x + 2y) = 4(34)$

Add the two equations together to get rid of x $\quad\quad$ $-(12x + 9y) + 12x + 8y = -144 + 136$

Simplify to find y $\quad\quad$ $y = 8$

Substitute y back in: $\quad\quad$ $4x + 3(8) = 48$

Simplify to find x $\quad\quad$ $x = 6$

54. E

Don't be fooled, this is an easy question, just obey BODMAS and don't skip steps.

$\frac{-(25-28)^2}{-36+14} = \frac{-(-3)^2}{-22}$

This gives: $\frac{-(9)}{-22} = \frac{9}{22}$

55. E

Since there are 26 possible letters for each of the 3 letters in the license plate, and there are 10 possible numbers (0 to 9) for each of the 3 numbers in the same plate, then the number of license plates would be:
$26 \times 26 \times 26 \times 10 \times 10 \times 10 = 17{,}576{,}000$

Because the range of answers is wide instead of calculating 26^3 you can also save time by realising that to $20^3 \times 10^3 = 8{,}000{,}000$ and $30^3 \times 10^3 = 27{,}000{,}000$ so the correct answer must be between these two figures.

56. B

Expand the brackets to give: $4x^2 - 12x + 9 = 0$.
Factorise: $(2x - 3)(2x - 3) = 0$.
Thus, only one solution exists, $x = 1.5$
Note that you could also use the fact that the discriminant, $b^2 - 4ac = 0$ to get the answer.

57. C

$$= \left(x^{\frac{1}{2}}\right)^{\frac{1}{2}} (y^{-3})^{\frac{1}{2}}$$

$$= x^{\frac{1}{4}} y^{-\frac{3}{2}} = \frac{x^{\frac{1}{4}}}{y^{\frac{3}{2}}}$$

58. A

Let x, y, and y represent the rent for the 1-bedroom, 2-bedroom, and 3-bedroom flats, respectively. We can write 3 different equations: 1 for the rent, 1 for the repairs, and the last one for the statement that the 3-bedroom unit costs twice as much as the 1-bedroom unit.

Rent for all three flats	$x + y + z = 1240$
Total cost of repairs	$0.1x + 0.2y + 0.3z = 276$
Rent of flat 1 relative to rent for flat 3	$z = 2x$

Substitute $z = 2x$ into the other equations to eliminate z.

Call this equation 4	$x + y + 2x = 1240$
Call this equation 5	$0.1x + 0.2y + 0.3(2x) = 276$
Multiply equation 4 by -2, we can call this equation 6.	$-6x - 2y = -1480$
Multiply equation 5 by 10, we can call this equation 7.	$10x + 2y + 6x = 2760$
Add equations 6 and 7	$10x + 2y + 6x - 6x - 2y = 2760 - 1480$
Now simplify for x	$x = 280$
We can now use equations 1 and 3 to solve for y and z	$z = 2(280) = 560$
	$280 + 560 + y = 1240$
	$y = 400$

59. C

Following BODMAS:

$$= 5 \left[5(6^2 - 5 \times 3) + 400^{\frac{1}{2}}\right]^{\frac{1}{3}} + 7$$

$$= 5 \left[5(36 - 15) + 20\right]^{\frac{1}{3}} + 7$$

$$= 5 \left[5(21) + 20\right]^{\frac{1}{3}} + 7$$

$$= 5(105 + 20)^{\frac{1}{3}} + 7$$

$$= 5(125)^{\frac{1}{3}} + 7$$

$$= 5(5) + 7$$

$$= 25 + 7 = 32$$

60. B

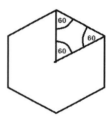

Consider a triangle formed by joining the centre to two adjacent vertices. Six similar triangles can be made around the centre – thus, the central angle is 60 degrees. Since the two lines forming the triangle are of equal length, we have 6 identical equilateral triangles in the hexagon. If this intuition is not clear remember that since the lines are of equal length their opposing angles must be the same and since the other angle is $60°$ then the remaining two angles are also $60°$ (i.e., $\frac{180° - 60°}{2} = 60°$).

Now split the triangle in half and apply Pythagoras' theorem:

$$1^2 = 0.5^2 + h^2$$

Thus, $h = \sqrt{\frac{3}{4}} = \frac{\sqrt{3}}{2}$

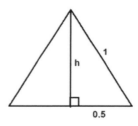

Thus, the area of the triangle is: $\frac{1}{2}bh = \frac{1}{2} \times 1 \times \frac{\sqrt{3}}{2} = \frac{\sqrt{3}}{4}$

Therefore, the area of the hexagon is: $\frac{\sqrt{3}}{4} \times 6 = \frac{3\sqrt{3}}{2}$

61. B

Let x be the width and $x + 19$ be the length.

Thus, the area of a rectangle is $x(x + 19) = 780$

Therefore:

$$x^2 + 19x^2 - 780 = 0$$

$$(x - 20)(x + 39) = 0$$

$$x = 20 \text{ or } x = -39$$

Since length can never be a negative number, we disregard $x = -39$ and use $x = 20$. So, the width is 20 and the length is 39 metres.

62. B

If you are familiar with Pythagorean triples you should be able to immediately identify the answer as B. The second quickest way to solve is by trial and error, substituting the provided options. However, if you're keen to do this algebraically, you can do the following.

Establish the equation for the perimeter	$2L + 2W = 34$
Establish the equation for the diagonal (using Pythagoras)	$L^2 + W^2 = 13^2$
Simplify and rearrange the equation for the perimeter	$W = 17 - L$
Substitute into the equation for the diagonal	$L^2 + (17 - L)^2 = 169$
Expand the brackets and rearrange	$L^2 + 289 - 34L + L^2 - 169 = 0$
Simplify and factorise	$2L^2 - 34L + 120 = 0$
	$(L-5)(L - 12) = 0$
	$L = 5, L = 12$
	$W = 12, W = 5$

63. C

Multiply both sides by 8:	$4(3x - 5) + 2(x + 5) = 8(x + 1)$
Remove brackets:	$12x - 20 + 2x + 10 = 8x + 8$
Simplify:	$14x - 10 = 8x + 8$
Add 10:	$14x = 8x + 18$
Subtract $8x$:	$6x = 18$
Therefore:	$x = 3$

64. C

Recognise that 1.742×3 is 5.226. Now, the original equation simplifies to: $= \frac{3\times10^6 + 3\times10^5}{10^{10}}$
$= 3 \times 10^{-4} + 3 \times 10^{-5} = 3.3 \times 10^{-4}$

65. A

$Area = \frac{(2 + \sqrt{2})(4 - \sqrt{2})}{2}$

$= \frac{8 - 2\sqrt{2} + 4\sqrt{2} - 2}{2}$

$= \frac{6 + 2\sqrt{2}}{2}$

$= 3 + \sqrt{2}$

66. C

Square both sides:	$\frac{4}{x} + 9 = (y - 2)^2$
Open the brackets and rearrange	$\frac{4}{x} = y^2 - 4y + 4 - 9$
Factorise	$\frac{4}{x} = (y + 1)(y - 5)$
Rearrange	$x = \frac{4}{(y+1)(y-5)}$

67. D

Set up the equation: $5x - 5 = 0.5(6x + 2)$

$10x - 10 = 6x + 2$

$4x = 12$

$x = 3$

68. C

Round numbers appropriately: $\dfrac{55 + (\frac{9}{4})^2}{\sqrt{900}} = \dfrac{55 + \frac{81}{16}}{30}$

81 rounds to 80 to give: $\dfrac{55 + 5}{30} = \dfrac{60}{30} = 2$

69. D

There are three outcomes from choosing the type of cheese in the crust. For each of the additional toppings to possibly add, there are 2 outcomes: 1 to include and another not to include a certain topping, for each of the 7 toppings.

Thus, the number of different kinds of pizza is: $3 \times 2^7 = 3 \times 128 = 384$

70. A

Although it is possible to do this algebraically, by far the easiest way is via trial and error. The clue that you shouldn't attempt it algebraically is that rearranging the first equation to make x or y the subject leaves you with a difficult equation to work with (e.g., $x = \sqrt{1 - y^2}$) when you try to substitute in the second. Another way to solve is to notice that the equations are symmetric in x and y, i.e., the solution is when $x = y$. Thus $2x^2 = 1$ and $2x = \sqrt{2}$ which gives $\dfrac{\sqrt{2}}{2}$ as the answer.

71. C

$f(x) = 0 = 16x^4 + 32x^3 + 24x^2 + 8x + 1$

$(2x + 1)^4 = x^4$

This means that $2x + 1 = \pm x \implies x = -\dfrac{1}{3}$ or -1

72. B

Rearrange the equation: $x^2 + x - 6 \geq 0$

Factorise: $(x + 3)(x - 2) \geq 0$

You can also do a quick sketch to ensure you don't make a silly mistake with which way the sign is.

Thus, $y = 0$ when $x = 2$ and $x = -3$. $y > 0$ when $x > 2$ or $x < -3$.

Thus, the solution is: $x \leq -3$ and $x \geq 2$.

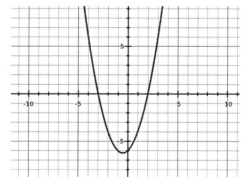

73. B

Using Pythagoras: $a^2 + b^2 = x^2$

Since the triangle is equilateral: $a = b$, so $2a^2 = x^2$

Area $= \frac{1}{2} base \times height = \frac{1}{2} a^2$. From above, $a^2 = \frac{x^2}{2}$

Thus, the area $= \frac{1}{2} x \frac{x^2}{2} = \frac{x^2}{4}$

74. A

If X and Y are doubled, the value of Q increases by 4. Halving the value of A reduces this to 2. Finally, tripling the value of B reduces this to $\frac{2}{3}$, i.e., the value decreases by $\frac{1}{3}$.

75. C

The quickest way to do this is to sketch the curves. This requires you to factorise both equations by completing the square:

$x^2 - 2x + 3 = (x - 1)^2 + 2$

$x^2 - 6x - 10 = (x - 3)^2 - 19$

Thus, the first equation has a turning point at $(1, 2)$ and doesn't cross the x-axis. The second equation has a turning point at $(3, -19)$ and crosses the x-axis twice.

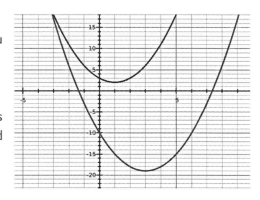

76. B

Let tail $= T$, body and legs $= B$ and head $= H$. We have already been told that $T = 30$kg.

As described in the question $H = T + 0.5B$ and $B = T + H$.

Therefore, substitute the second equation into the first as $H = 30 + 0.5(30 + H)$.

Re-arranging reveals that $0.5H = 45$kg and therefore the weight of the head is 90kg, the body and legs 120kg and as we were told the tail weighs 30kg.

Thus, giving a total weight of 240kg.

77. B

Expand the larger scientific number so that it reads 10 to the power 6 like so: $4.2 \times 10^{10} = 42000 \times 10^6$. Now that the powers are the same across the numerators, a simple subtraction can be performed $(42000 - 4.2) \times 10^6 = 41995.8 \times 10^6$ which can be simplified to 4.19958×10^{10}. Next consider the division which can be competed in a two-step process, first divide the numerator by 2 like so $\frac{4.19958}{2} \times 10^{10} = 2.09979 \times 10^{10}$ and then subtract the powers like so $2.09979 \times 10^{10-3} = 2.09979 \times 10^7$.

78. A

Note the triangle formed by the right-angle lines and the tangent. Recall that as this is a right-angle triangle then the other two angles must be 45°. As angles along a straight line add up to 180°, a must equal $180 - 45 = 135^0$. Angles around the origin must add up to 360° and therefore $b = \frac{360 - 90}{2} = 135^0$. Therefore, the correct answer is A.

79. B

The probability of drawing a blue ball is $\frac{1}{21}$ and the probability of drawing a black ball once the blue ball has been removed is $\frac{1}{20}$. So, the probability of drawing a blue ball and then a black ball is $\frac{1}{21} \times \frac{1}{20} = \frac{1}{420}$. However, note that it is also possible that these balls could also be drawn out in the opposite order. Therefore, the probability must be multiplied by two giving an answer of $\frac{1}{420} \times 2 = \frac{2}{420} = \frac{1}{210}$.

80. D

To answer this, you need to change one equivalent function to another:

$$y = 9x^{-\frac{1}{3}} = \frac{9}{x^{\frac{1}{3}}} = \frac{9}{\sqrt[3]{x}}$$

81. B

Start by multiplying each term by ax to give: $a(y + x) = x^2 + a^2$

Expand the brackets: $ay + ax = x^2 + a^2$

Subtract ax from both sides $ay = x^2 + a^2 - ax$

Lastly, divide the both sides by a to get: $y = \frac{x^2 + a^2 - ax}{a}$

82. A

The equation for a circle, with centre at the origin and radius r is $x^2 + y^2 = r^2$

The equation of this circle is therefore $x^2 + y^2 = 25$

Solve the problem using simultaneous equations or by drawing the line onto the graph.

$x^2 + (3x - 5)^2 = 25$

This simplifies to $10x^2 - 30x = 0$

$10x(x - 3) = 0$

So $x = 3$ or $x = 0$ where the two graphs intersect

83. C

Number of annual flights = Flights per hour × Number of hours in one year × Number of airports

$= 4 \times (24 \times 365) \times 1000$

$= 96 \times 365 \times (1000)$

$\approx 100 \times 365 \times 10 \times 100$

$= 365 \times 10^5 = 36.5$ million

84. E

The way to solve this is to break the calculation down into parts, almost working backwards.

The number of seconds in 66 weeks is given by: $= 60 \times 60 \times 24 \times 7 \times 66$: ($i.e., seconds \times minutes \times hours \times days \times weeks$).

From there you can break the numbers down by their factors and rearrange them to get the correct factorial.

$= (2 \times 3 \times 10) \times (12 \times 5) \times (4 \times 6) \times 7 \times (11 \times 6)$

Because you know that 11 is a prime number you can infer that it will have to be part of the final factorial – i.e., the final factorial has to be at least 11! To determine whether the answer is 11! or 12! continue to rearrange.

$= 2 \times 3 \times 4 \times 5 \times 6 \times 7 \times 10 \times 11 \times (12 \times 6)$

$= 2 \times 3 \times 4 \times 5 \times 6 \times 7 \times 10 \times 11 \times (3 \times 4 \times 2 \times 3)$

$= 2 \times 3 \times 4 \times 5 \times 6 \times 7 \times 10 \times 11 \times (9 \times 8)$

Because $\times 1$ is a factor of all our numbers and the product will remain the same we can introduce a $\times 1$ to make the factorial complete

$= 1 \times 2 \times 3 \times 4 \times 5 \times 6 \times 7 \times 8 \times 9 \times 10 \times 11 = 11!$

85. A

Write $\frac{\sqrt{20}-2}{\sqrt{5}+3}$ in the form $p\sqrt{5} + q$

When asked to simplify an equation a good place to start is by simplifying any square root functions.

In this case you can write $\sqrt{20}$ as $2\sqrt{5}$ because $\sqrt{20} = \sqrt{4 \times 5}$ and $\sqrt{4} = 2$.

Now you have an equation in the form $\frac{2\sqrt{5}-2}{\sqrt{5}+3}$

To convert this equation from a fraction to you can multiply the term by $\frac{\sqrt{5}-3}{\sqrt{5}-3}$ (i.e., 1) this will make the equation easier to rearrange.

$\frac{(2\sqrt{5}\times\sqrt{5})+(-3\times2\sqrt{5})+(-2\times\sqrt{5})+(-2\times-3)}{(\sqrt{5}\times\sqrt{5})+(3\sqrt{5})-(3\sqrt{5})+(3\times-3)} = \frac{10-6\sqrt{5}-2\sqrt{5}+6}{5-9}$

$\frac{16-8\sqrt{5}}{-4}$

$2\sqrt{5} - 4$

Therefore $p = 2$ and $q = -4$

86. C

ABC and DBE are similar triangles because all of the angles are equal.

Therefore: $\frac{BE}{BC} = \frac{DE}{AC}$

This is the case because the side lengths of the small and large triangles are in proportion to each other. Substitute the side lengths into the expression:

$\frac{4}{6} = \frac{DE}{9}$

$DE = 6$cm

87. C

The formula for calculating compound interest can be given as

$Final\ Amount = Investment \times (1 + \frac{annual\ interest\ rate}{n})^{nt}$

Where n = number of times interest is compounded per unit of time t, and t = the unit of time over which the investment is made. Because in this case the interest compounds annually (i.e., n = 1) we can simplify this to

$Final\ Amount = Investment \times (1 + annual\ interest\ rate)^{years}$

By substituting the numbers given in the question into this equation we get

$1687.5 = 500 \times (1 + annual\ interest\ rate)^3$

As you can see rearranging this formula to $\sqrt[3]{\frac{1687.5}{500}} = (1 + annual\ interest\ rate)$ does not make it easy for you

to find an answer without a calculator. Instead try plugging the answers into $500 \times (1 + annual\ interest\ rate)^3$ and work by a process of elimination starting from the median answer, if the answer is too high, try a lower interest rate, if the answer is too low, try a higher interest rate.

In this instance this tactic would lead you to

$500 \times (1 + 0.5)^3$

$500 \times 3.375 = 1687.5$

88. B

To win one game, Rupert must win one squash game and one tennis game. In order to calculate the probability one winning one game, it is necessary to add the probability of winning one tennis game and losing one squash game to the probability of losing one tennis game and winning one squash game. So $(\frac{3}{4} \times \frac{2}{3}) + (\frac{1}{4} \times \frac{1}{3}) = \frac{7}{12}$

89. C

The formula for the sum of internal angles in a regular polygon is given by: $180(n - 2)$, where n is the number of sides of the polygon.

$180(n - 2) = 150 \times n$

$180n - 360 = 150n$

$3n = 36$

$n = 12$

Each side is 15cm so the perimeter is $12 \times 15cm = 180cm$

90. C

Put the numerator and the denominator in like terms: $2.5 \times 10^8 = 2 \times (1.25 \times 10^8)$

$\frac{(1.25\times10^{10}) + (1.25\times10^9)}{2\times(1.25\times10^8)}$

$\frac{10^2+10}{2} = \frac{110}{2} = 55$

Alternatively, if you recognise that all the terms share the common factor of 1.25×10^8 you could let

$y = 1.25 \times 10^8$ and solve for $\frac{100y + 10y}{2y} = 55$.

91. A

Equate y to give:

$2x - 1 = x^2 - 1$

$x^2 - 2x = 0$

$x(x - 2) = 0$

Thus, $x = 2$ and $x = 0$

There is no need to substitute back to get the y values as only option A satisfies the x values.

92. E

Firstly, deal with the term in the brackets: $3^3 = 27$.

$(x^{\frac{1}{2}})^3 = x^{1.5}$

$(3x^{\frac{1}{2}})^3 = 27x^{1.5}$

Next, divide by $3x^2$: $\frac{27}{3} = 9$

$\frac{x^{1.5}}{x^2} = x^{-0.5} = \frac{1}{\sqrt{x}}$

Answer $= \frac{9}{\sqrt{x}}$

93. C

The formula for the sum of internal angles in a regular polygon is given by the number of internal triangles in the shape. This can also be expressed as $180°(n - 2)$, where n is the number of sides of the polygon. So, the sum of interior angles of a pentagon can be calculated as $180°(5 - 2) = 540°$.

If the sum of the interior angles is $540°$ then each interior angle in the (regular) polygon is: $\frac{540°}{5} = 108°$

Therefore, angle a is $108°$.

Since angles around a point add up $360°$ we can calculate larger angle in the central quadrilateral by subtracting the two angles of a polygon $2 \times 108°$ from $360°$ this will give us $360° - (2 \times 108°) = 144°$.

Recalling that angles within a quadrilateral sum to $360°$, we can now calculate b. Because the quadrilateral has identical length sides (they are formed from the sides of the polygons) we also know that opposing angles will be of identical sizes.

Therefore, b can be calculated as $\frac{360° - (2 \times 144°)}{2} = 36°$.

The product of $36°$ and $108°$ is $3,888°$.

94. B

The ruler and the cruise ship look to be the same size because their edges are in line with Tim's line of sight. His eyes form the apex of two similar triangles. All the sides of two similar triangles are in the same ratio since the angles are the same, therefore:

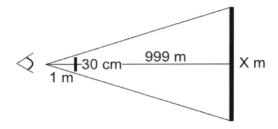

$$\frac{0.3 \text{ meters}}{x \text{ meters}} = \frac{1 \text{ meters}}{1 \text{ meters} + 999 \text{ meters}}$$

Thus, x meters $= 1000$ meters $\times \frac{0.3 \text{ meters}}{1 \text{ meters}}$

$1000 \times 0.3 = 300$ meters

95. C

Let Bob $= B$, Kerry $= K$ and Son $= S$.

$B = 2K$, $K = 3S$ and $B + K + S = 50$

$50 = 2K + K + \frac{K}{3} = \frac{6K}{3} + \frac{3K}{3} + \frac{K}{3}$

$50 = \frac{10K}{3}$

Hence: $10K = 150$

$K = 15$

$B = 2 \times 15 = 30$

$S = \frac{15}{3} = 5$

So: Bob's age when his son was born $= 30 - 5 = 25$.

96. B

The mean is the sum of all the numbers in the set divided by the number of members in the set. The sum of all the numbers in the original set must be: $11 \; numbers \times mean \; of \; 6 = 66$. The sum of all the numbers once two are removed must then be: $9 \; numbers \times mean \; of \; 5 = 45$. Thus, any two numbers which sum to $66 - 45 = 21$ could have been removed from the set. 6 and 9 are the only two number option available which does not sum to 21. This answer can also be obtained faster by skipping deriving the correct answer and simply noting that all correct answers will all sum to the same number and only B does not sum to 21.

97. B

Let $y = 3.4 \times 10^{10}$; this is not necessary, but helpful, as the question can then be expressed as:

$\frac{10y + y}{200y} = \frac{11y}{200y} = \frac{11}{200} = \frac{5.5}{100}$

$= 5.5 \times 10^{-2}$

98. C

The radius and tangent to a circle always form a right angle, so using Pythagoras:

$3^2 + 4^2 = x^2$

$x = 5$

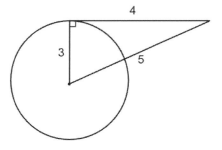

99. C
Solve as simultaneous equations
Start by rearranging equation A to $x = \frac{y}{3}$ and then substitute it into equation B.
This gives $y = \frac{18}{y} - 7$
Multiply every term by y to give:
$0 = y^2 + 7y - 18$
Factorise this quadratic to give:
$0 = (y + 9)(y - 2)$
Where the graphs meet, y is equal to 2 and -9.
Then $y = 3x$ so the graphs meet when $x = \frac{2}{3}$ and $x = -3$

100. B
Equate the volume with the surface area in the proportion instructed by the question. $3(\frac{4}{3}\pi r^3) = 4\pi r^2$, simplifies to $r = 1$.

101. B
The shortest distance between points A and B is a direct line. Using Pythagoras:
The diagonal of a sports field $= \sqrt{40^2 + 30^2} = \sqrt{1,600 + 900} = \sqrt{2,500} = 50$.
The diagonal between the sports fields $= \sqrt{4^2 + 3^2} = \sqrt{16 + 9} = \sqrt{25} = 5$.
Thus, the shortest distance between A and B $= 50 + 5 + 50 = 105$m.

102. F
$1 + (3\sqrt{2} - 1)^2 + (3 + \sqrt{2})^2$
$= 1 + (18 - 2(3\sqrt{2}) + 1) + (9 + 2(3\sqrt{2}) + 2)$
$= 31 - 6\sqrt{2} + 6\sqrt{2} = 31$

103. D
It is extremely helpful to draw diagrams to simplify this.
Shaded area = area of circle − area of square
The area of the circle is $\pi r^2 = 3 \times 12 = 3$cm^2.
We don't know the side length of the square, but we do know the length of the diagonal is 2cm, splitting the shape into two triangles.
The hypotenuse is therefore $= radius \times 2 = 2$
Using Pythagoras' theorem, $2^2 = x^2 + x^2$ (where $x = $ *length and width of square*)
Hence $2x^2 = 4$
$x^2 = 2 = $ the area of the square
Therefore, the shaded area $= 3 - 2 = 1$cm².

104. D

The first step is to multiply out $(3p + 5)^2$

$(3p + 5)(3p + 5) = 24p + 49$

$9p^2 + 30p + 25 = 24p + 49$

$9p^2 + 6p - 24 = 0$

Then put the quadratic into brackets.

$(3p + 6)(3p - 4) = 0$

Therefore, p must equal -6 or 4.

105. E

From the rules of angles made by intersections with parallel lines, all of the angles marked with the same letter are equal. There is no way to find if $d = 90°$, only that $b + d = c = 180° - a = 135°$, so b is unknown.

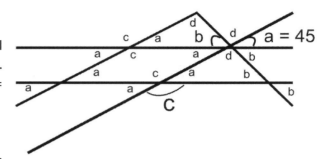

106. B

We know that the product of slopes of perpendicular lines equals -1. Therefore:

$(n + 1)(n + 3) = -1.$

$n^2 + 4n + 3 = -1$

$n^2 + 4n + 4 = 0$

Factorising gives $(n + 2)(n + 2)$, therefore $n = -2$ for the lines to be perpendicular.

107. C

The numerator of the fraction consists of 3 distinct terms all measured in metres (a unit of length). As this shows these 3 terms (all with units of metres) being multiplied together, we can assume the product of them results in a volume. (e.g., the volume of a cube is expressed as xyz)

108. E

Begin by drawing your line of best fit, remembering not to force it through the origin. Begin fitting the general equation $y = mx + c$ to your line. Calculate the gradient as $\frac{\Delta y}{\Delta x}$ and read the y intercept off your annotated graph.

109. C

Rather than converting all the fractions to decimals you just need to figure out the median of 7 numbers. Order the numbers by using their *relative* size to infer their position relative to the decimals.

$$0.25; \frac{7}{36}; 0.\dot{3}; \frac{11}{18}; 0.75; \frac{62}{72}; \frac{7}{7}$$

110. D

Working by orders of magnitude, multiply all the bacteria tested on the numerator and the number of resistances on the denominator. This gives an order of 10^{25}, which is the solution.

111. B

Solve $y = x^2 - 3x + 4$ and $y - x = 1$ as (x, y).

Substitute the quadratic expression into the other non-quadratic. You will get another equation.

$x + 1 = x^2 - 3x + 4$

Rearrange to get a quadratic equation and solve.

$x^2 - 4x + 3 = 0$

$(x - 1)(x - 3) = 0$

Therefore $x = 1$ or $x = 3$

Substitute your x values into the equation, $y - x = 1$ and solve to work out y values.

$y = 2$ or $y = 4$

Therefore, the coordinates are $(1, 2)$ and $(3, 4)$.

112. C

Transform all numbers into fractions then follow the order of operations to simplify. Move the surds next to each other and evaluate systematically:

$$= \left(\left(\frac{6}{8} \times \frac{7}{3}\right) \div \left(\frac{7}{5} \times \frac{2}{6}\right) \right) \times \frac{4}{10} \times \frac{15}{100} \times \frac{5}{100} \times \frac{5}{25} \times \pi \times \left(\sqrt{e^2}\right) \times e\pi^{-1}$$

$$= \left(\frac{42}{24} \div \frac{14}{30}\right) \times \frac{4 \times 3 \times 25}{10 \times 20 \times 100 \times 25} \times \pi \times \pi^{-1} \times e^{-1} \times e$$

$$= \left(\frac{21}{12} \div \frac{7}{15}\right) \times \frac{12}{200 \times 100} \times \frac{\pi}{\pi} \times \frac{e}{e}$$

$$= \left(\frac{21}{12} \times \frac{15}{7}\right) \times \frac{3}{50 \times 100}$$

$$= \frac{45}{12} \times \frac{3}{5000}$$

$$= \frac{9}{4} \times \frac{1}{1000}$$

$$= \frac{9}{4000}$$

113. B

There are several steps to working out this problem. The first is to work out the area of the entire floor, minus the fish tank and the cut out corner. The length of the room is 8m and the width is 4m. So, the area of the entire room is 32m².

The cut out corner is a square with the dimension 2×2m. Thus, the area of the cut out corner is 4m².

The fish tank is a circle, and thus its area can be worked out using πr^2. π is taken to be 3 and thus $3 \times 1^2 = 3$m². Therefore, the floor area, Bill needs to cover is $32 - (4 + 3) = 25$m².

We then need to work out the area of one plank. The dimensions of this are in cm and so we need to convert to m. 1m is 100cm and so we can say that the length of the plank is 0.6m and the width is 0.1m. Thus, the area is $0.6 \times 0.1 = 0.06$m².

To work out the number of planks, required, we need to divide the area of the floor space by the area of the plank. A quick way of doing this would be rounding the area of the room down to 24 and multiplying the area of the plank by 100 so it becomes 6. $24 \div 6 = 4$, then because we multiplied the area of the plank by 100, we then multiply the answer by 100 which gives us 400 planks. The closest answer to our solution is 417, which is listed as B.

114. A

$\frac{(16x+11)}{(4x+5)} = 4y^2 + 2$

$16x + 11 = (4y^2 + 2)(4x + 5)$

$16x + 11 = 4x(4y^2 + 2) + 5(4y^2 + 2)$

$16x - 4x(4y^2 + 2) = 5(4y^2 + 2) - 11$

$x(16 - 4(4y^2 + 2) = 20y^2 - 1$

$x = \frac{20y^2 - 1}{[16 - 4(4y^2 + 2)]}$

115. C

The question asks about the probability of getting at most 2 heads, with 4 coins. There are 16 total outcomes, with the distribution 1,4,6,4,1.

Therefore, the total probability is the sum of the following probabilities:

P(0 heads) $= \frac{1}{16}$

P(1 heads) $= \frac{1}{16} \times 4 = \frac{4}{16}$

P(2 heads) $= \frac{1}{16} \times 6 = \frac{6}{16}$

P(2 at most heads) $= \frac{1}{16} + \frac{4}{16} + \frac{6}{16} = \frac{11}{16}$

116. C

The probability of any 3 given throws giving the same given number is $\left(\frac{1}{6}\right)^3$. Now any number can be repeated 3 times, giving us $\left(\frac{1}{6}\right)^3 \times 6$. Now we count the ways we can place these 3 throws in the 5, this is just 5 choose 3, 10, giving $\left(\frac{1}{6}\right)^3 \times 6 \times 10 = \frac{10}{36}$. Now we have to discount the times that the other two numbers are the same as our given number. Fix a number n. The probability that in two throws, at least one of those yields n is just $\frac{11}{36}$, by counting the possibilities. (say n is 1, we get 11,12,13,14,15,16,21,31,41,51,61) for instance. So, the probability it is not is $\frac{25}{36}$, which we multiply our previous probability by, so our answer is $\frac{10}{36} \times \frac{25}{36} = \frac{125}{648}$

117. B

Obviously, this question could be done by brute force, but there is a much quicker way. $301^5 = (1 + 3 \times 10^2)^5$. If we treat this like a binomial expansion, we are looking for the coefficient of 10^5. If we look at the first few terms, $(301)^5 = 1 + 5 \times 3 \times 10^2 + 10 \times 9 \times 10^4 + 10 \times 27 \times 10^6 + \cdots$. The later terms will be too large, and it is clear here the only 10^5 term here will have coefficient 9.

118. A

This question relies on noticing the reason for not combining the constant terms inside each large square root: they are both square numbers. The expression is equal to $\sqrt{\left(5 - 2\sqrt{5}\right)^2} + \sqrt{\left(\sqrt{5} - 4\right)^2}$. As $\sqrt{}$ implies taking the positive root, we do have to determine whether these are positive or negative; $\sqrt{5} < \sqrt{9} = 3 < 4$, so it is clear that $4 - \sqrt{5} > 0$ but for the first, it is slightly closer. However, $2 < \sqrt{5}$ which means that $2\sqrt{5} < \left(\sqrt{5}\right)^2 = 5$, so $5 - 2\sqrt{5} > 0$. This means our sum is equal to $5 - 2\sqrt{5} + 4 - \sqrt{5} = 9 - 3\sqrt{5}$.

119. D

Possibly the simplest way to consider this problem is to look at the number of patients who will survive. From splitting the wards up, we know that the number of patients who will survive is $\frac{3p}{5} + \frac{q}{9}$. We also know it is $\frac{p+q}{4}$ by taking the number of people in the whole hospital, and the overall survival rate. By rearranging the fractions, we get $108p + 20q = 45p + 45q$; $63p = 25q$; $q = \frac{63p}{25}$.

120. C

The first thing to notice is these events are not mutually exclusive, so we cannot find their independent probabilities and multiply them. The easier to work with is the latter; the probability that we get 2 heads in the last three tosses is simply the probability the last three tosses come up as one of HHT, HTH or THH. Each of these is equally likely, with probability $\frac{1}{8}$, so the probability of this is $\frac{3}{8}$. If we know that both events occurred, then we must have gotten more than $(4 - 2) = 2$ heads in the first 4 tosses. This just means getting $2, 3$ or 4 heads in 4 tosses.

Each sequence is equally likely (with probability $\frac{1}{16}$) and the sequences which we care about are $HHHH$, $HHHT, HHTH, HTHH, THHH$, $HHTT, HTTH, HTHT, TTHH, THTH, THHT$. There are 11 of these.

Now, with this event described as "getting more than 2 heads in the first 4 tosses and 2 in the last 3 tosses", the events are independent, because there is no dependence of any 1 toss on any other. This means we can multiply probabilities, and we get the answer to be $\frac{11}{16} \times \frac{3}{8} = \frac{33}{128}$.

121. D

This is a problem about counting. The boxes are indistinguishable, which means we only care about how the balls are distributed, not specifically which boxes they are in. A good way to approach this is to have an order to the counting. We shall do it based on how many boxes are empty at the end:

No empty boxes– This is only true if there is 1 ball in each box, and there is only one way to do this.

One empty box – There must be two balls in 1 box and 1 in the other 3. The two balls could both be blue, both be red, or be 1 of each. (3 possible combinations).

2 – There are two possibilities here, a $3, 1, 1$ split, or a $2, 2, 1$ split. In the former case, the 3 balls could be all red, 2 red 1 blue, or all blue. Either way they uniquely determine the other balls. In the latter case, we consider where the two blue balls are; they could be in the same box, one could be in each of the boxes with 2 balls in, or one could be in a 2 box and the other in the 1 box. As there are no other ways to distribute the blue balls, this is an exhaustive list (6 possible combinations).

3 – All balls being only in 2 boxes means they are split $1, 4$ or $2, 3$. In the former, there are 2 possibilities, the single ball is red, or it is blue. In the latter, there are 3 possibilities for the box with two balls in, RR, BB or RB, but no matter what this also determines what is in the other box (5 possible combinations).

4 – Only one way, all the balls are in the same box (1 possible combination). Summing these possibilities, we have 16 ways.

122. B

The time between $08\!:\!34$ am and $11\!:\!12$ am is 158 minutes. For each minute that passes, the minute hand turns an angle of $360 \div 60 = 6°$. Therefore, the total angle turned is 158 mins $\times 6° = 948°$, and the answer is B.

123. D

The inflated football is spherical, so its volume is given by $\frac{4}{3}\pi r^3$ whilst the volume of the box containing the football is given by $(2r)^3 = 8r^3$. The ratio of the volume of the football to the volume of the box is therefore $\left(\frac{4}{3}\right)\pi r^3 : 8r^3$. This simplifies to $\frac{\pi}{6} : 1$, so the answer is D.

124. D

First, the scaling factor between the similar triangles must be calculated which is given by $24\text{m} \div 14\text{m}$. The length of the base of the larger triangle, x, can then be calculated by multiplying the length of the smaller triangle's base by the scaling factor: $4\text{m} \times 24\text{m} \div 14\text{m}$. Therefore, $x = 96 \div 14$ which is simplified to $48 \div 7$ or $6\frac{6}{7}$ m, so the answer is D.

125. D

The external angle of a pentagon is $360° \div 5 = 72°$. Which means that the internal angle is $180° - 72° = 108$. Drawing a line from point 4 to point 2 creates an isosceles triangle. The small opposite angles are therefore $\frac{180°-108°}{2} = 36°$. From point 4 to point 3 is due east (or 90° degrees), point 4 to 2 is 36° degrees less than this $(90° - 36°) = 54°$ degrees. To find the opposite bearing on a compass (point 2 to point 4) simply add 180° degrees to give 234° degrees. Therefore, the answer is D.

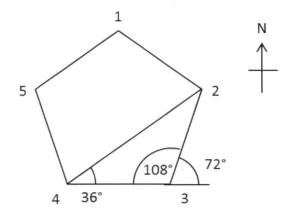

126. C

First x must be found:

$$(7x)^2 = \left(3\sqrt{6}\right)^2 - \left(2\sqrt{10}\right)^2$$

$$7x = \sqrt{54 - 40}$$

$$x = \frac{\sqrt{14}}{7}$$

Thus, the triangles base is:

$$9x = \frac{9\sqrt{14}}{7}$$

Therefore, to calculate the area, use $\frac{1}{2} \times base \times height$:

$$= \frac{9\sqrt{14}}{7} \times 2\sqrt{10} \times \frac{1}{2}$$

$$= \frac{18\sqrt{140}}{14}$$

$$= \frac{9 \times \sqrt{4} \times \sqrt{35}}{7} = \frac{18\sqrt{35}}{7}$$

Therefore, C is the correct answer.

127. B

First, the total area of the garden must be determined, and is calculated by $30m \times 20m = 600m^2$. The total white space is then calculated by calculating the area of each of the white rectangles and adding them together. The area of the larger rectangle is $8m \times 10m = 80m^2$, and the area of the smaller rectangle is $(20m - 8m) \times 4m = 48m^2$. The area of the grey space is then determined by subtracting the white area from the total area: $600m^2 - (80m^2 + 48m^2) = 472m^2$. The number of rolls of grass is then determined by dividing the grey area by $10m^2$ (as the rolls are 1m wide and 10m long so the area of each roll is $10m^2$): $472m^2 \div 10m^2 = 47.2$. As it is not possible to buy 0.2 rolls, 47.2 must be rounded up. Therefore, 48 rolls are required to cover the garden, and the answer is B.

128. B

There are $(3 + 2) \times 2 \times 4 = 40$ single shoes, half of which are left and half of which are right. After a left size 11 has been removed, there are 39 left. There are still $3 \times 4 = 12$ right size 11 shoes in the bag. Therefore, the probability of picking a size 11 right shoe is $\frac{12}{39}$ and the answer is B.

129. C

First, the surface area of a cylinder with radius 'r' and length '$3r$' is calculated by summing the surface area of each end and the middle section: $(2 \times \pi r^2) + (\pi \times 2r \times 3r) = 8\pi r^2$. The volume is given by the area of the cylinder end multiplied by the length: $(\pi \times r^2) \times 3r = 3\pi r^3$. Therefore, the surface area to volume ratio is $8\pi r^2 : 3\pi r^3$, which simplifies to $8 : 3r$. The answer is C.

130. C

The volume of a cylinder of radius r, height h, is $\pi r^2 h$. The surface area is made up of two circles of area πr^2 each and the curved surface area, which is equivalent to a rectangle of side lengths h & $2\pi r$. Thus, from the question, we know that $2 \times (2\pi r^2 + 2\pi rh) \leq \pi r^2 h \leq 3 \times (2\pi r^2 + 2\pi rh)$. We can cancel some terms here which are positive to get $2 \times 2(r + h) \leq rh \leq 3 \times 2(r + h)$. By substituting in the value known for h, we know that $4(r + 8) \leq 8r \leq 6(r + 8)$. By splitting this up into two inequalities, we can get two conditions for r; $4(r + 8) \leq 8r$ implies that $32 \leq 4r; r \geq 8$ and $8r \leq 6(r + 8)$ implies that $2r \leq 48; r \leq 24$. These must both be true simultaneously so $8 \leq r \leq 24$.

131. E

A tree diagram is very helpful in this situation.

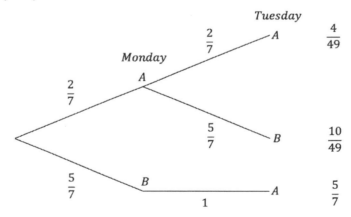

It can be seen that we have a $\frac{39}{49}$ chance of picking A on Tuesday. We also know we have a $\frac{4}{49}$ chance of picking A on Monday and picking it on Tuesday.

Because we know we picked A on Tuesday, we are only concerned with the outcomes AA and BA, as we know the other two did not occur. The probability that it was AA out of these two is then $\frac{P(AA)}{P(AA)+P(BA)} = \frac{\frac{4}{49}}{\frac{39}{49}} = \frac{4}{39}$.

132. B

For the man to walk his dog "at least once every two days", we know he never had two consecutive days which he <u>did not</u> walk the dog. So, representing going for a walk as W, and not going as N, the possible ways he spent his 4 days are $WWWW, WWWN, WWNW, WNWW, NWWW, NWNW, NWWN, WNWN$. These are not all equally likely as each W has $\frac{1}{3}$ chance of appearing, and each N has a $\frac{2}{3}$ chance. Thus, the probability that each set of 4 days occurred is $\frac{1}{81}, \frac{2}{81}, \frac{2}{81}, \frac{2}{81}, \frac{2}{81}, \frac{4}{81}, \frac{4}{81}, \frac{4}{81}$. As we only want to know the probability any one of these occurred, we can sum them, to get $\frac{1+2\times4+3\times4}{81} = \frac{21}{81} = \frac{7}{27}$.

133. B

The maximum straight line distance is from the front-bottom-left corner to the back-top-right corner (or another symmetrical orientation). The hypotenuse along the bottom face is calculated as $\sqrt{(3^2 + 4^2)} = 5$. The hypotenuse corresponding to the longest stick is $\sqrt{(5^2 + 5^2)} = \sqrt{50}$. This simplifies to $5\sqrt{2}$, so the answer is B.

134. A

Having already thrown a 6 is irrelevant. A fair die has equal probability $P = \frac{1}{6}$ for every throw.

For three throws: $P(6 \cap 6 \cap 6) = \left(\frac{1}{6}\right)^3 = \frac{1}{216}$

135. D

Total probability is sum of all probabilities:
$$= P(Y \cap Y \cap Y) + P(Y \cap Y \cap N) + P(Y \cap N \cap Y) + P(N \cap Y \cap Y)$$
$$= \frac{1}{60} + \frac{2}{60} + \frac{3}{60} + \frac{4}{60} = \frac{10}{60} = \frac{1}{6}$$

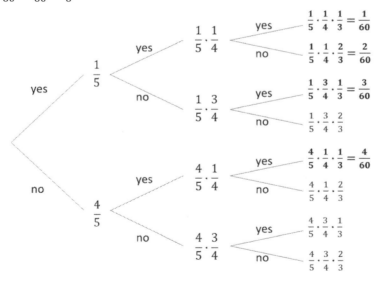

136. C

$$P[(A \cup B)'] = 1 - P[(A \cup B)]$$
$$= 1 - \{P(A) + P(B) - P(A \cap B)\}$$
$$= 1 - \frac{2+6-1}{8} = \frac{3}{8}$$

Worked Answers: Advanced Maths

1.   B

Factoring the given expression will prove fruitless. Instead, identify its stationary points. Differentiating, we see that $f'(x) = 4(x^3 - 6x^2 + 11x - 6) = 4(x - 1)(x - 2)(x - 3)$, which we factorise by inspection (or by using the factor theorem). Now we can establish $f(1), f(2), f(3)$, and using the asymptotic limits of $+\infty$ for both large positive and negative x, and the obvious root at 0, we have the following sketch., from which we see one positive root.

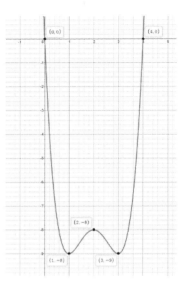

2.   A

We can factor the numerator as a difference of two squares $(\sqrt{x} + 2)(\sqrt{x} - 2)$, so

we the integral is just $\int_0^1 1 - 2x^{\frac{1}{2}} dx = \left[x - 4x^{-\frac{1}{2}}\right]_0^1 = -3$

3.   A

In the first expansion, the coefficient of x^4 is given by $\binom{7}{4}3^4 b^3 = 2835b^3$ and in the second, the coefficient of x^2 is $\binom{4}{2}(3b)^2 = 54b^2$, and equating, we see that $b = \frac{54}{2835} = \frac{2}{105}$

4.   D

First calculate the equation of the tangent. By differentiating, we find $\frac{dy}{dx} = 2x + b$, and so at $x = 2, \frac{dy}{dx} = 4 + b$. The equation is this $y - (4 + 2b) = (4 + b)(x - 2)$ using the equation for a straight line though the point $(2, 4 + 2b)$. Now the x intercept is found by setting y = 0, and we find this to be at $\frac{4}{4+b}$. Now letting this be greater than 4, we find that $b < -3$

5.   C

Note that the inside of the bracket is a perfect square and is simply $\left(3x + \frac{2}{x}\right)^2$.

So $f(x) = 3x + \frac{2}{x}$

$f'(x) = 3 - \frac{2}{x^2}$ and $f'(2) = \frac{5}{2}$

$f''(x) = \frac{4}{x^3}$ and $f''(2) = \frac{1}{2}$

$f'''(x) = -\frac{12}{x^4}$, and so $f'''(2) = -\frac{3}{4}$

6.   C

We may factorise the function as $(x-1)(x+1)(x+2)(x+4)$, which allows us to graph it.

From the graph we can see that in the range provided by option C, $-2 < x < -1$, correctly describes some of the solutions to this equation.

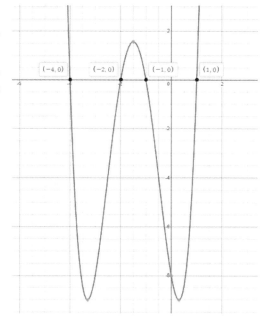

7.   A

Note $0.04 = \frac{1}{25}$. Consider the arithmetic series: $2 + 4 + 6 + \cdots + 2x = 2(1 + \cdots + x) = x(x+1)$, so the exponent on the left is $x(x+1) - 2$ So $5^{x(x+1)-2} = (5^{-2})^{-14} = 5^{28}$. Taking logs (to base 5): $x(x+1) - 2 = 28$, giving $x^2 + x - 30 = 0$, which has positive root $x = 5$.

8.   E

We have an arithmetic progression, and $x_{100} = x_1 + 99q$, giving $q = \frac{1}{9}$. The sum to infinity is thus $\frac{a}{1-r} = \frac{5}{1-\frac{1}{9}} = \frac{45}{8}$

9.   B

The roots are given by $\frac{-3 \pm \sqrt{9 - 4(c-2)}}{2}$, making the difference $\sqrt{9 - 4(c-2)} = 7$, gives $c = -8$

10.   D

The line of symmetry of $\sin(x)$ lie at $\frac{\pi}{2} + n\pi$, and so of $\sin(4x + \frac{\pi}{3})$ at $\frac{1}{4}\left(\frac{\pi}{2} + n\pi - \frac{\pi}{3}\right) = \frac{1}{4}\left(\frac{\pi}{6} + n\pi\right)$. Taking $n = 2$ gives $\frac{13\pi}{24}$

11.   A

This is an example of the Collatz Conjecture. Applying the rule a few times we get the sequence 12, 6, 3, 10, 5, 16, 8, 4, 2, 1, 4, 2, 1... and we see it repeats. We see $x_8 = 4, x_9 = 2, x_{10} = 1$, and from then on x_n depends only on the remainder when n is divided by 3. Since the remainder is 1 when dividing 100 by 3, we see the answer is 1.

12.   E

Let $x = \sqrt{2}^y$. Substituting in gives $x^2 - 10x + 24 = 0 \rightarrow (x-6)(x-4) = 0$, so $x = 4, 6$. Now $x = 2^{\frac{y}{2}}$ and so $y = 2\log_2 x$, so the sum of roots is $2(\log_2 4 + \log_2 6) = 2(2 + \log_2 2 + \log_2 3) = 2(2 + 1 + \log_2 3) = 6 + 2\log_2 3$

13. C

A good sketch will help. First find the intercept.

At the intercept $x = py^2 = p(px^2)^2 = p^3x^4$, and so $x(p^3x^3 - 1) =$ 0. Excluding the 0 solution, we see that $x = \frac{1}{p}$.

Now we must compute the area, which is the difference of two integrals.

We must invert $x = py^2$ to get $y = \sqrt{\frac{x}{p}}$, from which we compute the

area as $\int_0^{1/p} \sqrt{\frac{x}{p}} - px^2 dx$, which one can compute to give $\frac{1}{3p^2}$.

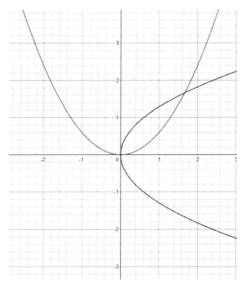

14. D

We can rewrite $\frac{x^2 + 2x}{\sqrt{x^3}}$ as $x^{\frac{1}{2}} + 2x^{-\frac{1}{2}}$.

Now differentiating we get $\frac{1}{2}x^{-\frac{1}{2}} - x^{-\left(\frac{3}{2}\right)}$.

We want this to be positive, i.e., $\frac{1}{2\sqrt{x}} - \frac{1}{x\sqrt{x}} > 0$

$\frac{1}{2} - \frac{1}{x} > 0$

$x > 2$

15. C

These are clearly circles. Completing the square on both gives equations of the circles

$(x - 2)^2 + (y - 4)^2 = 8$ and $(x + 2)^2 + (y + 3)^2 = 3$

So we have centre $(2,4)$ radius $2\sqrt{2}$, and centre $(-2,-3)$ radius $\sqrt{3}$.

The shortest distance lies on the line between the two centres, which has length $\sqrt{4^2 + 7^2} = \sqrt{65}$.

Now subtract the two radii.

So, the answer is $\sqrt{65} - 2\sqrt{2} - \sqrt{3}$.

16. C

Note that we may divide through by $\cos 2x$ to obtain the equation $\log x = \tan 2x$. We have to be careful though that we have no solutions when $\cos 2x = 0$, but this is clear since if $\cos 2x = 0$ then $\sin 2x = \pm 1$. Now draw a graph of $\log x$, and of $\tan 2x$ and count the number of intersections in the range. There are 5.

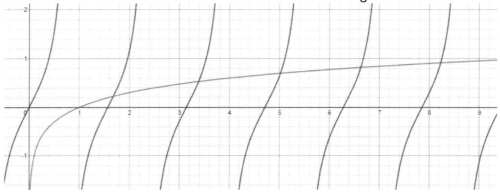

17. E

Let the first term of the GP be a and the ratio be r.

We have a system of two equations in 2 unknowns: $\frac{a}{1-r} = 4$ and $\frac{a^2}{1-r^2} = 10$. We want to find r. Rearrange the 2 equations as $a = 4(1-r)$ and $a^2 = 10(1-r^2)$.

Divide the second by the first to get $a = \frac{10}{4}\frac{(1-r^2)}{1-r} = \frac{10}{4}(1+r)$.

Now sub this back into our first equation to get $\frac{10}{4}(1+r) = 4(1-r)$

$10 + 10r = 16 - 16r$

$r = \frac{6}{26} = \frac{3}{13}$

18. B

If you know the chain rule, the integration is slightly less tedious, but if not, by expanding and then integrating we see that $V(t) = \frac{t^5}{5} + t^4 + 2t^3 + 2t^2 + t + c$.

$V(1) = 5$ gives $c = -\frac{6}{5}$.

Then $V(2) = \frac{236}{5}$

19. B

$S_3 = 18 = 3a + 3d$, so $a + d = 6$, which is also $a = 6 - d$.

We also know that $a + 4d = k$.

Thus $3d = k - 6$, $d = \frac{k}{3} - 2$.

The formula for $S_n = na + \frac{n(n-1)}{2}d = 6n - nd + \frac{n^2d}{2} - \frac{nd}{2}$

$6n - \frac{nk}{3} + 2n + \frac{n^2k}{6} - n^2 - \frac{nk}{6} + n = 9n - \frac{nk}{3} + \frac{kn^2}{6} - n^2$ (using the substitutions of a and d).

This last expression has only two terms which might be non-integers, $\frac{nk}{3}$ and $\frac{kn^2}{6}$.

To make the latter an integer for every value of n, k must be a multiple of 6, which also implies it is a multiple of 3. It is not necessary for k to have a factor of 18, as $k = 24$ works (common difference is 1, all terms integers which means all sums are integers). It is not necessary for k to be odd as it's a multiple of 6. Thus, the answer is I only.

20. A

Use trigonometric identities, $\cos 2x = 1 - 2\sin^2 x$, $\sin 2x = 2\sin x \cos x$.

This means that $\frac{\sin 2x}{1 - \cos 2x} = \frac{\cos x}{\sin x}$.

We then know the critical values of x are when $\cos x$ is equal to 0 ($x = \frac{n\pi}{2}$).

The other part of the expression has only 1 critical value at $x = \log_3 2$. All that's left to determine is whether they are positive or negative around these values.

$(3^x - 2)$ is increasing, so it must be below the x-axis before $x = \log_3 2$ and positive after.

We only need to consider $\frac{\pi}{2}$ which is the only critical value in range for this problem, and both $\sin x$ and $\cos x$ are positive at $x = 0$, so the graph must be positive before $x = \frac{\pi}{2}$ and negative after.

We are looking for where they have the same sign, and we know that $\log_3 2 < 1$ (as $\log_3 3 = 1$) so it must be $\log_3 2 \le x \le \frac{\pi}{2}$.

21. A

$25^{x-1} = 5^{2x-2} = \frac{(5^x)^2}{25}$ so, we make the substitution $y = 5^x$. This gives us $\frac{y^2}{25} + \frac{96}{25} = y$.

We can then immediately use the quadratic formula to get $y = \dfrac{1 \pm \sqrt{1 - 4 \times \frac{96}{25}}}{\frac{2}{25}} = \dfrac{25 \pm \sqrt{25^2 - 24^2}}{2}$.

Which means $y = 10$ or $y = 15$. i.e., $5^x = 10$ or $5^x = 15$.

$\log_5 10 = \log_5 5 + \log_5 2$ and $\log_5 15 = \log_5 5 + \log_5 3$

So, the difference is $\log_5 3 - \log_5 2 = \log_5 \left(\frac{3}{2}\right)$.

22. B

To find an equidistant line, we must find the line which joins the two centres, take its midpoint, and find the line through it with the perpendicular gradient.

The circles can be rearranged to be $(y+3)^2 + (x-2)^2 + 12 - 9 - 4 = 0 : (y+3)^2 + (x-2)^2 = 1$ and $(y-1)^2 + x^2 = 9^2$.

This means their centres are at $(2,-3)$ and $(0,1)$.

The joining line then has gradient $\frac{-3-1}{2-0} = -2$, so its perpendicular has gradient $\frac{1}{2}$.

We also know its midpoint is $\left(\frac{2+0}{2}, \frac{1-3}{2}\right) = (1,-1)$.

Finally, the line must be $y + 1 = \frac{1}{2}(x - 1)$

$y = \frac{x}{2} - \frac{3}{2}$.

23. B

To find the former, we follow the marble's path and calculate distances with Pythagoras.

The first movement has distance $\sqrt{(7-4)^2 + (2-6)^2 + (12-0)^2} = \sqrt{9 + 16 + 144} = \sqrt{169} = 13$.

The second movement has distance $\sqrt{81 + 169 + 25} = \sqrt{275} = 5\sqrt{11}$.

The overall distance is simply the distance from the first to the third point which is $\sqrt{144 + 81 + 49} = \sqrt{274}$.

The difference of the square of these distances is $\left(13 + 5\sqrt{11}\right)^2 - 274 = 169 + 130\sqrt{11} + 275 - 274$

$170 + 130\sqrt{11} = 10(17 + 13\sqrt{11})$.

24. A

We must first find the stationary points. So, as usual we differentiate, set to 0 and solve for x. $f'(x) = 15x^2 - 5 = 0$ tells us that $x^2 = \frac{5}{15}$

$x = \pm \frac{1}{\sqrt{3}}$.

To find the co-ordinates of the stationary points, we then find the corresponding y values.

$f\left(\frac{1}{\sqrt{3}}\right) = \frac{5}{3\sqrt{3}} - \frac{5}{\sqrt{3}} + 6 = 6 - \frac{10}{3\sqrt{3}}$ and $f\left(\frac{-1}{\sqrt{3}}\right) = \frac{-5}{3\sqrt{3}} + \frac{5}{\sqrt{3}} + 6 = 6 + \frac{10}{3\sqrt{3}}$.

The distance between the 2 points is found via Pythagoras as distance $= \sqrt{\left(\frac{2}{\sqrt{3}}\right)^2 + \left(\frac{20}{3\sqrt{3}}\right)^2} = \frac{2}{\sqrt{3}}\sqrt{1 + \frac{100}{9}} = \frac{2\sqrt{109}}{3\sqrt{3}}$.

25. D

The formula for x_{n+1} can be rewritten in the form $x_{n+1} = x_n^{-\frac{1}{2}}$.

We can then say that $x_{n+2} = (x_{n+1})^{-\frac{1}{2}} = x_n^{\frac{1}{4}}$.

What we have found is that $x_{n+k} = (x_n)^{\left(-\frac{1}{2}\right)^k}$.
As we know that $1000 = 999 + 1$,

$x_{1000} = (x_1)^{\frac{-1}{2^{999}}}$

$(10^3)^{-2^{-999}} = 10^{-3 \times 2^{-999}}$

26. A

We first determine what $f(x)$ is:

$(4x^2 - 7x + 1)(2x - q) = 8x^3 - 14x^2 + 2x - 4qx^2 + 7qx - q$

$f(x)$ divided by $(x + 2)$ is the same as

$f(-2) = 8 \times -8 - (14 + 4q) \times 4 + (2 + 7q) \times (-2) - q$

$= -31q - 124 = -31^2$

This gives us $q + 4 = 31$, so $q = 27$.

27. A

With integrals with modulus signs in, we typically split the integral range into the parts where the modulus function is defined properly.

$\int_0^2 |x - 1|(3\sqrt{x} - x\sqrt{x})dx = \int_0^1 (1 - x)(3\sqrt{x} - x\sqrt{x})dx + \int_1^2 (x - 1)(3\sqrt{x} - x\sqrt{x})dx.$

You can notice here that the integrand is identical except for a minus sign in the 2 integrals on the right. This means we don't have to integrate two different functions, only 1, and change what we substitute in as limits.

If we take the first integral, $\int_0^1 (1 - x)(3\sqrt{x} - x\sqrt{x})dx = \int_0^1 x^{\frac{5}{2}} - 4x^{\frac{3}{2}} + 3x^{\frac{1}{2}} dx = \left[\frac{2x^{\frac{7}{2}}}{7} - \frac{8x^{\frac{5}{2}}}{5} + 2x^{\frac{3}{2}}\right]_0^1.$

But we then know that the second integral is just $\left[\frac{2x^{\frac{7}{2}}}{7} - \frac{8x^{\frac{5}{2}}}{5} + 2x^{\frac{3}{2}}\right]_2^1.$

So, we simply calculate $2\left(\frac{2}{7} - \frac{8}{5} + 2\right) - \left(\frac{2 \times 2^{\frac{7}{2}}}{7} - \frac{8 \times 2^{\frac{5}{2}}}{5} + 2 \times 2^{\frac{3}{2}}\right) = 2\left(\frac{24}{35}\right) - \sqrt{2}\left(\frac{4}{35}\right) = \frac{48 - 4\sqrt{2}}{35}.$

28. B

The function is symmetric about 1, which means $\int_1^2 f(x)dx = \int_0^1 f(x)dx.$

This implies that $\int_0^2 f(x)dx = 2\int_0^1 f(x)dx.$

Making this substitution, we get a quadratic in $\int_0^1 f(x)dx$ with

$\left(\int_0^1 f(x)dx\right)^2 + 4\int_0^1 f(x)dx - 12 = 0 = (\int_0^1 f(x)dx + 6)(\int_0^1 f(x)dx - 2).$

This gives us $\int_0^1 f(x)dx = \int_1^2 f(x)dx = 2$ or $\int_1^2 f(x)dx = -6.$

29. A

It is not strictly necessary to expand these brackets to find the answer to this question, however that is how we'll solve it. $\left(\frac{x}{2}+1\right)^3 = \frac{x^3}{8} + \frac{3x^2}{4} + \frac{3x}{2} + 1$.

$f'(x) = \frac{3x^2}{8} + \frac{3x}{2} + \frac{3}{2}; f''(x) = \frac{3x}{4} + \frac{3}{2}$.

Then, to find $f''(2)$, we substitute in to get our answer; 3.

30. C

Instead of trying to calculate sums involving 5^3, we can treat this like a factorisation problem. We are told that $(4x-3)$ & $(x-5)$ are the only roots, so we can deduce their powers in the factorisation of $f(x)$ by looking at the constant term. $75 = 5^2 \times 3$ which means our polynomial must be equal to $(4x-3)(x-5)^2$. From here, we can simply expand this and find our answer; $(4x-3)(x-5)^2 = (4x-3)(x^2-10x+25) = 4x^3 + 53x^2 + 58x - 75$. Then our average is $\frac{4+53+58}{3} = \frac{115}{3}$.

31. D

We first differentiate the function, to get $f'(x) = 5ax^4 + 2x^3 + c$.

We are told this at $x = 1; 5a + 2 + c = -a^2$.

Our integral can be found in terms of a and c as well; $\int_0^2 f(x)dx = \left[\frac{ax^6}{6} + \frac{x^5}{10} + \frac{cx^2}{2}\right]_0^2 = \frac{32a}{3} + \frac{32}{10} + 2c$. First of all,

we can substitute for c to get $\int_0^2 f(x)dx = \frac{32a}{3} + \frac{32}{10} - 2a^2 - 10a - 4 = \frac{2a}{3} - \frac{4}{5} - 2a^2$.

This is a negative quadratic, so we can find its maximum point by completing the square. $\frac{2a}{3} - \frac{4}{5} - 2a^2 =$

$-2\left(a^2 - \frac{a}{3} + \frac{2}{5}\right) = -2\left(\left(a - \frac{1}{6}\right)^2 - \frac{1}{36} + \frac{2}{5}\right)$. The maximum value of this is therefore $\left(\frac{2}{5} - \frac{1}{36}\right) \times -2 = \frac{67}{18}$.

32. C

It cannot be $\frac{9+3\sqrt{6}}{2}$.

These three terms must be of the form ar^n for some a and some r, with $n \leq 7$. The ratio between any two of

them is $\frac{2}{3}$, which means $r = \frac{2}{3}$ or $r = \sqrt{\frac{2}{3}}$, as the terms could be consecutive or spaced two apart (they must be

evenly spaced due to the ratio between $1 : \frac{2}{3}$ and $\frac{2}{3} : \frac{4}{9}$ being equal).

If $r = \frac{2}{3}$, and if $a_0 = 1, S_\infty = \frac{1}{1-\frac{2}{3}} = 3$. But it may not start at 1. Starting at the term <u>before 1</u>, i.e., $\frac{3}{2}$, the sum would

be $3 + \frac{3}{2} = \frac{9}{2}$, and another further back $S_\infty = \frac{9}{2} + \frac{9}{4} = \frac{27}{4}$.

Alternatively, if we consider the starting point of 1 with $r = \sqrt{\frac{2}{3}}, S_\infty = \frac{1}{1-\sqrt{\frac{2}{3}}} = \frac{\sqrt{3}}{\sqrt{3}-\sqrt{2}} = \frac{3+\sqrt{6}}{3-2} = 3 + \sqrt{6}$. If we

consider starting at terms earlier than 1 as we did in the previous case, we must remember we can only take one

step backwards before $\frac{4}{9}$ is the 7th term. Thus, $3 + \sqrt{6} + \sqrt{\frac{3}{2}}$ is a possible solution but $S_\infty = \frac{\frac{3}{2}}{1-\sqrt{\frac{2}{3}}} = \frac{3\sqrt{3}}{2\sqrt{3}-2\sqrt{2}} =$

$\frac{3}{2}\left(3 + \sqrt{6}\right) = \frac{9+3\sqrt{6}}{2}$ is not a possible solution, as it would force $\frac{4}{9}$ to be the 8th term.

33. A

The right-hand side can be converted, by combining the fractions, into $\frac{6}{1-\sin^2 t}$, which is $6\sec^2 t$. Then, by integrating, we get $x = 6\tan t + A$.

Using the initial condition, $A = -\frac{6}{\sqrt{3}}$. Then, substituting $x = 6\left(\sqrt{3} - \frac{1}{\sqrt{3}}\right)$ at $t = \frac{\pi}{3}$. This simplifies to $4\sqrt{3}$, by combining and rationalising the denominator.

34. C

To find crossing points, we equate the two lines.

$mx + c = (x-3)^2 - 4 = x^2 - 6x + 5$

$0 = x^2 - (m+6)x + 5 - c$

The lines do not cross so there are no real solutions, thus $b^2 - 4ac < 0$

i.e., $(m+6)^2 - 20 + 4c = m^2 + 12m + 16 + 4c < 0$.

We want the values of m which are at the edges of the interval which are $m = \frac{-12 \pm \sqrt{144 - 64 - 16c}}{2} = -6 \pm \sqrt{20 - 4c}$.

Thus, the size of the interval is $R = 4\sqrt{5 - c}$. Rearranging we get $c = 5 - \frac{R^2}{16}$.

35. C

$f(1) = 0$ which means $(x-1)$ divides f.

We can get the rest of the polynomial by long division or inspection from

$3x^5 + 8x^4 + x^3 - 4x - 16 = (x-1)(ax^4 + bx^3 + cx^2 + dx + e)$.

By looking at the edge cases, $a = 3, e = 16$.

Then $b - a = 8, c - b = 1$ and $d - c = -4$.

From this we derive that $\frac{f(x)}{x-1} = g(x) = 3x^4 + 11x^3 + 12x^2 + 8x + 16$.

We then divide by $(x+2)$ in the same way, $3x^4 + 11x^3 + 12x^2 + 8x + 16 = (x+2)(ax^3 + bx^2 + cx + d)$ and again we find $a = 3, b + 2a = 11, c + 2b = 12, d + 2c = 8, 2d = 16$ to get $\frac{g(x)}{x-2} = h(x) = 3x^3 + 5x^2 + 2x + 8$.

Now, we are unsure what to do. However, knowing $f(a) = 0$ for some a does not mean it has only a simple root there. $h(-2) = 0$ still, so we can divide by $(x+2)$ again.

By inspection, or the previous method, this is $\frac{h(x)}{x+2} = j(x) = 3x^2 - x + 4$.

Checking the discriminant, $b^2 - 4ac = 1 - 48 < 0$ so this quadratic has no real roots.

Thus, 2 distinct real roots total, $x = 1, -2$.

36. G

$S_5 = 5a_0 + 10d$ (by the formula for sum of an arithmetic series) and $a_{10} = a_0 + 9d$.

This means, in the case of I, $a_0 = -\frac{d}{4}$.

This means that, whichever value a_0 has, the sequence will advance towards 0 initially.

This means that, eventually, a_n will have the opposite sign to a_0, which means the product of this term and a_0 would be < 0.

In the case of II, $a_0 = \frac{d}{4}$.

In this case and in III, this means that the sequence progresses away from 0 at all times. Thus, if the sequence began negative, it would remain so, and vice versa.

So, the product of any two terms will always be positive. So, the answer is II & III.

37. D

$(1 + 2kx)^2 = 1 + 4kx + 4k^2x^2$ is much smaller and easier to work with. If two of these coefficients are equal, either $1 = 4k$ $\left(so\ k = \frac{1}{4}\right), 1 = 4k^2 \left(so\ k = \pm\frac{1}{2}\right)$ or $4k = 4k^2 (so\ k = 0\ or\ 1)$.

We must then only check these values in the expansion of $(k + x)^5 = k^5 + 5k^4x + 10k^3x^2 + 10k^2x^3 + 5kx^4 + x^5$.

It is clear if $k = 0$ or $k = 1$ that there are equal coefficients here.

If $k = \frac{1}{4}$, the coefficients are $\frac{1}{1024}, \frac{5}{256}, \frac{5}{32}, \frac{5}{8}, \frac{5}{4}$ and 1, of which no two are equal.

If $k = \pm\frac{1}{2}$, the coefficients are $\pm\frac{1}{32}, \frac{5}{16}, \pm\frac{5}{4}, \frac{5}{2}, \pm\frac{5}{2}, 1$.

It is clear that there is in fact an equality, but only for $k = \frac{1}{2}$.

Thus, there are 3 valid values of k.

38. D

We can rearrange this equation to $3^{\tan 2x} = \frac{1}{x}$, which can then be turned into $\tan 2x = -\log_3 x$. We can count the number of solutions by the number of intersections of the respective graphs of these functions. As a note, we know that the x-intersection of $y = -\log_3 x$ is before the intersection of $y = \tan 2x$ purely because the former is always 1, the latter must be $\frac{\pi}{2}$, and $\frac{\pi}{2} > \frac{3}{2} > 1$. This then has 3 solutions in the given range.

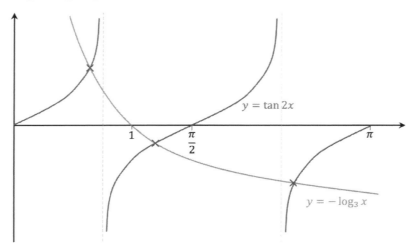

39. C

Knowing that the highest point of $y = 5 - |x - 1|$ will be at $x = 1$ tells you that point is at $(1, 5)$, which is above the line $y = |x - 4|$ as it is at $(1, 3)$ there. This tells you there are two intersection points, with a quick sketch.

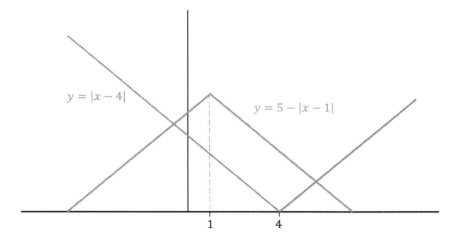

While this may or may not be to scale, it doesn't matter; we can see from the sketch that there is one intersection when both are in their first half, and one in their second half, whether the apex or base of either two graphs should be closer or further apart is irrelevant.

Thus, we solve $5 - (x - 1) = x - 4$ (gives $x = 5$) and $5 + x - 1 = 4 - x$ (gives $x = 0$).

These points are $(5, 1)$ and $(0, 4)$ respectively and using Pythagoras' Theorem tells us their distance is $\sqrt{(5 - 0)^2 + (1 - 4)^2} = \sqrt{25 + 9} = \sqrt{34}$.

40. A

The first integral will give us a relationship between a and b.

We have that $\left[\frac{x^4}{4} + \frac{ax^3}{3} + \frac{bx^2}{2} + x\right]$ which must be evaluated at 4 (as at 0, it is 0).

So, we have $64 + \frac{64a}{3} + 8b + 4 = 17 + \frac{16a}{3} + 2b = 0$ i.e., $b = -\frac{51 + 16a}{6}$.

We can then find the value of the 2nd integral in terms of a by evaluating our integrated expression at 3 and substituting for b.

We get $\frac{81}{4} + 9a - \frac{3}{4}(51 + 16a) + 3 = \frac{93}{4} - \frac{153}{4} - 3a = -3(a + 5)$.

We don't even have to differentiate here, this decreases as a increases, which means we want the smallest a possible. As the question says that $a \le 0$, this means we take $a = 0$ and get the integral to be -15.

41. D

$f(x) = \frac{x^4 - 2x + x^{-2}}{x^{\frac{1}{3}}} = x^{\frac{11}{3}} - 2x^{\frac{2}{3}} + x^{-\frac{7}{3}}$.

Then, $f'(x) = \frac{11x^{\frac{8}{3}}}{3} - \frac{4x^{-\frac{1}{3}}}{3} - \frac{7x^{-\frac{10}{3}}}{3} = \frac{x^{\frac{2}{3}}}{3}[11x^2 - 4x^{-1} - 7x^{-4}]$. Thus, $abc + pqr = 11(-4)(-7) + 2(-1)(-4) = 316$.

42. D

From the values given for the angles, we know that the angle at B is $45°$ or $135°$, and at C it is $60°$ or $120°$. This would imply at most 4 different triangles (if the length AB was not specified, it would be infinitely many as the size of the triangle wouldn't be specified), however we cannot be sure each exists. For example, if B and C take the larger values, the angles inside the triangle would sum to more than $180°$, which cannot occur. By drawing them out, with a side of fixed length and approximate angles at B and C, it can be seen the other three are all plausible. So, the answer is 3.

43. D

Typically, it is good to find out whether each of the values you have is larger or smaller than some reference value.
$1.4^2 = \frac{14^2}{100} = 1.96$, so perhaps 2 is a good reference value. $\sqrt{6} > \sqrt{4} = 2$; $\log_3 8 < \log_3 9 = 2$, $\frac{\sqrt{15}}{\sqrt{5}+1} < \frac{4}{\sqrt{5}+1} < \frac{4}{3} < 2$.

And $\frac{13}{6}$ is just greater than $\frac{12}{6} = 2$.

So, only two of our values are even greater than 2, so must only really compare them i.e., $\sqrt{6}$ and $\frac{13}{6}$.

We can simply square both to see that $\left(\frac{13}{6}\right)^2 = \frac{169}{36} = 4 + \frac{25}{36} < 5 < 6 = \left(\sqrt{6}\right)^2$.

So, as both are positive, we know $\sqrt{6}$ is the largest.

44. C

It is first crucial to find the equation of l_2. It is perpendicular to l so has gradient -3, and we know it intersects l at $y = 8$.
The x coordinate here is $3(8 - 3) = 15$.
So, the equation of l_2 is $y - 8 = -3(x - 15)$.
We can now split the area we are calculating into two triangles and a rectangle; the rectangle will be the simplest, with opposing corners at $(0,0)$ and $(15,3)$.
This lets our triangles be from the y-intersect of l to this corner to $(15,8)$, and from $(15,8)$ to $(15,0)$ to the x-intersect of l_2.
These have respective areas $3 \times 15 = 45$, $15 \times \frac{8-3}{2} = \frac{75}{2}$ and $\frac{8}{2} \times \left(\frac{53}{3} - 15\right) = \frac{32}{3}$.
The sum of these areas is our goal, which is $\frac{559}{6}$.

45. B

$\log_8 xy = \frac{1}{2} = \log_8 x + \log_8 y$

We can then substitute for $\log_8 y$ in the 2nd equation to get $(\log_8 x)(\frac{1}{2} - \log_8 x) = -5 = -(\log_8 x)^2 + \frac{\log_8 x}{2}$.

Making the substitution $z = \log_8 x$, we have a simple quadratic with solutions $z = \frac{-\frac{1}{2} \pm \sqrt{\frac{1}{4} + 20}}{2} = \frac{5}{2}\, or - 2$. This gives us solutions for x of $8^{\frac{5}{2}}$ and 8^{-2} which are $2^{\frac{15}{2}}$ and 2^{-6}.

46. E

This question is mostly an exercise in number manipulation. We first want to find out the area of the triangle. We would like to use $\frac{1}{2}ab\sin C$ but we have only one side length.

It is easiest to first use the sine rule to calculate side length $BC = a$.

This is then $\frac{a}{\sin 45} = \frac{500}{\sin 30}$

$a = 500\sqrt{2}\, mm$.

We can then use the cosine rule to calculate side length $AC = b$

$500^2 = 2 \times 500^2 + b^2 - 2 \times 500b\sqrt{2}\cos 30$

$0 = 500^2 + b^2 - 500b\sqrt{6}$.

This is a quadratic for b, where we get $b = 250\sqrt{6} \pm \sqrt{6 \times 250^2 - 4 \times 250^2} = 250(\sqrt{6} \pm \sqrt{2})$.

We know that the angle opposite this side is the largest angle in the triangle, so this must be the largest side, which means we take the positive root here.

So, $b = 250(\sqrt{6} + \sqrt{2})$.

We then use our formula for the area, to get area $= 250^2(\sqrt{6} + \sqrt{2})\sqrt{2} \times \sin 30 = 250^2(\sqrt{3} + 1)$.

47. D

The length of an arc of a circle is simply $r\theta$ where θ is the angle in radians of the sector and r is the radius. We know the radius of this circle is 2, so the angle between the lines from the centre of the circle to the two points this line intersects the circle is $\theta = \frac{7\pi}{12}$. This may not seem helpful initially, however we also can deduce the angle between the y-axis and the radius to the one intersection point we already know.

The intersection is at $x = \sqrt{3}$, the it is at $(\sqrt{3}, 3)$ or $(\sqrt{3}, 1)$. It is the lower point so $(\sqrt{3}, 1)$.

As the centre is on the y-axis, the angle a radius makes with the centre from this point is $\arctan\frac{\sqrt{3}}{1} = \frac{\pi}{3}$.

So, the angle it must make on the other side of the y-axis is $\frac{7\pi}{12} - \frac{\pi}{3} = \frac{\pi}{4}$. This means the right triangle to the intersection point is isosceles, and the hypotenuse is still 2 (it is a radius) so the 2nd intersection is at $(-\sqrt{2}, 2 - \sqrt{2})$. We can now calculate the equation of the line like any other, finding the gradient between the points and using one in the formula $y - y_1 = m(x - x_1)$.

We get $y = (\sqrt{6} - \sqrt{3} + \sqrt{2} - 2)x - \sqrt{18} + 2 - \sqrt{6} + 3\sqrt{3}$.

48. B

The first thing to do is expand this equation so we are working with a simple polynomial in t i.e., $\frac{dy}{dt} = 2t^{-3} + 3t^2 - t^4$.

We can immediately integrate both sides of this equation to get $y = -\frac{t^{-4}}{2} + t^3 - \frac{t^5}{5} + c$.

Using the point that we do know, we can substitute to find c. $2 = -\frac{1}{2} + 1 - \frac{1}{5} + c$; $c = 1 + \frac{1}{2} + \frac{1}{5} = \frac{17}{10}$. Then, we simply put this into our formula for y.

$y = -\frac{t^{-4}}{2} + t^3 - \frac{t^5}{5} + \frac{17}{10}$.

49. D

A stretch by a scale factor of 8 parallel to the x-axis is equivalent to $\frac{\log_7 8x}{3}$.

We are told this is the same as a translation in the y direction, which is equivalent to $\frac{\log_7 x}{3} + d$ for some value d.

We can see that $\frac{\log_7 8x}{3} = \frac{1}{3}(\log_7 8 + \log_7 x)$.

This means we have translated by $\frac{\log_7 8}{3} = \frac{3\log_7 2}{3} = \log_7 2$.

50. D

The shortest distance between two lines is always a straight line, that must be perpendicular to both lines. This means that this "shortest distance line" for a circle must be an extension of a radius of the circle. Because we are comparing two circles, the shortest distance line is an extension of both of their radii; the only time these are the same line is on the line connecting the centres of the two circles.

We can complete the square on both equations to obtain $(x - 7)^2 + (y - 2)^2 = 3^2$ and $(x + 3)^2 + (y + 4)^2 = 5^2$.

We can read off the centres of the 2 circles as $(7, 2)$ and $(-3, -4)$.

We then need only calculate distance between these two points $\sqrt{(7 - (-3))^2 + (2 - (-4))^2} = \sqrt{100 + 36} = 2\sqrt{34}$.

This value, minus the lengths of the 2 radii, is the distance between the two circles i.e., $2\sqrt{34} - 8$.

51. C

We first need to expand each bracket, giving:

$(2 - x)^2 = 2^2 + 2(2)(-x) + (-x)^2 = 4 - 4x + x^2$

$(2 + x)^4 = (2)^4 + 4(2)^3(x) + 6(2)^2(x)^2 + 4(2)(x)^3 + (x)^4 = 16 + 32x + 24x^2 + 8x^3 + x^4$

$(x - 2)^2 = (x)^2 + 2(x)(-2) + (-2)^2 = x^2 - 4x + 4$

$(2 - x)^2(2 + x)^4(x - 2)^2 = (4 - 4x + x^2)(16 + 32x + 24x^2 + 8x^3 + x^4)(x^2 - 4x + 4)$

$= (64 + 128x + 96x^2 + 32x^3 + 4x^4 - 64x - 128x^2 - 96x^3 - 32x^4 - 4x^5 + 16x^2 + 32x^3 + 24x^4 + 8x^5 + x^6)(x^2 - 4x + 4)$

$= (64 + 64x - 16x^2 - 32x^3 - 4x^4 + 4x^5 + x^6)(x^2 - 4x + 4)$

From the above, we can see that the x^3 term will be comprised of

$(64x)(x^2) + (-16x^2)(-4x) + (-32x^3)(4) = 64x^3 + 64x^3 - 128x^3 = 0$

OR

We first need to realise that $(2 - x)^2 = \left(-(x - 2)\right)^2 = (x - 2)^2$

$(2 - x)^2(2 + x)^4(x - 2)^2 = (2 - x)^4(2 + x)^4$

$(2 - x)(2 + x)(2 - x)(2 + x)(2 - x)(2 + x)(2 - x)(2 + x) = (2^2 - x^2)^4$

From the above expression, we know that all x terms will have even power. Hence, x^3 is zero.

52. A

$$\frac{1}{x^2+x-6} = \frac{1}{(x+3)(x-2)} = \frac{a}{(x+3)} + \frac{b}{(x-2)}$$

To find a and b, it is then:

$$ax - 2a + bx + 3b = 1;$$
$$a = -b \qquad (1)$$
$$3b - 2a = 1 \qquad (2)$$

Substitute (1) into (2):

$$3b - 2(-b) = 5b = 1$$
$$b = 0.2$$
$$a = -0.2$$

Hence:

$$\int_3^4 \frac{1}{x^2+x-6} dx = \int_3^4 \left(\frac{-0.2}{x+3} + \frac{0.2}{x-2}\right) dx$$
$$-0.2\ln(x+3) + 0.2\ln(x-2)]_3^4 = [-0.2\ln(7) + 0.2\ln(2)] - [-0.2\ln(6) + 0.2\ln(1)]$$
$$0.2[\ln(2) + \ln(6) - \ln(7) - \ln(1)] = 0.2\ln\left(\frac{2*6}{7*1}\right)$$
$$0.2\ln\left(\frac{12}{7}\right)$$

53. A

$$f'(x) = (-2)e^{-2x} + 2x$$
$$f''(x) = (-2)(-2)e^{-2x} + 2 = 4e^{-2x} + 2$$

54. D

First, we need to find the gradient of the tangent:

$$m = \frac{dy}{dx} = 6x$$
put $x = 1 \rightarrow m = 6$

Equation of the line:

$$y - y_1 = m(x - x_1);$$
$$y - 3 = 6(x - 1)$$
$$y = 6x - 3$$

55. C

Using division rule:

$$\frac{dy}{dx} = \frac{2(\cos(2x+5))(x^2+6x) - \sin(2x+5)(2x+6)}{(x^2+6x)^2}$$

56. B

This is a geometric progression with first term 1 and common ratio $\frac{1}{2}$.

Hence: $S_\infty = \frac{a}{1-r}$

$$\frac{1}{1-\frac{1}{2}} = 2$$

57. C

By factorisation, we can see that $x^3 - 7x + 6 = (x^2 + x - 6)(x - 1) = (x + 3)(x - 2)(x - 1)$.
The roots are then $x = -3, 2$ and 1.

58. B

$f'(x) = -2\sin x + 2x$

59. A

We first need to find the gradient of the tangent:

$m = \frac{dy}{dx} = \frac{1}{2}(8x - 4x^2)^{-\frac{1}{2}}(8 - 8x);$ put $x = 2$:

$m = \frac{8 - 8(2)}{2\sqrt{8(2) - 4(2)^2}} = \frac{-8}{2\sqrt{0}} \to \infty$

From this, we know that the tangent is going to be a straight vertical line.
Hence, the tangent is a line $x = 2$.

60. B

Since $f(2x)$ is squashed horizontally, but we have scaled the integral by 2, we can immediately write down that $\int_1^3 f(x)dx = 1$. Now we are told that f is antisymmetric in $\frac{3}{2}$. By drawing a diagram, it is easy to convince yourself that this is equivalent to $\int_1^2 f(x)dx = 0$. So then combining integration ranges we see $\int_2^3 f(x)dx = 1$, and so $\int_2^3 f(x) + 1\, dx = 2$

61. C

Recall the definition of a prime: a positive integer whose only positive factors are itself and 1. I is false – 2 is a counterexample. II is false: 5 is a counterexample, it is prime and divisible by 5. III is true – no prime is divisible by 6, since then it must be divisible by both 2 and 3, neither of which can be p or 1.

62. C

As II→ III, III is true. As IV → not III the contrapositive is III → not IV so IV is false. The contrapositive of the implication Not I → II is Not II → I. But Not I is false, so we can't say anything about I.

63. D

Of the list, 1 maxima and 1 minima is the only allowed configuration. For large magnitude of x, the graph looks like ax^7, so we must have an equal number of turning points of each kind.

64.   D

Given that the highest order of x in the first bracket is two, we see 3 different ways for an x^2 term to emerge:

1)   A constant term from the first bracket, 1, multiplying an x^2 term from the second, $\binom{4}{3}\left(\frac{2}{x^2}\right)(-3x^2)^3 = -4 \times 2 \times 3^2 \times x^2 = -72x^2$

2)   An x term from the first bracket, and an x from the second. This can't happen as in the second bracket all powers of x are even

3)   An x^2 in the first bracket and a constant term in the second bracket. This gives $\binom{4}{2}\left(\frac{2}{x^2}\right)^2 (-3x^2)^2 = 216x^2$

Putting this together we get a coefficient of 144.

65.   B

We have the two conditions I → II, i.e., II if I and II → I, i.e. I if II. The contrapositive is equivalent to each, i.e., the first is equivalent to Not II → Not I, and the second to Not I → Not II. So, B is not an equivalent formulation.

66.   D

Substitute the linear equation into the quadratic, to get an equation in x only: $x^2 - 16x + (32 + a) = 0$. Use the positivity of the discriminant to get the condition $32 \leq a$

67.   E

We need to count the number of multiples of two, but not of four, in the range. So 50,54,58, … 98. There are 13.

68.   D

I is true, as we have just translated the function. II is true, as it is a stretch in x direction, translation and stretch in the y direction. III is false (can you come up with a counterexample?). IV is true – the equation holds exactly when $f(x) = 0$.

69.   C

Expand the numerator, to get 4 terms as powers of x. Then differentiate. Either try to factorise the derivative – (noting $(4x + 1)^2$ must be a factor as it is in every answer), or expand the given answers. Doing so carefully gives the answer as C. Note you can also use the chain rule to solve this problem.

70. F

This condition is convexity. You can see this by drawing a curve. At $t = 0$ both the left hand side and right hand side are at x_1, and at t=1 both at x_2. The left hand side is just the function evaluated between x_1 and x_2, while the right is the value of the straight line between $(x_1, f(x_1)), (x_2, f(x_2))$, at the same x value as the left. The diagram below shows it is sufficient for the function to be curving up – i.e., $f''(x) \geq 0$

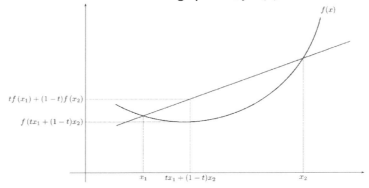

71. C

The 6th term can, with common ratio r, be written $ar^5 = \sqrt{32}r^5 = \frac{1}{32}$

$r = \frac{1}{2\sqrt{2}}$.

The sum to infinity is then $\frac{a}{1-r} = \frac{\sqrt{32}}{1-\frac{1}{2\sqrt{2}}}$. This can be rationalised to $\frac{16+32\sqrt{2}}{7}$.

72. C

Consider a set of 4 bulbs. Let 1 denote an on bulb and 0 an off. We start in 0000. Hit the second switch: 1010, now hit the 3rd: 1111. As 2020 is a multiple of 4 this strategy can turn on all the bulbs.

73. B

We have an infinite number of geometric series. The sum of the first is $\frac{1}{1-\frac{1}{3}}$. The second is $\frac{\frac{1}{3}}{1-\frac{1}{3}}$... so the sum is

$$\frac{1}{1-\frac{1}{3}}\left(1+\frac{1}{3}+\frac{1}{9}+\cdots\right) = \frac{1}{1-\frac{1}{3}} \times \frac{1}{1-\frac{1}{3}} = \frac{9}{4}$$

74. E

The error is in cancelling the numerator at the start. The numerator could be 0. We can amend this by instead beginning by cross multiplying: $(2x^2 - 3x - 2)(x^2 - 5x + 6) = (x^2 + x + 1)(x^2 - 5x + 6)$, and so $(x^2 - 5x + 6)(x^2 + 2x - 3) = 0$, $(x - 3)(x - 2)(x + 3)(x - 1) = 0$, giving 4 solutions.

75. D

Let's call $x = \sqrt{a - \sqrt{a - \sqrt{a - \cdots}}} = \cfrac{1}{a - \cfrac{1}{a - \cfrac{1}{a - \cdots}}}$, so that $x = \sqrt{a - x} = \frac{1}{a-x}$.

Now $x = \sqrt{a - x} \rightarrow x^2 = a - x$, and $x = \frac{1}{a-x} \rightarrow x^2 = ax - 1$. Combining these, we see that $ax - 1 = a - x \rightarrow$ $x(a + 1) = (a + 1)$. a clearly isn't -1, so we can divide through and see $x = 1$. Substituting back into a previous equation we see that $a = 2$ is necessary. To establish sufficiency, we need to check they are indeed equal when $a = 2$, but this is fairly obvious.

76. E

I is true. $n^3 - n = n(n + 1)(n - 1)$ Any 3 consecutive numbers will always contain a multiple of two and three, so hence the product is divisible by 6. However, it doesn't have to be divisible by 4, for example $n = 6$. III is true, because of I. You may worry about small numbers, (e.g., 5 is a prime, but is divisible by 5) but since 6 is not prime we don't run into issues.

77. E

We can't compute the integrals (yet), so we resort to graphical methods. We know the immediately $B < A$ and $D < C$, since squaring a number less than 1 makes it smaller, and integration gives the area under the curve.

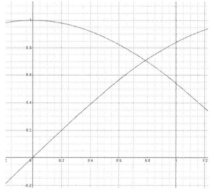

A good diagram clearly shows that the *cos* integral is larger than the *sin*, since the small triangle where sin is above cos is tiny compared to the section where *cos* is above *sin*: $A < C$. So now we have $B < A < C$, and just need to place D. One might suspect $D < B$ for the same reason as $A < C$. This is true:

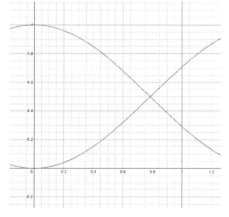

So, we have $D < B < A < C$

78. F

Begin by multiplying both sides by $\cos^2 3x$. This gives us $\sin^2 3x = \cos 3x$. Using $\sin^2 x + \cos^2 x = 1$, we can get a quadratic for $\cos 3x$ of $\cos^2 3x + \cos 3x - 1 = 0$. This has solutions $\cos 3x = \frac{-1 \pm \sqrt{5}}{2}$. However, $\cos y \geq -1$ for all values of y, which means only the positive root is taken. In the region 0 to 2π, we would normally have two solutions for any value of $\cos 3x = a$, so we have triple that amount in the case of $\cos 3x = a$, so we have 6 solutions.

79. D

$4^{-6} = 2^{-12} = (2^3)^{-4} = 8^{-4}$, not 8^{-3}. So, line III.

80. D

12 dividing a^2 does not imply that 12 divides a, take for example 6 squared. Thus, the error is in the line (IV).

81. D

$f(r) = 0$ so $f(x) - f(r) = f(x)$ which means II is never true, as $f(x)$ has three roots.

$f(x + r)$ is a shift of the whole curve r units to the left. This does now guarantee that all of the roots of the graph are at $x \leq 0$, but if it had no <u>positive</u> roots to begin with, the curve does not now have fewer positive roots, so statement I is only sometimes true.

The original statement also did not say that the polynomial was cubic; while a cubic polynomial cannot have zero roots, a quartic polynomial, where one of the roots is repeated, can easily satisfy the original assumptions on $f(x)$.

And, it is also possible the other stationary point on this graph had a y co-ordinate between 0 and -1, which would mean $f(x) + 1$ would have no real roots. So, III is sometimes true.
In all, II is never true, I and III are sometimes true.

82. G

If a decreases, then the graph will become flatter until the parabola turns upside down, thus I is possible.
II is not possible as b is not changing.

III is possible as despite changing, a and c do not have to change drastically, and without any markings on the graph a change in scale could make it look exactly the same.

IV is wrong as c must have decreased here, which it does not. So, it can't be II and IV.

83. D

We need only consider terms which have x powers which sum to 3. The first bracket gives x^6, x^4, x^2 and constant terms, while the 2nd bracket has constant, x^{-1}, x^{-2}, x^{-3} and x^{-4} terms. The only combinations here which make x^3 terms are $x^6 \times x^{-3}$ and $x^4 \times x^{-1}$. The coefficient of the first is $1 \times \frac{4}{3^3} = \frac{4}{27}$ and the latter is $3 \times (-2) \times \frac{4}{3} = -\frac{24}{3}$. Taking the sum, we get that the coefficient of x^3 is $\frac{4}{27} - \frac{24}{3} = \frac{4-216}{27} = -\frac{212}{27}$.

84. D

We seek a function which has 3 distinct roots and is not cubic. D. $(x-1)^2(x-2)(x-3)$ satisfies this as its only roots are 1,2 & 3, but it is quartic. We need not consider any others.

85. B

It is easy to check which of the roots are right by substituting into the original equation. We see that $x = 1$ is fine, but if $x = -\frac{2}{9}$, the right-hand side is less than 0, but the $\sqrt{x}$ symbol denotes taking the positive root. Thus, only $x = 1$ is correct. The error occurred in line (I) due to assuming no roots were generated from squaring both sides. This is what created the 2nd root.

86. F

We want the two graphs to intersect but equating the expressions won't get us very far. Instead, a sketch of both graphs is more illuminating. The line intersects the y-axis at 10, which is much higher than the other line. The gradient of $\log_2 x$ is decreasing, and as the gradient of the straight line is constant, if it begins large enough, they will never meet. 10 is one such value and so anything larger will also never meet the curve. However, there are also slightly smaller values which would also work, so it is not necessary. For m negative, the line must proceed downwards from $(0, 10)$. One can see that, as eventually $\log_2 x = 10$, even an almost flat decreasing straight line would intersect the curve. Thus, no matter the value of m, if it is negative, the lines must cross. So, 1 is sufficient, 2 is neither.

87. D

Usually, the easiest way to show a condition is "not necessary" is to find, or convince yourself you could find, a function which satisfies the condition that does not satisfy the alleged "necessary condition". However here, we know that $\int_0^1 f \, dx \le 0$ because $x \le 0$ for all the values of x we are considering. As $\int_{-1}^1 f \, dx = \int_0^1 f \, dx + \int_{-1}^0 f \, dx$, we also know that $\int_{-1}^0 f \, dx > 0$. This automatically satisfies D, for $a = -1$, so D is necessary, and we are only seeking one answer.

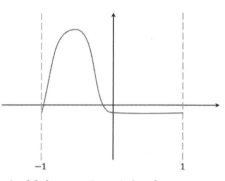

A is very nearly true, but any function which satisfies A actually has an integral of 0 from -1 to 1 (or from $-a$ to a for any a for that matter) because everything to the right of $x = 0$ perfectly cancels with that to the left.

For B, C and F consider the graph below. It has all the features of B,C and F, yet clearly the total area below the line is positive between -1 and 1.

For E, this in fact can never be true, as it forces all x values everywhere to be ≤ 0.

The only condition left is D.

88. F

We know that $f(x)$ is shaped roughly like the graphs shown. The 2nd graph is $f(x - b) - f(b)$, and the box in both graphs is the same size; it is $2b$ in length, and $f(b)$ in height. It is also clear to see that it encloses all of the area between the curve and the x-axis in the second picture. The excess being precisely what is described as R. Thus, the new area is $2bf(b) - R$.

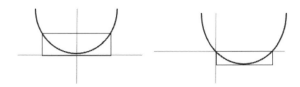

89. E

$\tan \theta$ has a root whenever $\theta = n\pi$ for some integer n. This means A has a root when $x = \frac{7n\pi}{5}$. Only one such integer n allows this to be in the given range, so $\tan \theta$ could be $f(x)$.

$\log x$ to any base always has 1 root at $x = 1$, and this is certainly in the range.

$\cos x = -1$ at precisely one point between 0 and 2π, at $x = \pi$, so $(\cos x) + 1$ has precisely one root. Similarly, for $(\sin x) - 1$, but at $x = \frac{\pi}{2}$.

3^x in fact, has no roots, anywhere, so cannot be $f(x)$ as it specifically has no roots in this range. So, this is the answer.

90. B

This is a relatively simple question if you pay very close attention, as the first error is in line I and if you spot it, you don't even need to check any other line due to the wording of the question. The question states "for non-negative n", but the base case checked is $n = 1$. This is not the smallest non-negative number, 0 is. In fact, for $n = 0$, this conjecture is false, as 6 is not divisible by 9. The answer is therefore line (I).

91. F

In case I, two of the 5 keys were correct each time. This means that in total, 6 guesses were right. Each character was in a different position each time, which means the characters that were right in each guess were different. However, that would imply that 6 different characters were right, but there are only 5. This is a contradiction, so this could not have occurred.

In case II, it is possible, with the code *cbead*.

In case III, because none of c, d and e moved between the guesses, whether they were correct or not must have remained the same as well. This means that the number of characters which were correct out of a and b also remained the same. However, they swapped places, which means if they were both right, they are now both wrong (a change in the number of correct guesses by 2), and if one of them was right the other cannot be right when they swap (else both are correct for the same position, which changes the number of correct guesses by 1). We are left with the possibility they were both initially wrong, but in this case all of c, d, e are right in the first guess. This means the code can only be *abcde* or *bacde*. So, one of the two should have been 5, not 3. Thus, this cannot occur.

Answer: I and III can never occur.

92. E

With integrals with modulus signs in, we typically split the integral range into the parts where the modulus function is defined properly i.e.

$$\int_0^7 |x - p| f(x) dx = \int_0^p (p - x) f(x) dx + \int_p^7 (x - p) f(x) dx$$

You can notice here that the integrand is identical except for a minus sign in the 2 integrals on the right. This means we don't have to integrate two different functions, only 1, and change what we substitute in as limits. By using the definition of F_1, we get $\int_0^7 |x - p| f(x) dx = F_1(7) - F_1(p) - F_1(p) + F_1(0) = F_1(0) + F_1(7) - 2F_1(p)$.

93. C

If the cylinder encasing the sphere is as small as possible, the radii of the two must be the same (so the sphere is touching all of the curved surface area of the cylinder) and it must be touching both top and bottom circle caps of the cylinder. This forces $2r = h$.

The surface area is made up of two circles of area πr^2 each and the curved surface area, which is equivalent to a rectangle of side lengths h & $2\pi r$. Thus $B = 2\pi r^2 + 2\pi r h = 2\pi r(r + 2r) = 6\pi r^2$. We can rearrange this to find that $r = \sqrt{\dfrac{B}{6\pi}}$. We substitute this into the equation for the volume of S and get $V = \dfrac{4}{3}\pi \left(\dfrac{B}{6\pi}\right)^{\frac{3}{2}} = \dfrac{4\pi B^{\frac{3}{2}}}{3 \times (6\pi)^{\frac{3}{2}}} = \dfrac{B^{\frac{3}{2}}\sqrt{2}}{9\sqrt{3\pi}}$.

94. D

A Venn diagram often helps in situations with probabilities which are not mutually exclusive.

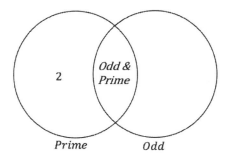

I is the same as the entire outside of the Venn diagram, but because the properties of being prime and being odd are not mutually exclusive, we cannot multiply them to obtain the probability they occur at the same time. So, this is not true unless the only prime number in the bag is 2, and we don't know whether this is true or not.

II is in fact the same statement as I, which is clear by looking at the Venn diagram. So, once again, as we do not know anything about the probability of picking 2 compared to an odd prime, we cannot determine this; it is not necessarily true.

III is the probability that the number picked is odd and not prime, which means it inhabits the "odd" circle in the diagram, minus the intersection. We know that the probability of being in this intersection is $P(prime) - P(2) = \frac{1}{5} - P(2)$. Thus, $P(not\ prime\ and\ odd) = \frac{1}{3} - \left(\frac{1}{5} - P(2)\right) = \frac{2}{15} + P(2)$.

Thus, only III is always true.

95. D

As usual for surds questions, we can start by squaring both sides to obtain $px = x^2 + 2x\sqrt{p} + p;\ 0 = x^2 + \left(2\sqrt{p} - p\right)x + p$. This has exactly one solution so its discriminant must be 0 i.e., $\left(2\sqrt{p} - p\right)^2 - 4p = 0 = p^2 - 4p\sqrt{p} + 4p - 4p = p\left(p - 4\sqrt{p}\right) = p\sqrt{p}\left(\sqrt{p} - 4\right)$. This tells us there are two solutions; $\sqrt{p} = 0$ or $4; p = 0\ or\ p = 16$. 0 is obviously a valid solution, but 16 might not be, since we may have generated extra solutions. If we substitute in $p = 16$, we must solve the equation $4\sqrt{x} = x + 4; 0 = x - 4\sqrt{x} + 4 = \left(\sqrt{x} - 2\right)^2 = 0$. This has precisely one solution, so $p = 16$ is a valid solution as well.

We have 2 valid solutions for p.

96.   F

For I, the probability you get more than 4 heads in 10 tosses is the same as getting 6 or fewer tails in 10 tosses. But, as getting a head or tail is equally likely, this is also the same as getting 6 or fewer heads in 10 tosses.

Every possible outcome falls into one of these two events, which means that
$P(more\ than\ 4\ heads) + P(fewer\ than\ 6\ heads) > 1$
$P(more\ than\ 4\ heads) + P(fewer\ than\ 6\ heads) = 2P(more\ than\ 4\ heads)$
$2P(more\ than\ 4\ heads) > 1$
$P(more\ than\ 4\ heads) > \frac{1}{2}$

For II, we know that the sequence we got appearing was one of the ways in which we could "get 7 tails", which means $P(get\ 7\ tails) > P(get\ our\ sequence) = p$.

For III, the next 10 coin tosses are completely independent of any previous coin tosses we made. Which means the probability of getting this exact sequence this time, is exactly the same as the probability we were going to get it last time. So, it is still equal to p.
Thus, I and III only are right.

97.   D

Quartic equations only have an odd number of solutions if there is a stationary point on the line $y = 0$. So, we differentiate to find $x(4x^3 - 3x - 1)$. Setting this equal to 0, we find stationary points at $x = 0, 1, -\frac{1}{4}$. Then, we substitute into the original equation, and find we have $a = 0, -\frac{1}{2}$ and $-\frac{11}{2^8}$. This means these are the values of a for which the stationary point is a solution, and thus there are an odd number. i.e., sum of values is $-\frac{139}{2^8}$.

98.   B

Use the product rule $\frac{df(x)g(x)}{dx} = f(x)\frac{dg(x)}{dx} + g(x)\frac{df(x)}{dx}$;
with $f(x) = 5x^2$ and $g(x) = \sin 2x$ in this case;
hence $\frac{df(x)g(x)}{dx} = (5x^2)(2\cos 2x) + (\sin 2x)(10x) = 10x(x\ cos2x + \sin 2x)$.

99.   D

If $x = 1$ is a root, then $(x - 1)$ is a factor. Hence, factorise $(x - 1)$ out of the polynomial we get:
$(x - 1)(2x^2 + 3x - 2) = (x - 1)(2x - 1)(x + 2) = 0$
Hence, the other two roots are $x = \frac{1}{2}$ and $x = -2$.

100. B

Expanding this sum we get $3^{-0} + 3^{-1} + 3^{-2} + 3^{-3} + 3^{-4}$. This is a geometric progression with first term of 1 and common ratio $\frac{1}{3}$. There are 5 terms in total, hence $S_5 = \frac{a(r^5 - 1)}{r - 1} = \frac{1\left(\left(\frac{1}{3}\right)^5 - 1\right)}{\left(\frac{1}{3}\right) - 1} = \frac{121}{81}$

101. A

$$\frac{\log_2 8^x}{\log_3 9^y} = \frac{x \log_2 8}{y \log_3 9} = 12\text{m},$$

Hence $\frac{3x}{2y} = 12$

$x = 8y$

Substitute this into the 2nd equation:

$3(8y) + 5y = 10$

$y = \frac{10}{29}$ and $x = 8\left(\frac{10}{29}\right) = \frac{80}{29}$

102. C

Take $3x^2 + 5 = u$

Then $\frac{du}{dx} = 6x$

Substitute u and dx into the integral:

$\int_0^5 \frac{6x}{3x^2+5} dx = \int_0^5 \frac{1}{u} du = \ln u = [\ln(3x^2 + 5)]_0^5$
$= \ln(80) - \ln(5) = \ln(16)$

103. C

First, we can see that this function has two roots, hence it is 2nd order polynomial;

$y = ax^2 + bx + c$

When $x = 0$:

$y = -8 = a(0)^2 + b(0) + c$

$c = -8$

When $x = 2$:

$0 = a(2)^2 + b(2) - 8$

$4a + 2b = 8 \qquad\qquad (1)$

When $x = -2$;

$0 = a(-2)^2 + b(-2) - 8$

$4a - 2b = 8 \quad (2)$

(1) - (2):

$4b = 0$

$b = 0$

Hence a = 2.

$y = ax^2 + bx + c = 2x^2 - 8$

104. C

The x^6 term comes from $(x^6)(x^4)$ and $(x^3)(x^3)$. Hence

$(3(1)(-2x)^2)(x^4) + (-2x)^3(4(2)(x^3)) = 12x^6 - 64x^6$
$= -52x^6$

105. C

$\log_4 \frac{1}{64} = \log_4 4^{-3} = -3$

Hence $\log_3 x^2 - 3 = 3$

$\log_3 x^2 = 6$;

$x^2 = 3^6 = 729$;

$x = 27$

106. D

Line equation can be obtained by:

$y - y_1 = \left(\frac{y_2 - y_1}{x_2 - x_1}\right)(x - x_1)$

$y - 5 = \frac{-6-5}{2-(-3)}\left(x - (-3)\right) = -\frac{11}{5}(x + 3)$

$5y + 11x = -8$

107. D

This is an arithmetic series, with first term 1 and common difference $+2$. We first need to find the nth term of 99.

$99 = 1 + (n - 1)2$;

$n = 50$

$S_{50} = \frac{n}{2}(2a + (n - 1)b) = \frac{50}{2}(2 + 49 \times 2) = 2500$

108. E

The numbers have to be either 4 digits or 5 digits:

4 digits: $3xxx, 4xxx$ and $5xxx$

5 digits: $1xxxx, 2xxxx, 3xxxx, 4xxxx, 5xxxx$

$3xxx =$ choose 3 digits from 4 possible number (1,2,4,5) so $4 \times 3 \times 2 = 24$

$4xxx =$ choose 3 digits from 4 possible number (1,2,3,5) so $4 \times 3 \times 2 = 24$

$5xxx =$ choose 3 digits from 4 possible number (1,2,3,4) so $4 \times 3 \times 2 = 24$

$1xxxx =$ choose 4 digits from 4 possible number (2,3,4,5) so $4 \times 3 \times 2 \times 1 = 24$

And so for $2xxxx, 3xxxx, 4xxxx$ and $5xxxx$

So total numbers are $24 \times 8 = 192$

109. E

$(6\sin x)(3\sin x) - (9\cos x)(-2\cos x) = 18\sin^2 x + 18\cos^2 x$

$18(\sin^2 x + \cos^2 x) = 18$

110. C

Define half the length of the inner equilateral triangle as x, and form a right-angled triangle by drawing a line from the centre of the inner circle to the inner triangle, defining the distance of that line as y.

$$\tan 30 = \frac{r}{x}$$

$$x = \frac{r}{\frac{1}{\sqrt{3}}} = \sqrt{3}r$$

$$\sin 30 = \frac{r}{y}$$

$$y = \frac{r}{\left(\frac{1}{2}\right)} = 2r$$

Using the formula for the area of a triangle, $Area = \frac{1}{2}ab\sin C$ in conjunction with the formula for area of a circle, $Area = \pi r^2$, we know that: $Area\ of\ the\ small\ circle = \pi r^2$

$Area\ of\ the\ big\ circle = \pi(2r)^2 = 4\pi r^2$

$Area\ of\ the\ small\ triangle = \frac{1}{2}\left(2\sqrt{3}r\right)\left(2\sqrt{3}r\right)\sin 60 = 12\sqrt{3}\ r^2$

Therefore, the shaded area is: $Shaded\ area = \left(12\sqrt{3} - 4\pi + 3\sqrt{3} - \pi\right)r^2$

$= \left(15\sqrt{3} - 5\pi\right)r^2$

$= 5r^2(3\sqrt{3} - \pi)$

111. A

$(3.12)^5 = (3 + 0.12)^5 = \left((3(1 + 0.04)\right)^5 = 3^5(1 + 0.04)^5$

$= 3^5\left(1 + 5(0.04) + 5\left(\frac{4}{2}\right)(0.04)^2 + \frac{5(4)(3)(0.04)^3}{6} + \cdots\right)$

$= 3^5(1 + 0.20 + 0.016 + 0.00064)$

$3^5 \times 0.00064 = 0.16$. Therefore, I must obtain 4 terms in the expansion.

112. B

$(\sin(\theta) + \sin(-\theta))(\cos(\theta) + \cos(-\theta))$

$= (\sin\theta + -\sin\theta)(\cos\theta + \cos\theta)$

$= 0(2\cos\theta) = 0$

113. C

$(2x - 5)^2 > \left(3(2x + 1)\right)^2$

$(2x - 5) = \pm 3(2x + 1)$

Critical values: -2 and $\frac{1}{4}$ such that $(2x - 5)^2 > \left(3(2x + 1)\right)^2$ within the range $-2 < x < \frac{1}{4}$

114. C

The distance between $(1, -4)$ and $(2,1)$ is $\sqrt{(2 - 1)^2 + \left(1 - (-4)\right)^2} = \sqrt{26}$. This is the radius of the circle.

The equation of the circle pre-reflection, therefore, is $(x - 2)^2 + (y - 1)^2 = 26$.

Upon reflection in the line $y = x$, the x and y coordinates of the circle change places, but the radius remains the same. Thus, the equation of the circle becomes $(x - 1)^2 + (y - 2)^2 = 26$.

115. D

Since the new computer does a calculations in b hours, it does $\frac{a}{60b}$ calculations in one minute. Simply add the individual rates together and multiply their sum by m minutes total to receive: $m\left(\frac{a}{60b} + \frac{c}{d}\right)$.

116. D

Since -1 is a zero of the function, $(x+1)$ is a factor of the overall polynomial. By long division or synthetic division, we can determine that $\frac{2x^3+3x^2-20x-21}{x+1} = 2x^2 + x - 21$.

Factoring $2x^2 + x - 21 = 0$, we get: $(2x+7)(x-3) = 0$

The roots are $x = -\frac{7}{2}$ or $x = 3$.

117. D

From these roots, we can find the factor of the polynomial:

$(x+1)(x)(x-1) = 0$

Opening the bracket gives us:

$f(x) = (x+1)(x)(x-1) = (x^2+x)(x-1) = (x^3 - x^2 + x^2 - x) = x^3 - x$

118. A

The expansion of $y_1 = (1-x)^6 = 1 - 6x + 15x^2$

The expansion of $y_2 = (1+2x)^6 = 1 + 12x + 60x^2$

The ratio of the second coefficient of y_1 to the third coefficient of y_2 is $-\frac{6}{60} = -\frac{1}{10}$.

119. C

These integers form an arithmetic progression with 300 terms, where $n = 300$, $a_1 = 1$, and $a_n = 300$. If you substitute these values into the formula for the sum of a finite arithmetic sequence, you will get:

$S_n = 1 + 2 + 3 + 4 + 5 + \cdots + 300$

$S_n = \frac{n}{2}(a_1 + a_n)$

$S_n = \frac{300}{2}(1 + 300)$

$S_n = 150(301) = 45150$

120. D

Recall the double angle formula for sine,

$\sin 2\theta = 2\sin\theta\cos\theta$

Since $\sin 2\theta = \frac{2}{5}$, $2\sin\theta\cos\theta = \frac{2}{5}$, $\sin\theta\cos\theta = \frac{1}{5}$

$\frac{1}{\sin\theta\cos\theta} = \left(\frac{1}{\frac{1}{5}}\right) = 5$

121. D

$-11 + 4\lfloor n \rfloor = 5$

$4\lfloor n \rfloor = 16$

$\lfloor n \rfloor = 4$

Since 4 is the greatest integer less than or equal to n, n must be on the interval $4 \leq n < 5$.

122. B

$$\left(\frac{T}{4\pi}\right)^2 = \frac{\text{l}(\text{M} + 3\text{m})}{3\text{g}(\text{M} + 2\text{m})}$$

$$\frac{T^2}{16\pi^2} \times \frac{3g}{l} = \frac{\text{M} + 3\text{m}}{\text{M} + 2\text{m}}$$

$3gT^2(M + 2m) = 16l\pi^2(\text{M} + 3\text{m})$

$3gT^2M + 6gT^2m = 16l\pi^2\text{M} + 48l\pi^2\text{m}$

$6gT^2m - 48l\pi^2\text{m} = 16l\pi^2\text{M} - 3gT^2M$

$m(6gT^2 - 48l\pi^2) = 16l\pi^2\text{M} - 3gT^2M$

$m = \frac{16l\pi^2\text{M} - 3gT^2M}{6gT^2 - 48l\pi^2}$

123. B

First, we set the two equations equal to one another: $k(x + 4) = 8 - 4x - 2x^2$

$2x^2 + kx + 4x + 4k - 8 = 0$

$2x^2 + (k + 4)x + 4(k - 2) = 0$

Subsequently, we set $b^2 - 4ac = 0$,

As follows: $(k + 4)^2 - 4 \times 2 \times 4(k - 2) = 0$

$k^2 - 24k + 80 = 0$

Solving this equation yields: $k = 4, k = 20$

124. A

We can find the common ratio of the series by dividing the second term of the series by the first, yielding the common ratio $r = \left(-\frac{1}{2}\right)x$

Since we know that the fifth coefficient is equivalent to $\frac{1}{32}$, we can solve for the value of x, the first term in the series, by equating $\frac{1}{32}$ to the formula for the fifth term of a geometric series:

$$\frac{1}{32} = ar^4$$

$$\frac{1}{32} = x\left(\left(-\frac{1}{2}\right)x\right)^4$$

$$\frac{1}{32} = \left(\frac{1}{16}\right)x^5$$

$$x^5 = \left(\frac{16}{32}\right)$$

$$x = \frac{(16)^{\left(\frac{1}{5}\right)}}{2}$$

This is an infinite geometric series with a first term of $a = x = \frac{(16)^{\left(\frac{1}{5}\right)}}{2}$.

We can simply find the common ratio by substituting $r = \left(-\frac{1}{2}\right)x = \left(-\frac{1}{2}\right)\frac{(16)^{\left(\frac{1}{5}\right)}}{2}$.

The sum to infinity of a geometric series is given by $S_\infty = \frac{a}{1-r}$.

Therefore, the sum of the series is given by: $S_\infty = \dfrac{\left(\frac{16^{\frac{1}{5}}}{2}\right)}{1-\left(-\frac{1}{2}\right)\left(\frac{(16)^{\left(\frac{1}{5}\right)}}{2}\right)}$

$$S_\infty = \frac{16^{\frac{1}{5}}}{2+\frac{(16^{\frac{1}{5}})}{2}}$$

125. D

$$\log_2 3 \times \frac{\log_2 4}{\log_2 3} \times \frac{\log_2 5}{\log_2 4} \dots \frac{\log_2(n+1)}{\log_2 n} \le 10$$

Solving the above equation, we have that $\log_2(n + 1) \le 10$. Consequently, $n + 1 \le 1024$. The largest value of n that satisfies this equation is 1023.

126. B

We have:

$(a + b + c)^2 = a^2 + b^2 + c^2 + 2(ab + bc + ca) = 364 + 2(ab + bc + ca) = 26^2 = 676$ so $ab + bc + ca = 156$
.

Since b and c are the second and third terms of a geometric progression respectively.

Let us denote $b = ar,$ and $c = ar^2,$

We have $a + b + c = a + ar + ar^2 = 26$ and $ab + bc + ca = a^2r + a^2r^3 + a^2r^2 = 156$

$a(1 + r + r^2) = 26$ and $a^2r(1 + r + r^2) = 156 = 6 \cdot 26.$

We can divide both equations to get

$a^2r(1 + r + r2)/a(1 + r + r^2) = 6$, or $ar = b = 6.$

127. A

$f(x)$ is a parabola, which is opened up (since its leading coefficient is $a^2 + 1 > 0$), so it has only one extremum and it is a global minimum. $f'(x) = 0 <=> 2(a^2 + 1)x - 2a = 0$ or $x = \frac{a}{a^2+1}$.

Luckily for us, $\frac{a}{a^2+1} = \frac{1}{2} \times \frac{2a}{a^2+1} \le \frac{1}{2}$ (since $0 \le \frac{2a}{a^2+1} \le 1$ for any positive a).

As a result, the minimum in the interval is reached for $x = \frac{a}{a^2+1}$.

We substitute into $f(x)$ to reach

$$fmin(x) = f\left(\frac{a}{a^2+1}\right) = (a^2+1).\left(\frac{a}{a^2+1}\right)^2 - 2a \times \frac{a}{a^2+1} + 10$$
$$= \frac{a^2}{a^2+1} - \frac{2a^2}{a^2+1} + 10 = 10 - \frac{a^2}{a^2+1} = \frac{9a^2+10}{a^2+1}$$

We want this value to be equal to $\frac{451}{50}$.

$\frac{9a^2+10}{a^2+1} = \frac{451}{50}$, so we cross multiply: $\quad 450a^2 + 500 = 451a^2 + 451$ or $a^2 = 49$.
Which means that $a = 7$, since $a > 0$.

128. B

We know that rain and snow are independent events. If the probability that it will rain is $\frac{2}{3}$ and the probability that it will both rain and snow the following day is $\frac{1}{5}$, we can find the probability that it will snow the day after tomorrow by simply solving the equation: $\frac{2}{3}x = \frac{1}{5}$

Which yields: $x = \frac{3}{10}$

129. A

Let us use the double angle formula, $\cos 2\theta = \cos^2\theta - \sin^2\theta$.

Given we know that $\cos 2\theta = \frac{3}{4} = \cos^2\theta - \sin^2\theta$, we know that $\frac{1}{\cos^2\theta - \sin^2\theta} = \frac{1}{\frac{3}{4}} = \frac{4}{3}$.

130. B

If you draw the graphs, you will notice that the two graphs are the reflections of one another in the y-axis.

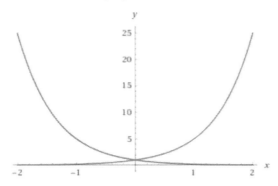

131. C

Note that $1 = \log_4(4)$.

$\log_4(2x+3) + \log_4(2x+15) - \log_4(4) = \log_4(14x+5)$

$\log_4(2x+3)(2x+15) = \log_4 4(14x+5)$

$(2x+3)(2x+15) = 56x + 20$

$4x^2 + 36x + 45 = 56x + 20$

$4x^2 - 20x + 25 = 0$

By factoring,

$4x^2 - 20x + 25 = 0$

$(2x-5)^2 = 0$

Hence, $x = \dfrac{5}{2}$

132. E

Begin by subtracting the integral from both sides producing $x - \int_{-z}^{z} 9a - 7 = \dfrac{\sqrt{b^3 - 9st}}{13j}$. Next multiply both sides by

$13j$ and square, rendering $[13j(x - \int_{-z}^{z} 9a - 7)]^2 = b^3 - 9st$. Finally subtract b^3 from both sides and divide by

$-9s$ leaving the correct answer: $\dfrac{[13j(x - \int_{-z}^{z} 9a - 7)]^2 - b^3}{-9s} = t$.

133. E

In order to start rearranging the fraction begin by adding m to both sides and squaring to yield

$$4m^2 = \frac{9xy^3z^5}{3x^9yz^4}$$

Now it is clear to see that this can be most simply displayed in terms of powers. Therefore, E is the correct answer

134. A

The gradient of the curve is $\dfrac{dy}{dx} = 2e^{2x-5}$.

We know that the gradient of the normal to the curve is $-\dfrac{1}{\frac{dy}{dx}}$.

Consequently, the equation of the normal is $y - e^{-1} = -\dfrac{e}{2}(x-2)$.

At the point A, where $y = 0$, $\quad x = 2 + \left(\dfrac{2}{e^2}\right)$

At point B, where $x = 0, y = e + \dfrac{1}{e} = \dfrac{e^2+1}{e}$

Since the area of a triangle is $\dfrac{1}{2} \times Base \times Height$, the area of the triangle OAB is:

$Area = \dfrac{1}{2} \times \dfrac{e^2+1}{e} \times 2 \times \dfrac{1+e^2}{e^2} = \dfrac{(e^2+1)^2}{e^3}$

135. D

We know that $(\sec x + \tan x)(\sec x - \tan x) = \sec^2 x - \tan^2 x$.

Using the trigonometric identity $\sec^2 x - \tan^2 x = 1$, as well as the information provided in the question, we know that:

$-5(\sec x + \tan x) = 1$

Therefore,

$(\sec x + \tan x) = -\frac{1}{5}$

By substitution, we know that $\sec x - \tan x + (\sec x + \tan x) = -5 + \left(-\frac{1}{5}\right)$

$2\sec x = -5.2$

$\sec x = -\frac{5.2}{2} = -2.6 = -\frac{13}{5}$

Since $\sec x = \frac{1}{\cos x}$,

$\cos x = \frac{1}{\sec x} = -\frac{5}{13}$

136. B

First, let us find the points along which any potential intersection between the line and the curve would take place, by setting the two equations equal to one another.

$x^2 + (3k - 4)x + 13 = 2x + k$

$x^2 + 3kx - 6x + 13 - k = 0$

$x^2 + 3(k - 2)x + 13 - k = 0$

Since the line and the curve do not intersect, we know that there must not be any real roots.

As such, by the discriminant condition, we know that $b^2 - 4ac < 0$.

Therefore:

$\left(3(k - 2)\right)^2 - 4(13 - k) < 0$

$9(k^2 - 4k + 4) - 52 + 4k < 0$

$9k^2 - 32k - 16 < 0$

$(9k + 4)(k - 4)$

We know that the critical values therefore extend from $-\frac{4}{9} < k < 4$.

137. A

The distance AC (equivalent to the radius of the circle) can be determined given the coordinates of A and C:

$A = (-2,1)\ C = (5,-3)$

Therefore $AC = \sqrt{(5 + 2)^2 + (1 + 3)^2} = \sqrt{65}$

To find the length of the line CT, we use Pythagoras' Theorem:

$CT^2 = AT^2 + AC^2$

$CT^2 = 4^2 + 65$

$CT^2 = 81$

$CT = 9$

138. B

At the stationary point, $\frac{dy}{dx} = 0$. Using the product rule: $\frac{dy}{dx} = x^2 e^x + e^x \times 2x$

When $\frac{dy}{dx} = 0$, $x^2 e^x + e^x \times 2x = 0$

Hence, $xe^x(x + 2) = 0$

Which shows that the x-coordinates passing through the stationary points of $y = x^2 e^x$ are $x = 0$ and $x = -2$ respectively. Therefore, the equation of the quadratic function is: $x(x + 2) = x^2 + 2x$.

139. B

The numerator of $\frac{x^2-16}{x^2-4x}$ is in the form $a^2 - b^2$, which means that it can be expressed as the quantity $(a + b)(a - b) = (x + 4)(x - 4)$

In turn, the numerator can be simplified into: $x(x - 4)$.

$\frac{x^2-16}{x^2-4x}$ can therefore be expressed as: $\frac{(x+4)(x-4)}{x(x-4)}$

Which simplifies to: $\frac{x+4}{x}$

140. B

We can use the inclusion-exclusion principle to find the probability that none of the balls are red. Since there are $2n$ blue balls, n red balls, and $3n$ balls altogether, the probability of drawing no red balls within the two draws is: $\frac{2n}{3n} \times \frac{(2n-1)}{(3n-1)} = \frac{4n-2}{3(3n-1)}$

Therefore, the probability of drawing at least one red ball is equal to:

$1 - \frac{4n-2}{3(3n-1)} = \frac{3(3n-1)-(4n-2)}{3(3n-1)}$

$= \frac{9n-3-4n+2}{3(3n-1)} = \frac{5n-1}{3(3n-1)}$

141. A

Recall the discriminant condition for the existence of real and distinct roots, $b^2 - 4ac > 0$

Using the coefficients in our question, this is: $(a - 2)^2 > 4a(-2)$

$a^2 + 4a + 4 > 0$

$(a + 2)^2 > 0$

Since this is a squared number, all values **but** $a = -2$ will satisfy this equation.

142. D

Let $y = 2^x$ then $y^2 - 8y + 15 = 0$

Solving this either using the quadratic equation or otherwise, we obtain $y = 3$ or $y = 5$.

If $3 = 2^x$

$x = \log_2 3 = \frac{\log_{10} 3}{\log_{10} 2}$

If $5 = 2^x$

$x = \frac{\log_{10} 5}{\log_{10} 2}$.

The sum of the roots is $\frac{\log_{10} 3}{\log_{10} 2} + \frac{\log_{10} 5}{\log_{10} 2} = \frac{\log_{10}(3*5)}{\log_{10} 2} = \frac{\log_{10} 15}{\log_{10} 2}$

143. C

Take logs of each side and separate out the LHS:

$3x \log_{10} a + x \log_{10} b + 4x \log_{10} c = \log_{10} 2$

$x (3 \log_{10} a + \log_{10} b + 4 \log_{10} c) = \log_{10} 2$

$x \log_{10}(a^3 b c^4) = \log_{10} 2$

$x = \dfrac{\log_{10} 2}{\log_{10}(a^3 b c^4)}$

144. B

Algebraically, we can find the result of reflecting the curve $y = x^2 + 3$ across the line $y = x$ by replacing y with x in the equation, and solving for the value of y in order to find the relevant equation, which is:

$x = f(y) = \sqrt{y - 3}$

Replacing y with x gives:

$y = \sqrt{x - 3}$

Translating the resulting equation by $\binom{4}{2}$ corresponds to introducing (-4) to the x term and $(+2)$ to the y:

$y + 2 = \sqrt{x - 4 - 3}$

$y = \sqrt{x - 7} + 2$

The x-intercept is found by setting $f(x) = 0$.

$\sqrt{x - 7} + 2 = 0$

$\sqrt{x - 7} = -2$

$x - 7 = 4$

$x = 11$

145. C

Segment area $= \dfrac{60}{360}\pi r^2 = \dfrac{1}{6}\pi r^2$

$\dfrac{x}{\sin 30°} = \dfrac{2r}{\sin 60°}$

$x = \dfrac{2r}{\sqrt{3}}$

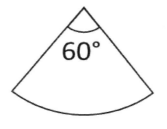
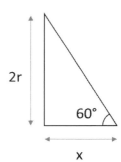

Total triangle area $= 2 \times \dfrac{1}{2} \times \dfrac{2r}{\sqrt{3}} \times 2r = \dfrac{4r^2}{\sqrt{3}}$

Proportion covered: $\dfrac{\frac{1}{6}\pi r^2}{\frac{4r^2}{\sqrt{3}}} = \dfrac{\sqrt{3}\pi}{24} \approx 23\%$

146. B

$(2r)^2 = r^2 + x^2$

$3r^2 = x^2$

$x = \sqrt{3}r$

$Total\ height = 2r + x = (2 + \sqrt{3})r$

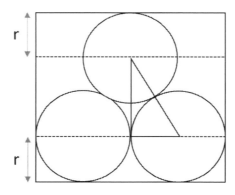
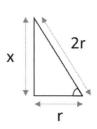

147. A

$V = \frac{1}{3}h \times$ base area

Therefore, base area must be equal if h and V are the same

Internal angle $= 180° -$ *external*

external $= \frac{360°}{6} = 60°$ giving internal angle $120°$.

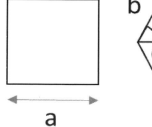
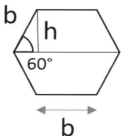

Hexagon is two trapezia of height h where: $\frac{b}{\sin 90°} = \frac{h}{\sin 60°}$

$h = \frac{\sqrt{3}}{2}b$

Trapezium area $= \frac{(2b+b)}{2}\frac{\sqrt{3}}{2}b = \frac{3\sqrt{3}}{4}b^2$

Total hexagon area $= \frac{3\sqrt{3}}{2}b^2$

So, from equal volumes: $a^2 = \frac{3\sqrt{3}}{2}b^2$

Ratio: $\sqrt{\frac{3\sqrt{3}}{2}}$

148. C

A cube has 6 sides so the area of 9 cm cube $= 6 \times 9^2$

9 cm cube splits into 3 cm cubes.

Area of 3 cm cubes $= 3^3 \times 6 \times 3^2$

$\frac{6 \times 3^2 \times 3^3}{6 \times 3^2 \times 3^2} = 3$

149. C

$x^2 = (4r)^2 + r^2$

$x = \sqrt{17}r$

$\frac{\sqrt{17}r}{\sin 90°} = \frac{r}{\sin\theta}$

$\theta = \sin^{-1}\left(\frac{1}{\sqrt{17}}\right)$

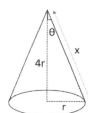

150. C

0 to 200 is 180 degrees so: $\frac{\theta}{180} = \frac{70}{200}$

$\theta = \frac{7 \times 180}{20} = 63°$

151. C

Since the rhombi are similar, the *ratio of angles* $= 1$

Length scales with square root of area so *length B* $= \sqrt{10}$ length A

$\frac{angle\,A/angle\,B}{length\,A/length\,B} = \frac{1}{\sqrt{10}/1} = \frac{1}{\sqrt{10}}$

152. E

$y = \ln(2x^2)$

$e^y = 2x^2$

$x = \sqrt{\dfrac{e^y}{2}}$

As the input is -x, the inverse function must be $f(x) = -\sqrt{\dfrac{e^y}{2}}$

153. C

$\log_8(x)$ and $\log_{10}(x) < 0$; $x^2 < 1$ $\sin(x) \leq 1$ and $1 < e^x < 2.72$

So e^x is largest over this range

154. C

$x \propto \sqrt{z}^3$

$\sqrt{2}^3 = 2\sqrt{2}$

155. A

The area of the shaded part, that is the difference between the area of the larger and smaller circles, is three times the area of the smaller so: $\pi r^2 - \pi x^2 = 3\pi x^2$. From this, we can see that the area of the larger circle, radius x, must be $4x$ the smaller one so: $4\pi r^2 = \pi x^2$

$4r^2 = x^2$

$x = 2r$

The gap is $x - r = 2r - r = r$

156. D

$x^2 + 3x - 4 \geq 0$

$(x - 1)(x + 4) \geq 0$

Hence, $x - 1 \geq 0$ or $x + 4 \geq 0$

So $x \geq 1$ or $x \geq -4$

157. C

$\dfrac{4}{3}\pi r^3 = \pi r^2$

$\dfrac{4}{3}r = 1$

$r = \dfrac{3}{4}$

158. B

When $x^2 = \frac{1}{x}$; $x = 1$

When $x > 1, x^2 > 1, \frac{1}{x} < 1$

When $x < 1, x^2 < 1, \frac{1}{x} > 1$

Range for $\frac{1}{x}$ is $x > 0$

Non-inclusive so: $0 < x < 1$

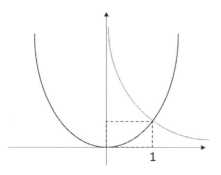

159. A

Don't be afraid of how difficult this initially looks. If you follow the pattern, you get $(e - e)$ which $= 0$. Anything multiplied by 0 gives zero.

160. C

For two vectors to be perpendicular their scalar product must be equal to 0.

Hence, $\begin{pmatrix} -1 \\ 6 \end{pmatrix} \cdot \begin{pmatrix} 2 \\ k \end{pmatrix} = 0$

$-2 + 6k = 0$

$k = \frac{1}{3}$

161. C

The point, q, in the plane meets the perpendicular line from the plane to the point p.

$q = -3i + j + \lambda_1(i + 2j)$

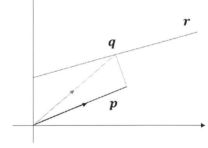

$\overrightarrow{PQ} = -3i + j + \lambda_1(i + 2j) + 4i + 5j$

$= \begin{pmatrix} -7 + \lambda_1 \\ -4 + 2\lambda_1 \end{pmatrix}$

PQ is perpendicular to the plane r therefore the dot product of $\overrightarrow{PQ}$ and a vector within the plane must be 0.

$\begin{pmatrix} -7 + \lambda_1 \\ -4 + 2\lambda_1 \end{pmatrix} \cdot \begin{pmatrix} 1 \\ 2 \end{pmatrix} = 0$

$-7 + \lambda_1 - 8 + 4 + \lambda_1 = 0$

$\lambda_1 = 3$

$\overrightarrow{PQ} = \begin{pmatrix} -4 \\ 2 \end{pmatrix}$

The perpendicular distance from the plane to point p is therefore the modulus of the vector joining the two $\overrightarrow{PQ}$:

$|\overrightarrow{PQ}| = \sqrt{(-4)^2 + 2^2} = \sqrt{20} = 2\sqrt{5}$

162. E

$-1 + 3\mu = -7 \; ; \; \mu = -2$

$2 + 4\lambda + 2\mu = 2 \; \therefore \; \lambda = 1$

$3 + \lambda + \mu = k \; \therefore \; k = 2$

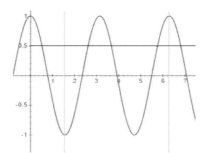

163. E

$\sin\left(\frac{\pi}{2} - 2\theta\right) = \cos(2\theta)$

Root solution to $\cos(\theta) = 0.5$

$\theta = \frac{\pi}{3}$

Solution to $\cos(2\theta) = 0.5$

$\theta = \frac{\pi}{6}$

Largest solution within range is: $2\pi - \frac{\pi}{6} = \frac{(12-1)\pi}{6} = \frac{11\pi}{6}$

164. A

$\cos^4(x) - \sin^4(x) \equiv \{\cos^2(x) - \sin^2(x)\}\{\cos^2(x) + \sin^2(x)\}$

From difference of two squares, then using Pythagorean identity $\cos^2(x) + \sin^2(x) = 1$

$\cos^4(x) - \sin^4(x) \equiv \cos^2(x) - \sin^2(x)$

But double angle formula says: $\cos(A + B) = \cos(A)\cos(B) - \sin(A)\sin(B)$

$\therefore if \; A = B, \cos(2A) = \cos(A)\cos(A) - \sin(A)\sin(A)$

$= \cos^2(A) - \sin^2(A)$

So, $\cos^4(x) - \sin^4(x) \equiv \cos(2x)$

165. C

Factorise: $(x + 1)(x + 2)(2x - 1)(x^2 + 2) = 0$

Three real roots at $x = -1, x = -2, x = 0.5$ and two imaginary roots at $2i$ and $-2i$

166. C

An arithmetic sequence has constant difference d so the sum increases by d more each time:

$u_n = u_1 + (n - 1)d$

$\sum_1^n u_n = \frac{n}{2}\{2u_1 + (n - 1)d\}$

$\sum_1^8 u_n = \frac{8}{2}\{4 + (8 - 1)3\} = 100$

167. E

$\binom{n}{k} 2^{n-k}(-x)^k = \binom{5}{2} 2^{5-2}(-x)^2$

$= 10 \times 2^3 x^2 = 80x^2$

168. D

Using the product rule: $\frac{dy}{dx} = x \cdot 4(x + 3)^3 + 1 \cdot (x + 3)^4$

$= 4x(x + 3)^3 + (x + 3)(x + 3)^3$

$= (5x + 3)(x + 3)^3$

169. A

$\int_1^2 \frac{2}{x^2} dx = \int_1^2 2x^{-2} dx =$

$\left[\frac{2x^{-1}}{-1}\right]_1^2 = \left[\frac{-2}{x}\right]_1^2$

$= \frac{-2}{2} - \frac{-2}{1} = -1$

170. D

Express $\frac{5i}{1+2i}$ in the form $a + bi$

$\frac{5i}{1+2i} \cdot \frac{1-2i}{1-2i}$

$= \frac{5i+10}{1+4} - \frac{5i+10}{5}$

$= i + 2$

171. B

$7\log_a(2) - 3\log_a(12) + 5\log_a(3)$

$7\log_a(2) = \log_a(2^7) = \log_a(128)$

$3\log_a(12) = \log_a(1728)$

$5\log_a(3) = \log_a(243)$

This gives: $\log_a(128) - \log_a(1728) + \log_a(243)$

$= \log_a\left(\frac{128 \times 243}{1728}\right) = \log_a(18)$

172. E

Functions of the form quadratic over quadratic have a horizontal asymptote.

Divide each term by the highest order in the polynomial i.e., x^2:

$\frac{2x^2 - x + 3}{x^2 + x - 2} = \frac{2 - \frac{1}{x} + \frac{3}{x^2}}{1 + \frac{1}{x} - \frac{2}{x^2}}$

$\lim_{x \to \infty} \left(\frac{2 - \frac{1}{x} + \frac{3}{x^2}}{1 + \frac{1}{x} - \frac{2}{x^2}}\right) = \frac{2}{1}$ i.e. $y \to 2$

So, the asymptote is $y = 2$

173. A

$1 - 3e^{-x} = e^x - 3$

$4 = e^x + 3e^{-x} = \frac{(e^x)^2}{e^x} + \frac{3}{e^x} = \frac{(e^x)^2 + 3}{e^x}$

This is a quadratic equation in (e^x): $(e^x)^2 - 4(e^x) + 3 = 0$

$(e^x - 3)(e^x - 1) = 0$

So $e^x = 3, x = \ln(3)$ or $e^x = 1, x = 0$

174. D

Rearrange into the format: $(x + a)^2 + (y + b)^2 = r^2$
$(x - 3)^2 + (y + 4)^2 - 25 = 12$
$(x - 3)^2 + (y + 4)^2 = 37$
$r = \sqrt{37}$

175. C

$\sin(-x) = -\sin(x)$
$\int_0^a 2\sin(-x)\,dx = -2\int_0^a \sin(x)\,dx = -2[\cos(x)]_0^a = \cos(a) - 1$
Solve $\cos(a) - 1 = 0$
So $a = 2k\pi$
Or simply the integral of any whole period of $\sin(x) = 0$ i.e., $a = 2k\pi$

176. E

$\frac{2x+3}{(x-2)(x-3)^2} = \frac{A}{(x-2)} + \frac{B}{(x-3)} + \frac{C}{(x-3)^2}$
$2x + 3 = A(x - 3)^2 + B(x - 2)(x - 3) + C(x - 2)$
When $x = 3, (x - 3) = 0$, $C = 9$
When $x = 2, (x - 2) = 0, A = 7$
$2x + 3 = 7(x - 3)^2 + B(x - 2)(x - 3) + 9(x - 2)$

For completeness: Equating coefficients of x^2 on either side: $0 = 7 + B$ which gives: $B = -7$

END OF SECTION

PAST PAPER WORKED SOLUTIONS

Hundreds of students take the ECAA exam each year. These exam papers are then released online to help future students prepare for the exam. Since the ECAA is such a new exam, past papers have become an invaluable resource in any student's preparation.

Where can I get ECAA Past Papers?

This book does not include ECAA past paper questions because it would be over 500 pages long if it did! However, all ECAA past papers since 2016 are available for free from the official ECAA website. To save you the hassle of downloading lots of files, we've put them all (including the specimen paper) into one easy-to-access folder for you at www.uniadmissions.co.uk/book.

How should I use ECAA Past Papers?

ECAA Past papers are one the best ways to prepare for the ECAA. Careful use of them can dramatically boost your scores in a short period of time. The way you use them will depend on your learning style and how much time you have until the exam date but here are some general pointers:

- Four to eight weeks of preparation is usually sufficient for most students.
- Make sure you are completely comfortable with the ECAA syllabus before attempting past papers – they are a scare resource and you shouldn't 'waste them' if you're not fully prepared to take them.
- Its best to start working through practice questions before tackling full papers under time conditions.

How should I use past papers?

This book is designed to accelerate your learning from ECAA past papers. Avoid the urge to have this book open alongside a past paper you're seeing for the first time. The ECAA is difficult because of the intense time pressure it puts you under – the best way of replicating this is by doing past papers under strict exam conditions (no half measures!). Don't start out by doing past papers (see previous page) as this 'wastes' papers.

Once you've finished, take a break and then mark your answers. Then, review the questions that you got wrong followed by ones which you found tough/spent too much time on. This is the best way to learn and with practice, you should find yourself steadily improving. You should keep a track of your scores on the next page so you can track your progress.

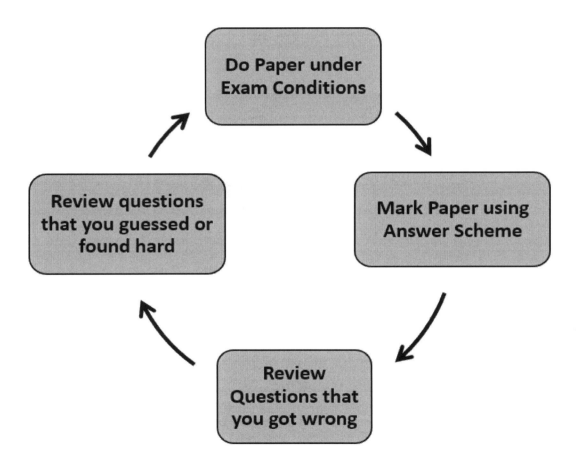

Scoring Tables

Use these to keep a record of your scores – you can then easily see which paper you should attempt next (always the one with the lowest score).

SECTION 1A	1st Attempt	2nd Attempt	3rd Attempt
Specimen			
2016			
2017			
2018			
2019			

SECTION 1B	1st Attempt	2nd Attempt	3rd Attempt
Specimen			
2016			
2017			
2018			
2019			

SECTION 2	1st Attempt	2nd Attempt	3rd Attempt
Specimen			
2016			
2017			
2018			
2019			

SPECIMEN

This is not the most recent specimen paper, but we have left it in the book because it is useful practice. The problem-solving questions are no longer in the specification so to make best use of your time we advise you start with Section 1B. This specimen paper can be found at **https://www.uniadmissions.co.uk/every-past-papers-answer-sheets/**. The most recent specimen paper can be found on the ECAA website.

Section 1A

1. C

The maximum number of days in a calendar month is 31. Each day of the week occurs four times during the first 28 days of every month. Two of these days will be working Saturdays. If the 29th, 30th and 31st of a 31-day month are all weekdays, or if the 31st is a working Saturday, the number of working days during the month will be $(4 \times 5) + 2 + 3 = 25$. In a month when the neighbours work the maximum 25 days, one of them will drive 12 times and the other one will drive 13 times.

2. D

The journey to work is 1800m, which would take $1800 \div 5 = 360 \; seconds = 6 \; minutes$ if there was no delay at either of the sets of lights. It takes $900 \div 5 = 180 \; seconds = 3 \; minutes$ to cycle from the first set of lights to the second. Because both sets change simultaneously, the maximum wait of 2 minutes at one of them will mean a wait of 1 minute at the other.
The longest journey time is therefore $6 + 2 + 1 = 9 \; minutes$.

3. B

There are eight possible side views of this paperweight: four with TLF uppermost (as shown in the question) and four with the reflection of TLF uppermost. You should visualise these views and eliminate the four options that are side views. From the side, a vertical line will be seen at each boundary between a projection and a recess. A and E are both views of the bases of the letters T, L and F. A is the view when TLF is uppermost and E is the view when the reflection of TLF is uppermost. C is the view of the tops of the letters T, L and F, with TLF uppermost. D is the view of the edge of the letter F, with the reflection of TLF uppermost. (Note that a view of the edge of the letter T would have a single vertical line one fifth of the way from one end.)

4. A

The energy values are for 100g of each food. The energy provided by the first four ingredients is:
Mealworms: $1.5 \times 150 = 225$ calories
Apples: $1.5 \times 350 = 525$ calories
Raisins: $2.5 \times 300 = 750$ calories
Suet: $1.25 \times 800 = 1000$ calories.
The total energy provided by these ingredients is $225 + 525 + 750 + 1000 = 2500$ calories. This means that the sunflower seeds must provide 2500 calories in order to make up the required total of 5000 calories. Sunflower seeds provide 500 calories per 100g, so $(2500 \div 500) \times 100 = 500g$ of sunflower seeds must be used.

5. B

The distance between Sue and Freya increases while Freya runs to collect the stick and decreases as she brings it back to Sue. Only options B and D show this situation. If Sue were to stand still, it would take the same amount of time for Freya to run 20m in both directions (assuming the same average speed both ways), but because Sue is walking towards her, the distance between them decreases from 20m to 0 in a shorter time than it increases from 0 to 20 m.

6. E

Because Alistair changes the code each time, you must not allow yourself to be distracted by the symbols making up his name. You simply need to identify which one of the options has repeated letters in the positions of the repeated symbols in the reply. Only SOMETIME has the 7th letter the same as the 3rd letter and the 8th letter the same as the 4th letter.

7. D

The two journeys took a total of $24 \div 32$ *hours*, which is 45 *minutes*. This means that on his second journey he travelled $24 - 15 = 9km$ in $45 - 30 = 15$ *minutes* ($\frac{1}{4}$ hour). *Speed = distance ÷ time*, so, his average speed on the second journey was $9km \div \frac{1}{4} hour = 36km/h$.

8. C

This question requires you to extract and process the relevant data from both the table and the narrative. You will need to compare the cost of silver membership for one year, which includes a free locker, with the cost of bronze membership for one year plus locker hire. The cost of silver membership for one year is the renewal price of £28. The cost of bronze membership for one year plus locker hire for 12 visits (one per month) is the renewal price of $£8 + (12 \times £2) = £32$. The cheaper option is silver membership for £28, which is £12 less than the £40 paid for gold membership 6 months ago as a new member.

9. A

To answer this question, you first need to establish that the number of 11-year olds who go swimming (104) is slightly greater than $\frac{2}{3}$ of the number of 16-year olds who go swimming. It is not necessary to carry out exact calculations for any of the sports; you only need to observe the following:

Football: $\frac{120}{181}$ is very close to $\frac{2}{3}$.

Cricket: $\frac{120}{133}$ is considerably greater than $\frac{2}{3}$.

Hockey: $\frac{55}{66}$ is considerably greater than $\frac{2}{3}$.

Tennis: $\frac{123}{149}$ is considerably greater than $\frac{2}{3}$.

Squash: $\frac{51}{97}$ is slightly greater than $\frac{1}{2}$.

10. B

The moving average of 13.82 beside 1913 means that $x + 13.3 + 14.9 + 13.7 + 14.2 = 13.82 \times 5$.
So $x + 56.1 = 69.1$ and $x = 13.0$.
y is therefore $(13.4 + 14.4 + 13.4 + 13.7 + 13.0) \div 5 = 67.9 \div 5 = 13.58$.

11. B

A group of 10 students would only require 2 instructors, who would be paid £12 each for 2 hours, but the extra £12 for a third instructor is much less than the extra income from a group of 18 students. A group of 18 students would pay a total of $18 \times (£7 + £5) = £216$ for 2 hours, so the maximum profit the centre can make from a group after paying the instructors for a two-hour session is £216– £36 = £180.

12. E

Grace has been late to lessons more than twice, so she can be eliminated. Andrew and Edward have both failed to complete more than two pieces of homework by the deadline set, so they can also be eliminated. Carole has 3 non-A-grade pieces of work, but Ian has only 2 pieces of non-A-grade work, so Ian will be awarded the prize.

13. B

Because each group involves the same number of people, this question can be approached by assuming that 400 people were surveyed altogether (100 in each age group) and then analysing the five statements as follows: In the age group 25 to 35, 32 people preferred Drink A and 33 people preferred Drink B, so conclusion A cannot be drawn. A total of 103 people preferred Drink B and 101 people had no preference, so conclusion B can be drawn. A total of 48 people in the age group 5 to 15 expressed a preference. This is less than half of the people in the group, so conclusion C cannot be drawn. A total of 225 people had a preference. This is more than half of the total number of people surveyed, so conclusion D cannot be drawn. A total of 74 people didn't know which they preferred. 20% of 400 = 80, so conclusion E cannot be drawn.

14. D

The fact that the bills for April and November are different amounts for the same number of units used means that the original tariff applies to at least the first four months of the year. From January to February (for instance) an increase of 25 units used increased the monthly charge by £2.50, so the original charge per unit was 10p per unit. From January to August the formula: $£30 + (units\ used) \times 10p$ consistently gives the monthly charge, but in September it doesn't. (The tariff changed to £20 standing charge per month plus 20p per unit used in September, but it is not necessary to calculate this in order to answer the question.)

15. C

The most efficient way of approaching this question is to solve the problem numerically. However, because it is the method of calculation that is important here and not the actual figures, time can be saved by using any number greater than 420 for the total number of desks available. The total number of desks available in the 12 rooms (including the sports hall, though it doesn't make any difference to the method if you don't include it) is 456, so there are 36 spare desks (456 – 420). The exams officer wants to leave the same number of empty desks in each room, so he should divide 36 by 12 and subtract the answer (3) from the number of desks in each room. This is the method described in option C.

16. D

The most efficient way of approaching this question is to work out your own answer from the graph and then select the option that is the closest. A reasonable estimate for the cumulative rainfall at the beginning of June is $175mm$ (three quarters of the way from $100mm$ to $200mm$) and it is clearly $400mm$ at the end of September. This gives an average of $225 \div 4 = 56.25 \ mm/month$ for the 4-month period. This is very close to $57mm/month$, which is option D.

17. B

The hot tap supplies $24 \ litres \ of \ water \ per \ minute$ ($360 \ litres \div 15 \ minutes$) and the cold tap supplies $36 \ litres \ of \ water \ per \ minute$ ($360 \ litres \div 10 \ minutes$). Together they supply a total of 90 litres in the $1\frac{1}{2}$ minutes before the cold tap is turned off, which makes the bath $\frac{1}{4}$ full. The hot tap then supplies another 180 litres to make the bath $\frac{3}{4}$ full, taking a further $180 \div 24 = 7\frac{1}{2}$ minutes. In all five options the graph rises from $(0, 0)$ to $(1, 1)$ as the two taps together make the bath $\frac{1}{4}$ full in the first $1\frac{1}{2}$ minutes. The correct graph then has to rise 2 units up the y-axis (from $\frac{1}{4}$ to $\frac{3}{4}$) as it advances 5 units along the x-axis ($7\frac{1}{2}$ minutes).

18. E

The reflection of 22:05, and therefore the correct time when the watch was reset to 22:05, is 20:55. This means that the watch is 1 hour 10 minutes ahead of the correct time. As a result, when the watch displayed the time as 10:09 this morning, the view of the digital clock that could be seen was the reflection of 08:59.

19. A

The bar chart reveals that the usage this year will be as follows (assuming it to be the same as last year, as instructed); January to March: 6,000; April to June: 7,000; July to September: 5,000; October to December: 6,000. There were 2,000 containers left at the end of last year, so it would appear that only 4,000 need to be delivered in January. However, this would mean that there would be none left at the end of March, and, because the maximum number that can be delivered at one time is 6,000, they would run out before the end of June. Ordering 5,000 in January would raise the total in stock to 7,000, with 1,000 left at the end of March. If 6,000 were then to be ordered in April there would be just enough to cover the usage of 7,000 from April to June. Following this, 5,000 could be ordered in July and 6,000 in October. This would result in there being none leftover at the end of the year.

20. E

To answer this question, you need to visualize the appearances of the trees from different parts of field Y. The most efficient approach is to imagine walking from one side of the field to the other. Starting from the extreme top left (for example), the order of the trees seen changes as follows: 4, 3, 2, 1 4, 1 (with 3 behind), 2 4, 1, 3, 2 1 (with 4 behind), 3, 2 1, 4, 3, 2 1, 4, 2 (with 3 behind) 1, 4, 2, 3 1, 2 (with 4 behind), 3 1, 2, 4, 3 Photographs were only taken when all four trees were visible, so there can be five different orders in the photographs

Section 1B

21. B

Use the product rule, such that:

$u = (3x - 2)^2, u' = 2(3x - 2)(2)$

$v = x^{-\frac{3}{2}}, v' = \left(-\frac{3}{2}\right)x^{-\frac{5}{2}}$

$\frac{dy}{dx} = (3x - 2)^2\left(-\frac{3}{2}x^{-\frac{5}{2}}\right) + \left(x^{-\frac{3}{2}}\right)(6)(3x - 2)$

Substituting $x = 2$ into this equation, we eventually find that

$\frac{dy}{dx} = (4^2)\left(-\frac{3}{2}\right)\left(\frac{1}{4\sqrt{2}}\right) + \left(\frac{1}{\sqrt{8}}(6(4))\right) + \left(\frac{1}{2\sqrt{2}}\right)(6)(4)$

$= -\frac{48}{8\sqrt{2}} + \frac{12}{\sqrt{2}} = \frac{6}{\sqrt{2}} = \frac{3 \times \sqrt{2}^2}{\sqrt{2}} = 3\sqrt{2}$

22. E

Because it is given that statement (*) is false, then it is not true that "every day next week, Fred will do at least one maths problem". Fred only needs to fail to do a maths problem on, say, Wednesday, for (*) to be false, even if he does maths problems every other day besides Wednesday.

23. F

$a^x b^{2x} c^{3x} = 2$

$\ln(a^x b^{2x} c^{3x}) = \ln(2)$

$\ln(a^x) + \ln(b^{2x}) + \ln(c^{3x}) = \ln(2)$

$x\ln(a^x) + x\ln(b^2) + x\ln(c^3) = \ln(2)$

$x(\ln(ab^2 c^3)) = \ln(2)$

$x = \frac{\ln(2)}{\ln(ab^2 c^3)}$

24. D

The roots differ by 2.

By the quadratic formula, the roots must be:

$$x = \frac{11 \pm \sqrt{(-11^2) - 4(2)c}}{4}$$

Since the roots differ by 2,

$$\frac{11 + \sqrt{(-11^2) - 4(2)c}}{4} - \frac{11 - \sqrt{(-11^2) - 4(2)c}}{4}$$

$$\frac{2\sqrt{(-11^2) - 4(2)c}}{4} = 2$$

$$\sqrt{121 - 8c} = 4$$

$$121 - 8c = 16$$

$$121 - 16 = 8c$$

$$105 = 8c$$

$$c = \frac{105}{8}$$

25. C

The answer is option C. Using just the runners' initials for simplicity, and writing ">" to mean "beat", we are told that: F > G, H > L, L > G, R > G It immediately follows that H > G, so G must have come last. Among the other four, we only know that H > L.

There are several ways to work out the number of orders from here:
There are $4! = 24$ ways to order the four runners.
In half of them H > L, in the other half, L > H. So, there are 12 orders with H > L.

26. E

Let $u = 2^x$

The equation becomes $u^2 - 8u + 15 = 0$

Solving the equation by factorizing, we get $(u - 3)(u - 5) = 0$

Which yields $u = 3 \ and \ u = 5$

Using $u = 2^x, 2^x = 3 \ and \ 2^x = 5$

$x \, lg_{10}2 = lg_{10}3 \ and \ x \, lg_{10}2 = lg_{10}5$

Hence,

$$x = \frac{lg_{10}3}{lg_{10}2}$$

and

$$x = \frac{lg_{10}5}{lg_{10}2}$$

The sum of the roots is $\frac{lg_{10}5}{lg_{10}2} + \frac{lg_{10}3}{lg_{10}2} = \frac{lg_{10}15}{lg_{10}2}$.

27. F

As the polynomial has degree 5, its derivative will have degree 4 so may have up to four real roots, and so our graph may have up to four stationary points. The graph of $dx\,dy$ either tends to $+\infty$ as $x \to \pm\infty$ or it tends to $-\infty$ for both; either way, it must cross the x-axis an even number of times. (Touching the axis without crossing results in a point of inflection, which we are not considering in this question.)

28. E

Statement 1 subtracts $a + b$ from both sides. Statement 2 can be written as $(a - b)^2 \geq 0$. This is always true. Statement 3 can be false if c is negative, for example $a = 2, b = 1, c = -1$.

29. C

This is a quartic graph and it will intersect the x-axis a minimum of two times, implying a minimum of two real roots. We differentiate the equation to find the turning points to see if the graph will cut the x-axis more times.
The derivative is:
$4x^3 - 12x^2 + 8x = 0$
$x(4x^2 - 12x + 8) = 0$
$4x(x^2 - 3x + 2) = 0$
$4x(x - 1)(x - 2) = 0$
Coordinates of the turning points are thus:
$(0, -10), (1, -9), (2, -10)$
None of the turning points are between the positive and negative sides of the y axis, implying that there are only two real roots.

30. D

The answer is $y = ax^b$. We can see this by taking logs of the equation and comparing it with the standard equation of a line,
$y = mx + c$ Taking logs gives: $\log y = \log a + b \log x$.
Comparing with $y = mx + c$, we can see that plotting $\log y$ on the Y-axis and $\log x$ on the X-axis would give us a straight line with a gradient of b and a Y-intercept of $\log a$.

31. A

Integrate directly to get:
$$\left[\frac{(x - a)^3}{3}\right]_0^1 = a^2 - a + \left(\frac{1}{3}\right)$$
Complete the square to get:
$$a^2 - a - \left(\frac{1}{2}\right)^2 + \left(\frac{1}{2}\right)^2 + \left(\frac{1}{3}\right)$$
$$\left(a - \frac{1}{2}\right)^2 + \frac{1}{2}$$
The minimum value of the integral as a varies is $\frac{1}{12}$.

32. E
The largest median will be if the middle number is as large as possible.

If the largest of the five numbers is u, then we will make the third number also u. Since the range is 20, the smallest number is $u - 20$.

To make the median u as large as possible, we want the second smallest number to be $u - 20$ too.

So, the five numbers are $u - 20, u - 20, u, u, u$.

Their sum is $5u - 40 = 0$ as the mean is 0, so $u = 8$, which is the largest possible median.

33. D
For real distinct roots the discriminant condition gives:

$(a - 2)^2 > 4a(-2)$

$a^2 + 4a + 4 > 0$

$(a + 2)^2 > 0$

Which is true for all values of a except -2.

34. C
$$P \propto \left(\frac{1}{Q^2}\right)$$

$P = \left(\frac{k}{Q^2}\right)$ for some k

When Q increases by 40%, the new value is 1.4Q.

$Q_{new} = 1.4Q$

Which yields:

$$P_{new} = \frac{k}{(1.4Q)^2} = \frac{k}{1.96Q^2} = \frac{1}{1.96}P$$

We then notice:

$$\frac{1}{1.96} \approx \frac{1}{2} \ and \ \frac{1}{1.96} > \frac{1}{2}$$

Hence P_{new} is slightly over 50% of P and we can deduce that P has decreased a little under 50%.

35. E
The probability that the first ball is red is $\frac{x}{x+y+z}$

The probability that the second ball is blue is $\frac{y}{x+y+z}$

The probability that the first ball is red and the second is blue is given by: $\frac{xy}{(x+y+z)^2}$

36. D

The first, second, and fourth terms of the GP are 4, $4r$, and $4r^3$ respectively.

Since the terms are also in arithmetic series, the common difference is constant.

$4r = 4 = 4r^3 - 4r$

Factorizing this, we get:

$4(r - 1) = 4r(r^2 - 1)$

Dividing by $4(r - 1)$ since $r =/= 1$

$1 = r(r + 1)$ yielding $r^2 + r - 1 = 0$

$r = \dfrac{1}{2}(\sqrt{5} - 1)$

Sum to infinity:

$\dfrac{a}{1 - r} = \dfrac{8}{3 - \sqrt{5}}$

Rationalizing this, we get: $2(3 + \sqrt{5})$

END OF SECTION

Section 2

What is understood by 'the Conventional Wisdom'? Discuss an example of an idea which qualifies as conventional wisdom.

An example of an idea that qualifies as conventional wisdom is the idea that individuals should choose university degrees that correspond to 'useful' professions in society such as law or medicine, and that students who do not choose such degrees effectively have shut themselves out of a future and will end up wasting their parents' money.

The reason that this constitutes a conventional wisdom is that it is an idea based on an assessment of stability and an assessment of the requirements of the real world, which is difficult and forbidding to engage with: The journey of an individual into the world of jobs and careers is a non-linear one, and upon first sight, degrees such as law and medicine provide a pathway into the job market that is secure and free from uncertainty, even if it is true that such a pathway does not correspond to the interests of a particular student.

The dangers of promoting only a small class of academic fields to the exclusion of others has its roots in practicality, but may not serve the populace well whether it is with respect to personal satisfaction or professional success: To choose an academic degree on the basis of what someone else has said is to effectively subjugate one's own decision to the judgment of others in order to make a call about what is best for oneself, and therefore to not pursue one's true passion in the pursuit of wealth from a path that has already been well-trodden and understood. While it is true that not every degree trains individuals to directly pursue a position within the job market directly as with law and medicine, education is not simply for the purpose of obtaining employment, but is also for the purpose of ensuring that one can achieve fulfilment in one's life, for the purpose of shaping the events of the world that have yet to occur and to understand their trends rather than to simply go along with the trends of society and follow along with the current.

To claim that a degree is useless for a particular purpose is to underestimate the value of the individual who stands behind the degree rather than to definitively state that the degree itself is useless, for each person who goes into the job market must make use of their skills, talents, and inclinations in order to stand and distinguish themselves in the job market: To designate a particular individual as being unemployable just because they have chosen a specific field of study is to place more credit on the past history of the individuals who have gone through a specific path rather than to give strength to the resolute determination of an individual who is driven to succeed in his or her chosen profession or pathway in life: Not everyone who is an investment banker or a management consultant has a degree in economics, and indeed, many people come to a disparate variety of professions from degrees in art history, commerce, and English literature with the skills, know-how, and preparation that is necessary to succeed in a career in virtue of their preparation and their desire for a career that is not at odds with their academic choices.

What the conventional wisdom proposes is a world where we remain in our lanes, pursuing what exists within the created world rather than rising up to create our own through the skills and experiences, the toolkits that we have developed in line with our specialization and interest to the exclusion of other worlds and pursuits, yet we live today in a world that is increasingly interconnected, where lines of knowledge seamlessly weave together, information is shared across worlds, and people step in and out of blurred boundaries across multiple streams of shared consciousness: This is a new world in which our contribution consists not simply in pushing into the workplace what we have learned in the academy, but also in piecing together what we see in order to make sense of a chaotic world.

While law and medicine are dreams that parents worldwide seek for their children, they are not the only dreams — For meaning is made from the pursuit of each path through a relentless process of action, a chase after success, and the cognition of a person as they progress through the world: Through choosing the academic and professional path that one truly desires, rather than a path that someone else has decided upon simply because it is 'stable', 'reputable', or 'desirable': Within the conscious pursuit of that path, even if it is not clear and the uncertainty is palpable, lies the answer to the questions that are posed within one's desire for self-fulfilment.

END OF PAPER

2016

Section 1A

1. B

I leave London at 17:30 GMT on August 19th, which is at this time 20th August in Auckland, at 5:30. I travel to Auckland and arrive at 6:15 on August 21st, which means that my entire journey must have taken 24 hours and 45 minutes. Accounting for my 1 hour stop in Los Angeles and 1.5 hour stop in Hawaii, it must be the case that I am due to spend 22 hours and 15 minutes in the air.

2. C

Of the options given, Kingda Ka is the only option that meets all the constraints:
Minimum height: 122cm
Speed: 128mph
Flight cost $\times 2 = \$56 \times 2 = \$102$
Average queue: 39 minutes

3. D

D is the only net that could be folded to make the above cube. A is not possible as the F will be in the wrong orientation. B is impossible because the E would be in the wrong position. C would not work because the E would be improperly aligned. F is eliminated from consideration because the B is in the wrong position.

4. C

Robert is on duty for three nights and is on duty on Friday night. Tom is on duty for four nights, and thus in order to satisfy the regulation of no more than two consecutive nights, he must be working on Monday, Tuesday, Thursday, and Friday. This leaves Monday, Tuesday, Wednesday, and Thursday as possible slots for Sheila. Sheila and Rob must work on Wednesday, as a minimum of two guards must guard the premises each day and Tom's slots are already occupied. Thus, Rob must also work on Tuesday, as if he worked on Thursday, this would violate the regulation. As a result, Sheila's slots must be Monday, Wednesday, and Thursday.

5. C

The cheapest possible option is to buy a concession family ticket for grandpa, dad, me, and for my brother who is two years older than me, although unfortunately, since we have decided to go on Saturday afternoon, we are subjected to peak hour prices. Buying a concession ticket is possible because grandpa is a senior citizen, my father is unemployed, and we are both children. This costs £4.80. Mother will pay for a £3.80 ticket, and grandma will pay £0.70 to observe. This yields a total cost of £9.30, and the answer is C.

6. B

B does not correspond to any of the tiles on the floor, even if it is rotated. Thus, the answer is B.

7. C

The fastest route is to travel from Essover to Yewton (20km), Yewton to Arford (18km), Arford to Teechester (25km), and then Teechester to Essover (23km). The sum of these distances is 86km.

8. A

We subtract the total number of fatal injuries in non-built-up areas (237) from the number of fatal or serious injuries (1724) to get a total of 1537 serious but not fatal injuries.

9. E

From the directional perspective indicated, the leftmost column should be one block high, the second column from the left should be two blocks high, the middle column is 3 units high, and the last column should be two blocks high. Hence, the answer is E.

10. B

The maximum score is 160, and we scored 138. If we answered 9 questions incorrectly and more frequently in Round 1 than any of the other rounds, the sole possibility for the distribution of our mistakes across rounds are:
Round 1: 5 mistakes (-5 points)
Round 2: 1 mistake (-2 points)
Round 3: 3 mistakes (-15 points)
If any other combination is tried, the numbers will not sum together such that we obtain 138 points in total.

11. D

I will buy a pack of 6 rolls at £20.94, as this is the most economical option.

12. A

W fits onto the right side of Y, to and X fits into the gap on the right. Z can then be rotated 180 degrees and placed in the resulting gap to create a carpet of width of 3 and length of 6. V does not participate in this arrangement.

13. A

The area of the entire flysheet is 24cm $\times$ 18cm $= 432$cm^2. The text must occupy half of the total area, and thus it occupies 216cm^2.
Let us denote the margin width as x.
We know that the area of the text is 216cm^2, and so to solve for x, we get:
$(24 - 2x) \times (18 - 2x) = 216$
$432 - 48x - 36x + 4x^2 - 216 = 0$
$216 - 84x + 4x^2 = 0$
Which yields $x = 3$ and $x = 18$ as possible roots
We select $x = 3$.
The answer is A, 3.00cm.

14. A

The cheapest option for them is to sit in the Balcony section between Monday to Friday, as the Dress Circle seats are more expensive even with the Dress circle group booking discount and the box seats are still more expensive than the Balcony section seats.

15. E

Pip: £54 × 28 = £1512
Eve: £56 × 27 = £1512
Nan: £72 × 21 = £1512
Bob: £63 × 24 = £1512
Viv: £68 × 22 = £1496
Viv is the only one with £1496. Hence, E is the answer.

16. D

The question specifies that charges for coffee and tea are whole number amounts. In other words, for:
$5c + s = 121$
$4t + s = 82$
s should be a number such that $121 - s$ and $82 - s$ are divisible by 5 and 4 into whole numbers respectively. The minimum number that satisfies this condition is $s = 6$.

17. A

The total area covered by the mushrooms is $100\text{m} \times 100\text{m} = 10000\text{m}^2$, and we observe that the area expands such that $A = (2n)^2$, where $n = 1,2,3....$
The area covered by the mushrooms equals to that of the field when $10000 = (2n)^2$, $100 = (2n)$, $n = 50$. On Wednesday, two days would have passed since the beginning, and thus 48 days remain until the field is completely covered.

18. D

A is represented by the second graph, B is represented by the fourth, C is represented by the first, and E is represented by the third. Only D is without representation.

19. C

We know that the quantity that Anna can obtain is the budget that she has allocated, divided by the respective prices. Dividing £3.00 by a weekday price of 20p, we have a quantity of 15. If we divide £3.00 by the Saturday morning price, 25p, we have a quantity of 12 (3 lower than the quantity obtained under weekday price), and if we divide £3.00 by the Saturday closing price, 15p, we get a quantity of 20 (5 larger than the quantity obtained under the weekday price). The answer is C.

20. A

The only cars that will satisfy the 4 to 5 door and 1.4 litre and above capacity constraint are the Rover 820 4 door, the Renault Laguna 5 door, Rover 825 4 door, and Ford Sierra 4 door.

Because he cares about lowest depreciation per mile, he will buy the Ford Sierra ($\frac{\$2000}{30,000 \text{ miles}} = \$0.067$ per mile).

21. D

D is not true. The sum total of individuals both male and female in the 80 to 84 age group is 1,332,700. The sum total of individuals both male and female in the 85+ age group is 1274300, which is less than 1,332,700. Therefore, not taking children below the age of 1 into consideration, the least numerous age group is the 85+ age group.

22. B

Imagine that the planets start off in alignment at time $t = 0$. One approach is to write expressions for the total full and partial revolutions that each planet will undergo in time, t:

$$p1 = \frac{t}{20}$$
$$p2 = \frac{t}{45}$$
$$p3 = \frac{t}{120}$$

Planets line up again when $p2 - p1$, $p3 - p2$, and $p3 - p1$ are all integer numbers of revolutions, i.e., all planets have moved the same amount round their orbits, give or take a whole number of revolutions.

$$p2 - p1 = \frac{t}{20} - \frac{t}{45} = \frac{25t}{20 \times 45} = N \text{ (i.e., some integer) for alignment}$$

$$t = \frac{N(20 \times 45)}{25} = N \times 36$$

So, Othello and Hamlet align every $36, 72, 108$ days etc.

Similarly, you get a sequence of values for $p3 - p2$ and for $p3 - p1$. The smallest value of t these all have in common is your answer.

Section 1B

23. D

The first three terms of a geometric progression are equivalent to the first, fifth, and sixth terms of an arithmetic progression. In other words,

$a = a$

$ar = a + 4d$

$ar^2 = a + 5d$

Rearranging the second equation to get r in terms of a and d, we get:

$ar = a + 4d$

$r = 1 + \dfrac{4d}{a}$

Using the value of r that we obtained in the rearrangement of the previous equation in the third equation, we get:

$a\left(\dfrac{a + 4d}{a}\right)\left(\dfrac{a + 4d}{a}\right) = a + 5d$

$\dfrac{a^2 + 8ad + 16d^2}{a} = a + 5d$

$a^2 + 8ad + 16d^2 = a^2 + 5ad$

$3ad + 16d^2 = 0$

$d(3a + 16d) = 0$

$3a + 16d = 0$

$3a = -16d$

$a = -\dfrac{16d}{3}$

Substituting a into the equation that we had earlier for r, we get

$r = 1 + \dfrac{4d}{\left(-\frac{16}{3}\right)d}$

$r = 1 - \dfrac{3}{4}$

$r = \dfrac{1}{4}$

24. D

The equation

$2x^2 + 9x - k = 0$

Has two roots, where one is more than the other by 4.

$2x^2 + 9x - k = 0$

$x^2 + \frac{9}{2}x - \frac{k}{2} = 0$

$x = \frac{-\left(\frac{9}{2}\right) \pm \sqrt{\left(\frac{9}{2}\right)^2 - 4(1)\left(-\frac{k}{2}\right)}}{2(1)}$

We know that one root is greater than the other by 4, and hence:

$\frac{-\left(\frac{9}{2}\right) + \sqrt{\left(\frac{9}{2}\right)^2 - 4(1)\left(-\frac{k}{2}\right)} - \left(-\left(\frac{9}{2}\right) - \sqrt{\left(\frac{9}{2}\right)^2 - 4(1)\left(-\frac{k}{2}\right)}\right)}{2(1)} = 4$

$-\left(\frac{9}{2}\right) + \sqrt{\left(\frac{9}{2}\right)^2 - 4(1)\left(-\frac{k}{2}\right)} + \left(\frac{9}{2}\right) + \sqrt{\left(\frac{9}{2}\right)^2 - 4(1)\left(-\frac{k}{2}\right)} = 8$

$2\sqrt{\left(\frac{9}{2}\right)^2 - 4(1)\left(-\frac{k}{2}\right)} = 8$

$\sqrt{\left(\frac{9}{2}\right)^2 - 4(1)\left(-\frac{k}{2}\right)} = 4$

$\sqrt{\left(\frac{9}{2}\right)^2 + 2k} = 4$

$\left(\frac{9}{2}\right)^2 + 2k = 16$

$\frac{81}{4} + 2k = \frac{64}{4}$

$2k = -\frac{17}{4}$

$k = -\frac{17}{8}$

25. D

The outer diameter of the roll is 11cm, or 110mm. The inner diameter is 5cm, or 50mm. The difference in diameter roughly attributable to the towels wrapping around the inner tube is 60mm.

Each towel is 250mm long, and there are 64 towels and thus 16000mm length of towel to wrap around the inner 5cm roll. Since the inner diameter is 5cm, the radius is 2.5cm, which is equivalent to 25mm, which means that the circumference is roughly 50π mm, which is roughly 150mm. In other words, the 16000mm length of towels will wrap around the inner roll approximately 100 times in total.

The 100 wraps account for about 60mm diameter difference, and hence each individual towel accounts for approximately 0.5mm of the thickness of the roll.

26. C

The initial value of the expression is:

$$\frac{abc(a+b+c)+2d(3bcd)}{2d(a+b+c)}$$

Thus, the value of the expression where a, b, c, and d are increased by 20% each is:

$$\frac{(1.2a)(1.2b)(1.2c)(1.2a+1.2b+1.2c)+2(1.2d)(3(1.2b)(1.2c)(1.2d)}{2(1.2d)\big((1.2a)+(1.2b)+(1.2c)\big)}$$

$$=\frac{(1.2^4)abc(a+b+c)+1.2^4\big(2d(3bcd)\big)}{2(1.2^2)d(a+b+c)}$$

$$=\frac{1.2^2(abc(a+b+c)+2d(3bcd))}{2d(a+b+c)}$$

1.2^2 is equivalent to 1.44.

Hence, we know that the percentage increase in the value of the expression is 44%.

27. F

We are given that the perimeter of the sector is 12cm, and the length of an arc subtended by an angle θ radians is $r\theta$. We know thus that: $x + x + x\theta = 12$ cm.

We know further that the area of the sector is defined by: $Area = \frac{1}{2}r^2\theta$.

Writing θ in terms of x:

$x + x + x\theta = 12cm$

$2x + x\theta = 12$

$\frac{12-2x}{x} = \theta$

$Area = \frac{1}{2}r^2\theta$

$Area = \frac{1}{2} \times r^2 \times \frac{12-2r}{r}$

$Area = \frac{1}{2}r(12 - 2r)$

$Area = 6r - r^2$

For maximum area, we set $\frac{d(Area)}{dr} = 0$

$\frac{d(Area)}{dr} = 6 - 2r = 0$

$r = 3$

Substituting the value of r into $\frac{12-2r}{r} = \theta$, we get $\theta = 2$.

Using the Area formula and the values of θ and r that we obtained…

$Maximum\ area = \frac{1}{2}r^2\theta$

$Maximum\ area = \frac{1}{2}(3^2)(2)$

$Maximum\ area = 9$

28. E

The equation of the gradient to the tangent to $y = 2x^3 - 9x^2 + 12x + p$ is $\frac{dy}{dx} = 6x^2 - 18x + 12$. To find the values of p, we can set $6x^2 - 18x + 12 = 0$ to find the points where the gradient to the tangent will be 0.

$6x^2 - 18x + 12 = 0$

$(3x - 6)(2x - 2) = 0$

$x = 2$

$x = 1$

Substituting these x-values into the original equation, we find that the corresponding y coordinates for these points would be:

$y = 5 + p$

$y = 4 + p$

We are given that the graph only cuts the x-axis at one point. If the graph is to do so, it follows that the bottom turning point should not touch the graph. In order for the turning point to not touch the graph, p should be greater than 4.

29. B

Using the properties of logarithms,

$2 + \log_5 x^2 = \log_5(24 + 10x)$

$= \log_5 25 + \log_5 x^2 = \log_5(24 + 10x)$

$= \log_5 25x^2 = \log_5(24 + 10x)$

So, we know that:

$25x^2 = 24 + 10x$

$x^2 - \frac{2}{5}x - \frac{24}{25} = 0$

Solving for the value of x using the quadratic formula, we find that:

$x = \frac{\left(\frac{2}{5}\right) \pm \sqrt{\left(\frac{4}{25}\right) - 4(1)\left(-\frac{24}{25}\right)}}{2}$

$x = \frac{\left(\frac{2}{5}\right) \pm \frac{10}{5}}{2}$

$x = \frac{6}{5}$, $x = -\frac{2}{5}$

$x = \frac{6}{5}$ is the positive value of x.

30. B

Jez cycled the first 5km at 10km/h, and therefore must have taken $\frac{1}{2}$ an hour to travel that distance. He travelled the remaining 10km at 30km/h, suggesting that he took $\frac{1}{3}$ of an hour to travel 10km. His average speed is his total distance travelled divided by the total number of hours, which is 15km divided by $\left(\frac{5}{6}\right)$ hours. His average speed is 18km/h.

31. D

The equation of the curve is:

$y = x(x + a)(x - 2a) = (x^2 + ax)(x - 2a)$
$= x^3 - 2ax^2 + ax^2 - 2a^2x = x^3 - ax^2 - 2a^2x$

The area of the curve enclosed within the curve and the lines $x = -a$ and $x = a$, where a is a positive constant, is:

$\int_{-a}^{a} x^3 - ax^2 - 2a^2x \, dx = \int_{0}^{a} x^3 - ax^2 - 2a^2x \, dx + \int_{-a}^{0} x^3 - ax^2 - 2a^2x \, dx$

$\int_{0}^{a} x^3 - ax^2 - 2a^2x \, dx = \left(\frac{a^4}{4}\right) - \frac{a^4}{3} - a^4 = -\frac{3a^4}{4} - \frac{4a^4}{12}$

$= -\frac{9a^4}{12} - \frac{4a^4}{12}$

$= -\frac{13a^4}{12}$

$\int_{-a}^{0} x^3 - ax^2 - 2a^2x \, dx = \frac{a^4}{4} - \frac{a(-a^3)}{3} - \frac{2a^2(-a^2)}{2}$

$= \frac{a^4}{4} + \frac{a^4}{3} - a^4$

$= -\frac{3a^4}{4} + \frac{a^4}{3}$

$= -\frac{9a^4}{12} + \frac{4a^4}{12}$

$= -\frac{5a^4}{12}$

$\int_{-a}^{a} x^3 - ax^2 - 2a^2x \, dx = \int_{0}^{a} x^3 - ax^2 - 2a^2x \, dx + \int_{-a}^{0} x^3 - ax^2 - 2a^2x \, dx$

$= -\frac{18a^4}{12} = -\frac{3}{2}a^4$

The total area is $\frac{3}{2}a^4 units^2$.

32. D

The x coordinates for points in the line will be the same. Distance will hence be:

$Distance = \sqrt{((3x^2 + 2) - (5x - 6))^2}$

$Distance = \sqrt{((3x^2 - 5x + 8))^2}$

$Distance = 3x^2 - 5x + 8$

For minimal distance, we take the derivative of the distance formula and set that equal to 0, as follows:

$\frac{d(Distance)}{dx} = 6x - 5 = 0$

$x = \frac{5}{6}$

For minimal distance, we substitute this value of x into the equation, yielding Distance $= \frac{71}{12}$.

33. E

We seek the probability that at least one of the balls will be red. In other words, we seek:

$P(at\ least\ one\ of\ the\ balls\ is\ red) = 1 - P(all\ the\ balls\ are\ blue)$.

$P(all\ the\ balls\ are\ blue) = \frac{2n}{3n} \times \frac{2n-1}{3n-1}$

$P(at\ least\ one\ of\ the\ balls\ is\ red) = 1 - P(all\ the\ balls\ are\ blue)$.

$= 1 - \frac{4n-2}{3(3n-1)}$

$= \frac{9n-3-4n+1}{3(3n-1)}$

$= \frac{5n-1}{3(3n-1)}$

34. A

Statement 1 could be false if a and b are negative.

Statement 2 must be true regardless of the circumstances. If a is less than or equal to b, the expression with a will always be smaller than the expression with b.

Statement 3 need not be true. If c is initially negative and a is less than or equal to b and is negative, the statement will be false.

35. E

We know that there is a maximum stationary point at $x = 0$ and a minimum stationary point in the 4th quadrant. Taking the derivative of the curve $y = ax^3 + bx^2 + c$, we find that:

$\frac{dy}{dx} = 3ax^2 + 2bx$

$\frac{d^2y}{dx^2} = 6ax + 2b$

In order that there be a maximum stationary point at $x = 0$, $\frac{d^2y}{dx^2} < 0$.

Hence, $6a(0) + 2b < 0$

Hence, $b < 0$.

In order that there be a minimum stationary point at a value in the fourth quadrant, $\frac{d^2y}{dx^2} > 0$.

$6ax + 2b > 0$

$6ax > -2b$

In the fourth quadrant, $x > 0$ and from the previous stationary point, we know that $b < 0$. The quantity $(-2b)$ can be represented therefore as a positive real number, which we can denote as c.

$6ax > c$

$a > \frac{c}{6x} > 0$

Hence, $a > 0$.

E is the only option that presents $a > 0$ and $b < 0$.

36. E

If bulb X is off or bulb Y is on, then bulb Z is on.

If bulb Z is off, then this is necessarily because bulb X is on or bulb Y is off.

37. E

The mean mass of the group is initially 84kg.

Thus, the total mass of the group of 20 individuals must be $84 \times 20 = 1680$kg.

We are asked for an expression for the mean mass of N individuals who leave the group and cause the mean to become 81kg.

We know thus that:

$\frac{1680 - N(\mu)}{20 - N} = 81$

$1680 - N(\mu) = 1620 - 81N$

$60 = N(\mu) - 81N$

$60 = N(\mu - 81)$

$\frac{60}{N} + 81 = \mu$

Hence, the answer is E.

END OF SECTION

Section 2

How does cooperation between people take place when no one is explicitly in charge?

Cooperation between people takes place when individuals cooperate to meet their best interests and needs through means that are self-interested in motivation, but socially beneficial to the world. Indeed, the famous Adam Smith quote, "It is not from the **benevolence of the butcher**, the brewer, or the **baker** that we expect our dinner, but from their regard to their own interest." Indeed, even if nobody is explicitly in charge of coordinating cooperation, the millions of decisions that people make throughout the world to fulfil their own needs creates the grand pattern of cooperation that we see throughout the world, as each person acts according to his own need, with the resources that are available at hand.

Take the example of the shirt that is provided in this essay, for example. As the author notes, "the shirt I bought, although a simple item by the standards of modern technology, represents a triumph of international cooperation. The cotton was grown in India, from seeds developed in the United States; the artificial fibre in the thread comes from Portugal and the material in the dyes from at least six other countries; the collar linings come from Brazil, and the machinery for the weaving, cutting, and sewing from Germany; the shirt itself was made up in Malaysia."

Why is it that these things occur, and how is it that individuals from such disparate geographical regions cooperate with one another over such a large scale in such a way? It is certainly not the case that a central entity is coordinating the production of these individual components - Rather, cooperation across these jurisdictions is the product of individuals making use of the idiosyncrasies of each location and translating them into products that it is most suited to make. People cooperate with one another when they can achieve specific goals, and one specific goal that most individuals have in mind is making a living: Each land has its own resources, capacities, and people of skill such that the land develops and people seek to make something of themselves.

Naturally, in a shared world, there are different kinds of lands, and different kinds of individuals, each with his own talents varying across the entire scope of human ability, as well as a differential ability to make use of those talents depending on the endowment of resources and market environment within a country. India, for example, has a climate that is especially suited for growing cotton, while Germany has a great industrial production operation that has been built on the back of engineering expertise, each of which has made these countries suited to performing the specific tasks that lead into the production of the shirt. If instead Germany had tried to grow cotton and India had tried to create machinery and neither of these countries had the expertise to do so, they would waste more time on these tasks rather than creating the products beforehand and exchanging them for the resources of other entities, as they would not have the people or the capacity necessary to participate in the market.

To the extent that human needs are common and are shared amongst individuals, it is possible for businesses to plan out the ways in which their labour will be distributed and sold with reasonable certainty of the ways in which these needs may be fulfilled, even if it is true that these individuals do not directly or explicitly cooperate with one another: To get the cheapest, most high quality material is the prerogative of the shirt manufacturer, who buys from the region where the product can be produced at both quality and cost in accordance with the specialization that arises from the development of a nation's comparative advantage, while providing the cheapest, highest quality material is the prerogative of the seller who has as his interest outcompeting other parties who would like to sell within the same market to other parties who are keen on converting the material into the infinitude of products that make up the sheer complexity that is our modern age market. None of this coordination requires the conscious will of a single individual and would certainly exceed the capacity of that individual if he were to attempt to replicate it.

END OF PAPER

2017

Section 1A

1. D

The height of the picture is 40cm, and the width of the frame it is contained in is 2cm. The mount is 6cm wide at the top, and 9cm wide at the bottom. The overall height of the picture is obtained by summing all the heights: $40cm + (2cm + 2cm)\ (height\ of\ the\ frame) + mount\ width\ (6cm + 9cm) = 59cm$.

2. D

Rhine is the answer. Look at the pairings across rows and columns — Rhine is the only team to a positive score for every single row and column pairing in which it appears.

3. A

The total area that Rosie needs to mow is $Area\ to\ mow = (10m \times 25m) - (2m \times 3m) = 244m^2$. With her old mower, she would have taken 244 minutes to mow the lawn at $1m^2$ per minute. With her new mower, she takes 122 minutes to mow the lawn at $2m^2$ per minute. The time savings that she sustains is $244 - 122 = 122\ minutes$.

4. C

My friend has a minimum of 1 coupon of each denomination, which make up a total of $(7p + 12p + 19p) = 38p$ value. To find the number of 19p coupons that he has, we can consider the case in which he has the fewest possible number of 19p coupons. Suppose that my friend had four 12p coupons in addition to the three he already has — His total coupon value would be 86p. In order that his total coupon value be 1 pound in total, it must be the case that two of the coupons have an individual value of 7p each. In other words, he needs three 19p coupons.

5. C

We need to find a difference in points that corresponds to 214 points for an 18cm record improvement. Looking at the table, we can see that the difference between 1.74m and 1.56m is 214 points. Hence, C is the answer.

6. D
We take the difference between car registrations for 2007 and 2012 for each month of the year.

January: 37.1
February: 10.1
March: 77.4
April: 29.9
May: 25.8
June: 35.1
July: 33.6
August: 18.7
September: 60.1
October: 18.3
November: 10.2
December: 16.7

The only graph provided that represents these totals accurately in terms of relative size is graph D.

7. A
To paint the wall and ceilings completely with the exception of the 10m² combined surface area occupied by the windows and door, I will need $2 \times (3m \times 8m) + 2 \times (3m \times 4m) + (8m \times 4m) - 10m^2 = 94m^2$ of paint. Each tin contains 8 litres of paint, and thus will allow me to cover $(8 \times 12m^2) = 96m^2$ of surface area.

Hence, one tin of paint is sufficient.

8. E
The friends' preferences are shown:
1st choices: Portugal Portugal Greece Majorca Tenerife
2nd choices: France France France France Tenerife
3rd choices: France Tenerife Tenerife Greece Majorca

Greece corresponds to one first choice and one third choice, and thus to $3 + 1 = 4$ points. Portugal corresponds to $3 + 3 = 6$ points. Majorca corresponds to $3 + 1$ points. Tenerife corresponds to one first choice, one second choice, and two third choices, and thus to $3 + 2 + 1 + 1 \, points = 7 \, points$. Hence, the friends go to Tenerife.

9. B
The vase is curved and concave, and thus the increase in height must be accelerating from the start and begin to decelerate as the vase becomes wider. The only graph that satisfies this condition is graph B.

10. B

The information given is that 6.0kg of the mixture contains $\frac{1}{4}$ of X and $\frac{3}{4}$ of Y, which means that there is 1.5kg of X and 4.5kg of Y in the solution. The technician wants to create a solution with the proportions 40% of X and 60% of Y, and hence the addition of a mass of X must result in a chemical 40% composed of X.

We can find this mass by solving the equation:
$\frac{1.5+x}{6+x} = 0.4$
Solving for x, we find that $x = 1.5$ kg.

11. D

Observe that the total mass of the package is 300g. Using the typical values per 100g, we can see that 300g of the material will contain 4.8g of sugars. Since each oatcake contains 0.3g of sugars, we can conclude that there is a total of $(\frac{4.8}{0.4}) = 24$ oatcakes.

12. B

We are given the totals for various variables, and can fill in the remainder of the information from there. The total number of boys and girls is 900, and thus the number of boys is $(900 - 460) = 440$. Using this, we can solve for the number of people who take the bus, which is $(440 - 80 - 130 - 200) = 30$. The total number of walkers is 410, and 200 boys walk. Therefore, 210 girls must walk. Hence, the number of girls who commute by car must be $(460 - 50 - 80 - 210) = 120$.

Thus, the total number of people who commute by car is $120 + 80 = 200$
The total number of people who commute by walking is 410
The total number of people who commute by biking is 210
The total number of people who commute by bus is $50 + 30 = 80$

The only graph that accurately represents this information is graph B.

13. C

To score 52 points, the Blues must have scored 8 majors and 4 minors, while to score 77 points, the Reds must have scored 7 majors and 14 minors. Hence, the total number of majors is $8 + 7 = 15$.

14. D

You can calculate three values. If you set up equations to represent each word, letting f, g, h, i represent each value:

$T + E + A + R = f$
$R + I + T + E = g$
$T + R + E + E = h$
$R + A + T = i$

You will see that E, A, I are the only equations that do not appear in all the equations and thus can be expressed in terms of the other variables. Hence, the answer is three variables.

15. D

D is not possible to make, as the long side of the L would have to be on the opposite side for shape D to be created and would require a backwards L shape: The other shapes can all be made.

16. C

If there were only three boats, they would respectively leave the island at 9:05am, 9:25am, and 9:45am, arrive at 9:45am, 10:05am and 10:25am, then take 40 minutes to return at 10:30 for departure at 10:35am, 10:50am for departure at 10:55am, and 11:10am for departure at 11:15am. However, the ferries begin leaving the island beginning from 9:15am, and if there were only three boats, it would be impossible to account for both the 9:15am and 9:35am departure time. Hence, a minimum of five boats is necessary.

17. A

We can solve this by creating simultaneous equations to represent the final total of legs, horns, and tails that we will obtain from the capture of all three types of creatures. Let A, O, and U represent the quantity caught of Arps, Orps, and Urps respectively.

$$3A + 2O = 99 \ horns$$
$$A + U = 33 \ tails$$
$$6A + 4O + 3U = 222 \ legs$$

Using the first equation, $A = \frac{99 - 2O}{3}$

Using the third equation,

$$6\left(99 - \frac{2O}{3}\right) + 4O + 3U = 222$$
$$198 - 4O + 4O + 3U = 222$$
$$198 + 3U = 222$$
$$3U = 24$$
$$U = 8$$

Hence, the answer is A.

18. C

Suppose that I consume aloe vera juice at my regular dosage per day. I will consume the entire 600ml bottle in (600ml/dosage per day) days.

If I consume aloe vera juice at the slowed rate after two regular doses and realising that the supplier has sold out, the entire bottle will take 6 days longer to consume. In other words, accounting for the first two dosages in each bottle, (2×dosage + ((3/4)×dosage×(n+6)) = (2×dosage + dosage×(n)).

Solving for the number of days that I would take to finish the entire bottle with a regular dosage beyond the first two dosages, I set ((3/4)×dosage×(n+6)) = (2×dosage + dosage×(n)), which yields a value of n = 18, and showcases that in a regular scenario with a regular dosage, I would finish the entire bottle in 20 days.

Thus, my normal daily dose of aloe vera juice must be 600ml/20 days = 30 ml per day. The answer is C.

19. B

The amount that Joan spends on cat food each day ($2\ sachets\ of\ wet\ food, 25g\ of\ dry\ food$) when she buys from the local pet store is

$$\frac{\text{£12.00 for 12 sachets}}{6} + \frac{\text{£4.00 for 400 grams}}{400 \times 25 \text{grams}} = \text{£2.25}$$

$$\frac{\frac{\text{£62.40 for four boxes}}{4}}{24\ sachets} + \frac{\text{£16 for 2 kgs}}{2000 \times 25} = \text{£1.50}$$

The cost savings is £2.25 − £1.50 = £0.75 = 75p.

20. D

At $8\!:\!00\ to\ 20\!:\!00$ local time, provided that London is used as the reference point, the siblings' availabilities are:

Nathan: $08\!:\!00\ to\ 20\!:\!00$

Mark: $00\!:\!00\ to\ 12\!:\!00$

Ben: $09\!:\!00\ to\ 21\!:\!00$

Isabel: $10\!:\!00\ to\ 22\!:\!00$

Between $00\!:\!00\ to\ 09\!:\!00$ only Nathan and Mark will be available. Beyond $20\!:\!00$, only Ben and Isabel will be available. Hence, at least three siblings will be available simultaneously throughout the course of $(24 - (9 + 4)) = 11\ hours$.

Section 1B:

21. D

The first price reduction brings the shirt to 70% of the original price. The second price reduction brings the shirt to 70% × 80% = 56% of the original price. The price reduction relative to the original price is therefore 44% and the answer is D.

22. E

$\int_1^2 \left(3x + \frac{1}{x}\right)\left(3x + \frac{1}{x}\right) dx$

$= \int_1^2 \left(9x^2 + 6 + \frac{1}{x^2}\right) dx$

$= \left(9(2)^2 + 6 + \frac{1}{(2)^2}\right) - \left(9(1)^2 + 6 + \frac{1}{(1)^2}\right) = 35.5 - 8 = 27.5$

23. E

The inequality is:

$x - \frac{3}{2} > \frac{1}{x}$

$\frac{2x-3}{2} > \frac{1}{x}$

$2x^2 - 3x > 2$

$x^2 - \frac{3}{2}x - 2 > 0$

By the quadratic formula, the roots are $-\frac{1}{2}$ and 2. Substituting the values into the equation, we find that the range of values is $-\frac{1}{2} < x < 0$, and $x > 2$.

24. D

The ratio of those who study both languages to those who do not is $5:3$. Therefore, the number of people who study no languages is 6. The intersection between French and German is 10 individuals, and therefore there must be 32 individuals who do not lie in the intersection and study only German and thus 75 − 32 − 6 = 37 individuals total who study French.

The probability that one pupil studies ONLY German is $\frac{32}{75}$.

25. A

$y = 3 + 2\left(\frac{x}{4} - 1\right)^2$

$y - 3 = 2\left(\frac{x}{4} - 1\right)^2$

$\frac{y-3}{2} = \left(\frac{x}{4} - 1\right)^2$

$\pm\sqrt{\frac{y-3}{2}} = \left(\frac{x}{4} - 1\right)$

$1 \pm \sqrt{\frac{y-3}{2}} = \frac{x}{4}$

$x = 4\left(1 \pm \sqrt{\frac{y-3}{2}}\right)$

26. A

By the remainder theorem, dividing $f(x)$ by $(x + 1)$ is analogous to evaluating $f(-1)$, and dividing by $(x - 1)$ is analogous to evaluating $f(1)$.

Hence,

$f(-1) = 12 = 2(-1) + p(1) + q(-1) + 6$

$p - q = 8$

$p = 8 - q$

$f(1) = -6 = 2(1) + p(1) + q(1) + 6$

$p + q = -14$

$(8 - q) + q = -14$

$q = -11$

$p = -3$

Identically, dividing $f(x)$ by $(2x - 1)$ to find the remainder is analogous to evaluating $f(\frac{1}{2})$, which we can now do since we know the values of p and q.

Hence, the remainder when $f(x)$ is divided by $(2x - 1)$ is:

$$f\left(\frac{1}{2}\right) = 2\left(\frac{1}{8}\right) - 3\left(\frac{1}{4}\right) - 11\left(\frac{1}{2}\right) + 6 = 0$$

27. F

The probability that the balls are not the same colour is:

$1 -$ *the probability that the balls are the same colour.*

The probability that the balls are the same colour is the probability that a red ball is chosen and a red ball is chosen again, added to the probability that a green ball is chosen and a green ball is chosen again. The probability that two balls chosen are the same colour is:

$$P(Same\ color) = \frac{n \times (n+1)}{(3n) \times (3n+1)} + \frac{(2n) \times (2n+1)}{(3n) \times (3n+1)}$$

$$= \frac{1}{3} \times \frac{n+1}{3n+1} + \frac{2}{3} \times \frac{2n+1}{3n+1}$$

The probability that two balls chosen are not the same colour is therefore:

$$P(Different\ color) = 1 - \left(\frac{1}{3} \times \frac{n+1}{3n+1} + \frac{2}{3} \times \frac{2n+1}{3n+1}\right)$$

$$P(Different\ color) = \frac{9n+3-n-1-4n-2}{9n+3} = \frac{4n}{3(3n+1)}$$

28. E

We observe that the graph cuts the positive x-axis at $x = 3$.

The gradient of the tangent is given by $\frac{dy}{dx} = 3x^2 - 7$

And thus, the gradient of the tangent at $x = 3$ is $\frac{dy}{dx} = 3(3)^2 - 7 = 20$.

The equation of the tangent is thus:

$\frac{y-0}{x-3} = 20$

$y = 20x - 60$

29. A

$2x - y = p$

$y = 2x - p$

$3x^2 - x(2x - p) = 4$

$3x^2 - 2x^2 + px = 4$

$x^2 + px = 4$

$x^2 + px - 4 = 0$

There are two distinct and real solutions for x, and thus by the quadratic formula.

$b^2 - 4ac > 0$

$p^2 - 4(1)(-4) > 0$

$p^2 > -16$

Since every square number is greater than 0, therefore the answer is A.

30. B

There are several un-surveyed individuals within the population. Looking at the totals, we can see that there are $94 - (34 + 12 + 29) = 19$ unsurveyed individuals in the population of category P employees, whereas there is a total of $86 - (30 + 21 + 27) = 9$ unsurveyed employees in category Q.

The probability that an employee who commutes by car is in category Q would be lowest if all the un-surveyed category P employees commuted by car, and all the un-surveyed category Q employees commuted another way.

The probability that an employee commuting by car is in category Q, in that scenario, would be $\frac{21}{21+31} = \frac{21}{52}$. The answer is D.

31. C

Since S and T are geometric progressions, and they have the same second term and sum to infinity, we can denote the first terms of S and T respectively as a_{1T} and a_{1S}, and the second terms of S and T as $T_{2S} = a_{1S}r_{1S}$ and $T_{2T} = a_{1T}r_{1T}$ and that both $T_{2S} = T_{2T} = 6$, but that $T_{1S} > T_{1T}$.

We know further that the sum to infinity of a geometric series, $S_\infty = \frac{a}{1-r}$ and that for S and T, , $S_\infty = \frac{a_{1T}}{1-r} = \frac{a_{1S}}{1-r} = 25$.

We know thus that $a_{1S} = 25 - 25r$.

Using $T_{2S} = a_{1S}r = 6$, we get:

$(25 - 25r)r = 6$

$(25r - 25r) = 6$

$25r - 25r + 6 = 0$

$r^2 - r + \left(\frac{6}{25}\right) = 0$

By the quadratic formula,

$r = \frac{1 \pm \sqrt{1 - 4(1)\left(\frac{6}{25}\right)}}{2}$

$r = \frac{1 \pm \frac{1}{5}}{2}$

$r = 0.6$

$r = 0.4$

Are two possible values for r.

Now, there are two possible values for r, and we know that $T_{2S} = a_{1S}r_{1S}$ and $T_{2T} = a_{1T}r_{1T}$, and that $T_{1S} > T_{1T}$. Substituting the value of r_{1S} into the equation, $a_{1S} = \frac{6}{0.4} = 15$, $a_{1T} = \frac{6}{0.6} = 10$.

The question asks for the fourth term of S, $T_{4S} = a_{1S}r_S^3 = 15 \times (0.4)^3 = \frac{24}{25}$

32. C

If 5 is added on to every term, then the sum of the series will have $5n$ added on to it, where n is the number of terms in the series, because each term is larger by 5 and there are still n terms in total in the new series, hence the answer is C.

33. A

To find the value of x, we can simply perform a substitution after performing a multiplication, by observing that the equation: $5^{2x+1} + 5^x - 4 = 0$

May be written as: $5(5^{2x}) + 5^x - 4 = 0$

Here, we can perform a substitution and solve the equation as a quadratic, such that: $u = 5^x$

The equation then becomes: $5u^2 + u - 4 = 0$

Which factors to: $(5u - 4)(u + 1)$

Which gives us roots $5u = 4$ and $u = -1$.

Here, we re-use our substitution, $u = 5^x$, and, observing that this exponential function can never be negative for any value of x, eliminate $u = -1$ as a root.

We thus use the root $5u = 4$.

$5u = 4$

$5(5^x) = 4$

$5^{x+1} = 4$

$(x + 1)\ln(5) = \ln(4)$

$(x + 1) = \dfrac{\ln(4)}{\ln(5)}$

Which, by change of base to base 2, becomes:

$(x + 1) = \dfrac{lg_2 4}{lg_2 5} \times \dfrac{lg_e 2}{lg_e 2}$

$(x + 1) = \dfrac{2}{lg_2 5}$

$x = \dfrac{2}{lg_2 5} - 1$

34. A

The intersections of the curves are located at $x = 1$ and $x = 2$.

The area between the two curves is:

$$\int_1^2 (-4 + 6x - 2x^2)dx = \frac{1}{3}$$

35. D

$y = f(x) + 2$ need not necessarily intersect the x-axis as the graph has been translated upwards and may not even touch it.

$y = f(x) - 2$ need not necessarily intersect the x-axis as the graph has been translated downwards and may not even touch it.

$y = f(x + 2)$ necessarily intersects the x-axis at the same points, as the graph has simply been shifted leftward by two units.

$y = 2f(x)$ necessarily intersects the x-axis twice, as the graph has simply undergone a vertical stretch that does not affect whether the axes are cut by the graph or not.

$y = 2 - f(x)$ need not necessarily intersect the x-axis as the graph has been shifted upward by two units.

$y = f(-2x)$ necessarily intersects the x-axis twice, as the graph has simply undergone a horizontal compression and this does not change the fact that it cuts the x -axis twice.

There are three scenarios above wherein the graphs necessarily intersect the graph at 2 distinct points. The answer is D.

36. Question 36: D

R is most definitely false, as I saw a pig with wings without horns.

P cannot be determined, as the pig had no horns and therefore, I cannot make a statement about causality here.

Q cannot be determined. The pig has wings and it breathes fire, but I can conclude nothing about whether breathing fire relates directly to the pig having wings.

END OF SECTION

Section 2

Evaluate two arguments for and two arguments against low interest rates.
To what extent does the case for low interest rates depend on other policy choices?

The passage provides a host of arguments against lowered interest rates, as well as arguments that support lowered interest rates within the context of a climate of austerity amongst central banks and national economies, during which governments have opted to undertake contractionary fiscal policy so as to mitigate the problems that arise from an overheating economy.

The article argues that a climate of low interest rates can be beneficial for the economy, particularly in a climate of contractionary fiscal policy. Contractionary fiscal policy results in a lowering of aggregate demand as a result of lowered government spending and low interest rates act as a form of monetary stimulus that serves to shift aggregate demand outward, mitigating the negative consequences of tight fiscal policy. Specifically, the effects of tight fiscal policy may result in a lowering of aggregate demand within the economy, but governments may wish to limit the extent to which spending decreases by decreasing the financial reward for saving, albeit accepting the spending stimulus thesis without question requires the assumption that capital that would have been saved under a higher interest rate regime would be spent instead, which is not necessarily going to be true.

Above and beyond considerations of the actual empirical effect of an interest rate decrease on the level of aggregate spending in the economy, it is desirable to think of lowering interest rates as a form of monetary stimulus that is easy to execute by a central bank without the necessity of breaking through legislative gridlock or obtaining bipartisan agreement - Indeed, apart from ease of use, another argument in favour of lowering interest rates close to zero is that low interest rates do not have an obvious cost, as the risk of inflation is low in large economies due to ample spare capacity, and central banks are not subjected to the political constraints that their companions in government face when making decisions about fiscal policy, during which they must minimally ensure bipartisan agreement across the political divide concerning taxation and public spending.

However, low interest rate policy is not always ideal under all circumstances. Central banks face a problem that is called the zero lower bound problem: Banks cannot lower rates beyond zero, and monetary policy has limited usefulness beyond this point. There are several immediate arguments against low interest rates. The first of these arguments is that low interest rates can have a distortionary effect on capital, specifically that low interest rates can cause individuals to allocate capital toward unproductive projects that do not maximally benefit society.

The second of these arguments is that low interest rates may incentivize destabilizing behaviour such as capital flight from countries with low interest rates to jurisdictions with higher ones, as investors seek to place their capital wherever they can obtain the highest possible rate of return, as well as induce banks to take the risk of borrowing debt with short maturities to capitalize on the low short-term rate to lend at higher-yield long term rates, and thereby make themselves susceptible to the vagaries of interest rate change.

Taking both the advantages and disadvantages of lowered interest rates into account, however, requires adequate consideration of the current policy mix, specifically the specific objectives of the country with respect to inflation and unemployment, which in turn will depend on the economic numbers for a particular quarter, election promises that were made in previous cycles, and the actions of external investors. If a country is, for example, trying to deal with inflation, it may try to increase its interest rate to encourage saving instead of spending within the economy, but correspondingly attract hot money from foreign destinations seeking the promise of higher returns.

It behoves governments to not simply consider the possibility of confounding effects, however, but also the possibility of supporting other objectives - A good example is mitigating the impact on aggregate demand from a tightening fiscal policy, an objective that governments can achieve by lowering the interest rate to help support the objective of increasing say, consumer spending so as to soften the impact from contractionary policies, albeit such a policy mix must also depend upon the mixture of stakeholders that a government must appeal to at any given point in time - It may be more attractive to countries to achieve their policy goals by increasing the interest rate than to cut government spending on a particular program so as to appeal to certain stakeholders just before an election.

END OF PAPER

2018

Section 1A

1. D

Woodchip: 27 rolls initially would need to be bought at £25 each, 5 rolls are free, so the total cost is $22 \times 25 = £550$

Vymura: 18 rolls initially would need to be bought at £35 each, 10% off is applied so the total cost is $18 \times 35 \times 0.9 = £567$

Anaglypta: 18 rolls initially would need to be bought at £40 each, 20% off is applied so the total cost is $18 \times 40 \times 0.8 = £576$

Embossed: 14 rolls initially would need to be bought at £50 each, 25% off is applied so the total cost is $14 \times 50 \times 0.75 = £525$

Fabric effect: 11 rolls initially would need to be bought at £100 each, buy one get one free is applied so the total cost is $6 \times 100 = £600$

2. C

Now there are 8 folded sheets on each block, on each half of the block the following page numbers will be shown since each page is double sided:

$Block\ 1\ Half\ 1\ -\ Pages\ 1\ to\ 16$
$Block\ 1\ Half\ 2\ -\ Pages\ 17\ to\ 32$
$Block\ 2\ Half\ 1\ -\ Pages\ 33\ to\ 48$
$Block\ 2\ Half\ 2\ -\ Pages\ 49\ to\ 64$
$Block\ 3\ Half\ 1\ -\ Pages\ 65\ to\ 80$
$Block\ 3\ Half\ 2\ -\ Pages\ 81\ to\ 96$

Therefore, the centre of the block will have pages 48 and 49

3. D

Initially there are 400 parts water and 100 parts concentrate. When 100ml is lost this represents a 20% decrease overall, so now there are 320 parts water and 80 parts concentrate. Adding 100ml of concentrate means the final ratio is 320 parts water and 180 parts concentrate.

$$\frac{180}{500} \times 100 = 36\%$$

4. D

From 2011 to 2012, since 4.2 is approximately 4, $\frac{4}{3}$ is roughly a 33% increase.

From 2012 to 2013, $6.3 - 4.2 = 2.1$ so there is a 50% increase.

From 2013 to 2014, $9.45 - 6.3 = 3.15$ so again there is a 50% increase.

From 2014 to 2015, approximately $15 - 9.5 = 5.5$ which is greater than a 50% increase.

From 2015 to 2016, approximately $22.5 - 15 = 7.5$ which is roughly a 50% increase.

As a result, from 2014 to 2015, the percentage increase is the biggest.

5. E

The item on the left has one large diagonal side and the item on the right has one large diagonal side and one small diagonal side. In combination E, both the large diagonal sides from each item are displayed, meaning the longest horizontal side on the item to the right must be connected to the item on the left, but then the small diagonal side must be visible too, which it is not therefore combination E is not possible.

6. D

Analysing training, Graham is eliminated.
Analysing penalties, David and Colin are eliminated.
Only John and Mike remain so by analysing goals, Mike scored the most so Mike wins.

7. B

Cube 2 is possible since both R & E are in the same position as initially therefore eliminate answers C, D, E.
Cube 3 is possible since both A & D are in the same position as initially therefore only answer B is possible.

8. B

Initially 4 girls have 22 shells and the youngest has x. The 4 girls each lose 3 shells so now 4 girls have 19 shells each and the youngest has $x + 12$. Since they all have the same $x + 12 = 19$ so $x = 7$

9. D

Looking at a general time $xy{:}ab$ and maximising the number of segments in b, we choose between numbers 0 to 9 and 8 has the most segments with 7. Maximising a, we choose between numbers 0 to 5 and 0 has the most segments with 6. Maximising y, we choose between numbers 0 to 9 and 8 has the most segments with 7. Maximising x, we choose between numbers 0 to 5 and 0 has the most segments with 6. Therefore, the time $08{:}08$ is shown with 26 segments.

10. A

Analysing the first 5 people in the queue, the photo development time is irreverent since the next person can insert their money while the photos are being developed. Therefore, the first person is finished in the booth after 3 minutes, the second after 6 minutes and so on until the 5th person is finished after 15 minutes. Therefore, despite you having to wait after you have inserted your money for your photos to be developed, the total waiting time before you can insert your money is still 15 minutes.

11. E

From Amy's view, we can label each pile from left to right as w, x, y, z respectively for reference. One of the 3 piles in x must be less than or equal to 6 boxes high since that is the number of boxes from Amy's view. But from Ben's view, he views that pile x should have 7 boxes which is a direct contradiction since then Amy's should see the tallest pile in x and view 7 boxes too, therefore combination E is not possible.

12. Question 12: C

Let x equal the number of 14p coupons, y equals the 9p coupons, and z the number of 20p coupons. As a result, we have the equation $14x + 9y + 20z = 150$.

We also have the inequality $x > y > z$. Since it is easier finding combinations of x and y that are multiples are 20 away from 150, we can start from there.

Starting off with $x = 8$ and $= 4$, $y = 14(6) + 9(4) = 120$ which is too small.

Next with $x = 8$ and $y = 2$, $14(8) + 9(2) = 130$ so z must therefore equal 1 giving the combination of $8 + 2 + 1 = 11$

13. E

Since we require the period 1900 to 1950, we can eliminate the books, Beginner's Guide too History and All About History. The cheapest is now History of the 20th Century at £45, so she withdraws that amount.

Now looking at the valid books at 20% off, History of the 20th Century is $45 \times 0.8 = 36$, The Illustrated Guide to History is $50 \times 0.8 = 40$ and History for All is $60 \times 0.8 = 48$, therefore she buys The Illustrated Guide to History at £45 leaving £5 left over.

14. B

Since $profit = revenue - total\ cost$, $and\ revenue = price \times quantity\ sold$, we can work out the profit for each item. Always round up for wholesale packs bought leaving some leftover.

	Revenue	Wholesale Packs bought	Total Cost	Profit
Crayon	$180 \times 10 = 1800$	$180 \div 12 = 15$	$15 \times 48 = 720$	$1800 - 720 = 1080$
Felt tips	$150 \times 12 = 1800$	$150 \div 12 = 12.5 = 13$	$13 \times 72 = 936$	$1800 - 936 = 864$
Pencils	$200 \times 6 = 1200$	$200 \div 24 = 8.3 = 9$	$9 \times 24 = 216$	$1200 - 216 = 984$
Pens	$150 \times 15 = 2250$	$150 \div 36 = 4.1 = 5$	$5 \times 36 = 180$	$2250 - 180 = 2070$
Rulers	$40 \times 30 = 1200$	$40 \div 12 = 3 \div 3 = 4$	$4 \times 60 = 240$	$1200 - 240 = 960$

Pens and Crayons produced the highest profit out of the five items sold

15. E

Since the total must be 10 digits, this means 4 numbers have 2 digits and 2 numbers have a single digit. The largest number should ideally end with a 0 and the smallest number should ideally end with a large digit. Since the largest number has 2 digits, this leaves 3 other numbers with 2 digits and 2 numbers with a single digit. Therefore, the 2 single digit numbers should be as large as possible, i.e. 8 and then 9. The next 3 numbers which are all 2 digits will have the first digit ascending and the second digit descending. Therefore, we have the following sequence: $8, 9, 17, 26, 35, 40$. This means the smallest range is $40 - 8 = 32$

16. C

One 8h ticket costs £6.20.

Testing increasing quantities of smaller length tickets, one 7h + one 1h ticket = £6

One 6h + one 2h = £5.40

One 5h + one 3h = £5.20

One 4h + one 3h + one 1h= £4.90

Four 2h = £4.80

Two 3h + one 2h = £4.60

Therefore, this is the smallest charge for parking for 8 hours, which is the minimum amount of time valid for a 7.5-hour period. Therefore, £6.20 − £4.60 = £1.60

17. D

Looking at the first leg of the journey, since speed equals distance divided by time, rearranging we have the time to be $\frac{15}{60} \times 60 = 15\ minutes.$

Looking at the second leg of the journey, the car travelled for 5 hours including two rest stops, but this is within the 5 hours, so the second leg took a total of 5 hours.

The third leg lasted for a total of $\frac{20}{40} \times 60 = 30\ minutes$, therefore the total time taken was 5 hours and 45 minutes. If the finish was at 12:00, then the journey therefore began at 6:15am.

18. C

Five shelves each 1.8m long and at least 40cm in depth means we can eliminate the columns in the table for 30cm since this isn't feasible, and 60cm since this will be too expensive for every option. Since the price per unit metre is falling as the length increases, prioritising longer pieces will be cheaper. Each 4m long piece can be cut into two 1.8m long pieces, therefore we can buy two 4m long pieces. This leaves us with one 1.8m piece so we need to buy a 2m long piece, all depth 45cm.

As a result, we find £9.30 + £9.30 + £4.95 = £23.55

19. C

Combination A all the smaller diagonal lines will cross over symmetrically about a vertical line midway and the long diagonal line will become horizontal, and thus symmetrical. Combination B, the bottom two lines on the left will form a symmetrical cross at the top. The top line on the left will become horizontal and the 2nd, 3rd, 4th lines will form a symmetrical cross thus combination B is symmetrical. If we draw combination C, we can see that by reversing the order of (in this case), the left axis, the chart is not symmetrical about a vertical line midway between the axes.

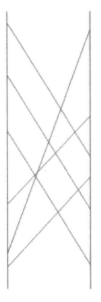

20. E

Labelling the x-axis time and the y-axis distance between the two trains, since the train from Weskham has to travel 11 miles to reach Orthorp and stop whereas the train leaving Eashon passes Orthorp after 7 miles, both trains therefore meet before one train stops, therefore the change in the gradient of the graph but occur after $y = 0$, this eliminates options A,C,D. When one train stops, the distance between the two trains still increases, just at a slower rate, therefore the gradient must be shallower, therefore eliminating option B meaning the only feasible option left is option E.

Section 1B

21. C
Since 25 is 5^2 and 125 is 5^3, the equation becomes $5^{x+1} \times 5^{6x} = 5^{57}$.
Using log laws and taking logs: $7x + 1 = 57$
$x = 8$

22. A
Let $T_n = a + (n-1)d$ where $T_1 = a$.
$T_5 = a^2 = a + 4d$
$T_{33} = a + 32d = 10(a + 2d)$
Rearranging gives $d = 0.75a$. Subbing back into T_5 we get $a = 4 \; and \; d = 3$.
Therefore, $T_{10} = a + 9d = 4 + 9(3) = 31$

23. D
Using the binomial theorem:
$(a + 2x)^6 = a^6 + 12a^5x^1 + 60a^4x^2 + 160a^3x^3 + 240a^2x^4 \dots$
Therefore $1200 = 240a^2$ which gives $a = \sqrt{5}$

24. D
Since $ax - 1$ is a factor, sub in $x = \frac{1}{a}$ into the equation.
This gives $3a(\frac{1}{a})^3 + (6a + 1)\left(\frac{1}{a}\right)^2 - 4$
This simplifies to $4a^{-1} + 6a^{-1} - 4$, so if we let $w = a^{-1}$ this gives the equation
$4w^2 + 6w - 4 = (2w - 1)(2w + 4)$
Therefore $w = 0.5 \; and \; w = -2$
So $a = 2 \; and \; a = -0.5$

25. D

Red \ Blue	1	2	3	4	5	6
1	–	0.5	–	–	–	–
2	–	–	–	0.5	–	–
3	–	–	–	–	–	0.5
4	–	–	–	–	–	–
5	–	–	–	–	–	–
6	–	–	–	–	–	–

Using a probability table dividing red by blue, we can see that the probability of achieving 0.5 is $\frac{3}{36} = \frac{1}{12}$

26. C
Using log laws
$$\log\left(\frac{4a}{b}\right) = 4$$
$$\log(2ab) = 3$$
This gives $\frac{4a}{b} = 2^4$ and $2ab = 2^3$.
Rearranging gives $a = 4b$ and therefore $b = 1$.
As a result, $a = 4$ which means $a - 2b = 4 - 2 = 2$

27. B
The probability the first three didn't get on at the same station equals one minus the probability the first three did get on at the same station.
This can be written as:
$$1 - \left(\frac{5\times4\times3}{12\times11\times10} + \frac{4\times3\times2}{12\times11\times10} + \frac{3\times2\times1}{12\times11\times10}\right) = 1 - \frac{90}{1320}$$
$$= 1 - \frac{3}{44} = \frac{41}{44}$$

28. F
Factorizing gives
$$x^2 + x - 6 = (x - 2)(x + 3) \geq 0$$
$$4 + 3x - x^2 = (x - 4)(x + 1) \leq 0$$
If we sketch this out, we can see that for the first equation, the inequality is only satisfied when $-3 \geq x$ and $x \geq 2$.
Looking at the second equation, the inequality is only satisfied when $x \geq 4$ and $-1 \geq x$.
As a result, both inequalities are only satisfied when $-3 \geq x$ and $x \geq 4$.

29. A
Dividing the first equation by $(1 + \sqrt{3})$ gives $y = \frac{p}{(1+\sqrt{3})}x + \frac{5}{(1+\sqrt{3})}$. Since the ratio of the gradients must equal -1,
since $(1 + \sqrt{3}) > 0$, $p < 0$ which only leaves answers A&C as possibilities.
Testing answer A by rationalising the denominator
$$\frac{5-3\sqrt{3}}{(1+\sqrt{3})} \times \frac{(1-\sqrt{3})}{(1-\sqrt{3})} = -\sqrt{3} - 2$$
Therefore, dividing the gradients gives $\frac{-\sqrt{3}-2}{(2-\sqrt{3})} = -1$ therefore the equations are perpendicular.

30. A

$$U_1 = \frac{2}{3}r^0$$

$$U_2 = \frac{2}{3}r^1$$

$$U_3 = \frac{2}{3}r^4 \ ..\ ..$$

$$U_n = \frac{2}{3}r^{n-1}$$

As a result, the sequence O is:

$$\frac{2}{3}, \frac{2}{3}r^2, \frac{2}{3}r^4$$

Meaning the first term is $\frac{2}{3}$ and the multiplier *is* r^2 therefore looking at the sum to infinity we have

$$\frac{8}{9} = \frac{\frac{2}{3}}{1-r^2}$$

Which leads to $r = \frac{1}{2}$

Similarly looking at the sum to infinity of E using $r = \frac{1}{2}$,

$$\frac{\frac{2}{3}r}{1-r^2} = \frac{4}{9}$$

31. C

Originally, $\sum x = n\bar{x} = 20 \times 70 = 1400$.

After the change, $\sum x = n\bar{x} = 25 \times 68 = 1700$

Which means the total marks for the new students are $1700 - 1400 = 300$.

This means the new students mean mark is 60 therefore statement 2 must be true.

Statements 1 and 3 do not necessarily have to be true given the information we have therefore only 2 must be true.

32. B

Factorising the equation gives $y = (x + 3)(x - 3)$ meaning the curve meets the x-axis at $(-3,0)$ $(3,0)$.

Differentiating gives $\frac{dy}{dx} = 2x$ which when evaluated at the given coordinates gives gradients of -6 and 6.

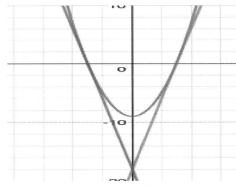

Forming the equation of each line,

$$y_1 = 6(x - 3)$$

$$y_1 = 6x - 18$$

$$y_2 = -6(x + 3)$$

$$y_2 = -6x - 18$$

Using the final form of y_1 and y_2 we can calculate the area of the triangle with coordinates $(-3,0)$ $(3,0)$ $(0,-18)$ which is 54.

Next, we need to subtract the area of the curve from the area of the triangle to obtain the answer which is $54 - \int_{-3}^{3} x^2 - 9\,dx = 54 - 36 = 18$.

33. B

Using $w = y^2$ transforms the equation into $w^2 - 15w + 36 = 0$ which can be factorised into $(w - 12)(w - 3) = 0$. As a result, $y = \pm 2\sqrt{3}$ or $y = \pm\sqrt{3}$.

Therefore $p = 2\sqrt{3}$ and $q = -2\sqrt{3}$ so this means $2p - q = 6\sqrt{3}$.

34. B

The statement looks at the region that is a mixture of both shaded colours red and black. Statement B looks at the region that is only shaded black and therefore does not include the region asked for in the statement and is directly a contradiction of the statement for the specified domain of x.

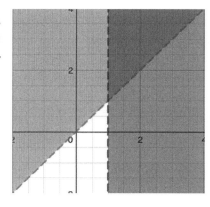

35. B

Analysing statement 2, this implies that $f(x) = x(x - 1)(x + 1)$ meaning that $x = 0$ is a solution, however $f(0) = d$ therefore this is not necessarily true. As a result only answers A,B,D,F remain. Statement 3 is not necessarily true for all values of b, c, d, for example if they all equal 1. So only A & B remain. Statement 1 must be necessarily true since at $x = 0$, then $f(0) = d$ (in the general case, k), so $f(d) = 0$, since $f(0) = d$, x has already been stated to equal 0, therefore 1 is true.

36. A

Analysing statement 3, if $x = -10$ and $y = -0.01$, $xy = 0.1$ therefore the statement is false.

Analysing statement 1, if $x = 5$ and $y = -1$ then $\frac{x}{y} = -5$ therefore the statement is false.

Analysing statement 2, using the wording "if and only if" implies that the condition is both necessary and sufficient yet $\frac{y}{x} < 1$ is not sufficient since the question had to specify certain restrictions on x and y (non-zero real numbers), therefore this statement is false.

END OF SECTION

Section 2

Read the article 'Drain or gain?' taken from The Economist (May 26th 2011). Based on this text, complete the task below.

Set out two ways in which emigration of skilled workers can harm developing countries, and two ways in which such countries can benefit.

How might you evaluate whether there was a net gain for a developing country from the emigration of skilled workers?

A skilled worker is a worker who has a competent level of knowledge in their field and will have often attended university or college. Skilled workers are discussed in the 'brain drain' hypothesis which sets out the theory of human capital flight whereby skilled workers in receipt of more advanced training domestically, emigrate abroad. Conversely, studies support the idea of a 'brain gain' hypothesis whereby the benefits of remittances and incentives to invest in education out way costs to developing countries such as a shortage of skilled workers and a loss of potential future entrepreneurs. Ultimately, there is great difficulty establishing a causing relationship between emigration and economic growth for developing countries but comparing two similar countries, one with high emigration and one with low emigration should provide an accurate assessment.

Firstly, the large-scale emigration of skilled workers can potentially harm developing countries due to a shortage of skilled workers generally across the economy, and more specifically in key industries. More generally, across the economy a lack of skilled workers will harm an economy's reputation if it is stuck in a cycle of producing low quality exports and faces a repeat of this for future generations due to a lack of quality teachers in the education system. As a result, in the international market there will be a lack of confidence surrounding the developing country, whether it be politically or for its firms, leading to worse terms of trade when negotiating, or higher rates of interest charged by international banks, increasing the costs of development projects in the country. More specifically, in industries such as healthcare, a lack of skilled workers, for example doctors could harm the population in the developing country as they face the consequences of poor access to quality healthcare.

However, the emigration of skilled workers can benefit developing countries through the effects of remittances. Remittances account for a significant proportion of developing countries GDP, reaching 'more than 20%' for countries such as Nepal and Lebanon, highlighting its crucial importance to developing economies. Moreover, the effect amount of remittance is even higher since while remittances totalled approximately '$325 billion n 2010', this doesn't factor into account the fact that some emigrants would have been jobless if they had stayed, meaning that when skilled workers leave, they form a more 'productive pairing' between their skills and jobs which lead to the vast figure previously quoted, but this figure doesn't highlight that although developing countries have some income per person, with high levels of unemployment many workers would have zero income and thus remittances are made much more valuable. For example, 'Romanian migrants 'earned almost $12,000 a year more in America' than their standard income per person of '$7,500', however if this skilled worker would have previously been unemployed then the remittances are even more valuable, highlighting the importance of skilled workers emigrating from developing countries.

Moreover, the 'brain drain' hypothesis is potentially harmful to developing countries due to the loss of potential entrepreneurs and ideas. If skilled workers wanted to become entrepreneurs or possessed the capacity to actively improve the production process in which they were working on, then the large-scale emigration of skilled workers would lead to a more inefficient production process. As a result, workers would become more unproductive that remain in the country and therefore increase the costs per unit output for firms. In addition, despite remittances proving important to supplement low skilled workers incomes in developing countries, the developing country would likely become dependent on these remittances to sustain the less efficient firms, leaving the developing country more prone to exogenous shocks.

A second benefit emigration of skilled workers brings to developing countries is an increased incentive to invest in education and more broadly the framework in which economies operate in. When young people perceive the chance of emigrating increasing, i.e., an increased likelihood to earn more in their lifetime and have access to better facilities than within their current country, they are more likely to progress further in education as seen by studies in Cape Verde, increasing the skill level of the general population if these young people decide not to emigrate in the end. Moreover, if these young people did emigrate, then they provide access for domestic firms to enter foreign, developed markets such as when Indian software firms were able to break into American markets easier due to the rise of Silicon Valley.

Upon evaluating whether there was a net gain for a developing country from the emigration of skilled workers, proving causality, or at least showing a correlation will be difficult due to the degree of other endogenous factors present. A developing country could analyse its rate of economic growth before large-scale emigration and after to see if there was truly a net gain involved, however this would simply show correlation, not necessarily implying causality. Comparing two similar developing countries, both experiencing similar GDP per capita, life expectancy and other baseline measures where one country is starting to experience large-scale emigration and one is still more isolated could lead to indicative results depending on if the country after more emigration is experiencing higher GDP per capita, and thus showing a net gain.

END OF PAPER

2019

Section 1A

1. C
We can immediately eliminate Roz who has the same tax rate but a different salary
Tim pays $10,000 \times 0.30 = \$3,000$
Neil $20,000 \times 0.25 = \$5,000$
Veronica $150,000 \times 0.03 = \$4,500$
David $50,000 \times 0.06 = \$3,000$

2. D
We know that the height is 2 because there is a square in the centre.
(In fact, because we are *purely* dealing with ratios here, it does not matter what we assume the height to be)
Total area $= 4 \times 2 = 8$
Red area $= 2 + 2 + 0.25 \times 4 = 5$
White area $= 8 - 5 = 3$.
Ratio of red to white is $5:3$.

3. C
We are looking for the lowest cost per km.
Option C is *both* longer and has lower cost than A and B, so we eliminate A and B.
Option D is the same cost as C, but the length is lower, so we eliminate D.
C will have a lower cost per km than E because $\frac{6}{75} < \frac{5}{46}$.

4. E
More tickets were sold on Friday *and* a larger % of these tickets were premium compared to Thursday. Sales income must have been higher on Friday than Thursday. This eliminates A, C and D.
More tickets were sold on Saturday than Friday (425 vs 375).

But less premium tickets sold on Saturday, which are more expensive. If premium tickets are much more expensive than standard tickets, Friday's sales income was probably higher.

If premium tickets are slightly more expensive, Saturday's sales income was probably higher. Without knowing how much more the premium tickets are, we cannot say for sure, therefore the answer is E.

N.B. it is possible (but very unlikely) that Thursday's sales income was higher than Saturday's. If premium tickets are much, *much* more expensive than standard ones then the extra income from premium tickets sold on Thursday could more than make up for lower total sales on Thursday. We know that Thursday's income was less than Friday, so the answer is still E. But it is possible for the ranking to be Friday, Thursday, Saturday.

5. B

The lowest common multiple of 3,5 and 6 is 30.

So, after 30 mins they cross the line together.

Alec has done 10 laps. Barry has done 6 laps.

Alec has done 4 more laps than Barry.

6. E

Scan down the table looking for big differences between the 1st and 3rd column.

Carbonda has a 100% increase, so eliminate A and B.

Grandia is 200% $\left(\left(\frac{60-20}{20}\right) \times 100\right)$, which is the highest % increase of the options shown

7. B

Diagram 1 shows that Car 2 is newer and more expensive.

Diagram 2 shows that Car 2 is bigger and faster.

Therefore Car 2 is newer, more expensive, bigger and faster than Car 1.

Option B says the cheaper car is bigger. This is wrong.

8. C

Picture the display switching from 1,2,3 etc.

The only number for which the bottom right segment does not light up is the number 2.

This means the maximum is 8, leaving us with options C and D.

The bottom left only lights up 3 times for numbers (2, 6 & 9).

9. C

Work out her cheapest option at each hotel.

Grand: Fri - Mon. $50 + 60 + 0 + 60 = 170$

Majestic: Fri - Mon. $40 + \frac{90}{2} + 40 + 40 = 165$

Palace: Fri - Mon. $50 + 90 + 80 + 60 = 280, \frac{280}{2} = 140$

Palms: Thurs - Sun. $50 + 0 + 50 + 60 = 160$

Plaza: Thurs − Sun. $60 + 50 + 70 + 50 - 50 = 180$

10. C

Andrew has 8 less votes in April – all the graphs show this

James gains 3 votes from Andrew, loses 1 vote overall to Roger

James gains 2 votes overall

In Option C James only receives 1 more vote in April compared to March, not 2 more.

11. E

A – Alex scores 7. Sue chooses 9 and 7 and scores 8. Sue wins

B – Alex scores 6. Sue chooses 6 and 7 and scores 6.5. Sue wins

C – Alex scores 1. Sue chooses 9 and 3 and scores 6. Sue wins.

D – Alex scores 2. Sue chooses 6 and 3 and scores 4.5 Sue wins.

E – Alex will win. With this hand, the player that chooses second will win. Thus, Alex should choose to play second.

12. B

On non-bank holiday weekdays: 3hrs and 50 mins of journey time.

First 3 journeys will take $3 \times 1 \text{ hr} = 3$ hrs. The ferry can then make 1 more 50 min journey

This is because cleaning is only required *between* crossings i.e. no cleaning is required if it is the last crossing of the day.

4 journeys are made. 21 days like this in the month. $4 \times 21 = 84$

On weekend and bank holidays: 6hrs 40 mins of journey time.

First 5 journeys (with cleaning) will take 1hr 10 mins $\times 5 = 5$hrs 50mins

Once again, no cleaning is required for this last journey, so the ferry can make one more 50 min journey after.

6 journeys made per day

10 days like this in May, $10 \times 6 = 60$

$84 + 60 = 144$

13. B

Nathan needs 4 rectangles of $15cm \times 38\ cm$

If Nathan chooses the $100cm$ width:

He will only be able to fit 2 rectangles along the width because $38cm \times 2\ rectangles = 76cm$ but $38cm \times 3\ rectangles = 114cm$ which is longer than the width of $100cm$.

Therefore, he will need to fit 2 rectangles along the length too.

So, he will need to buy $30cm$ of length. This will cost £$2 \times 0.3 = 60p$

If Nathan chooses $120cm$ of width:

He will only be able to fit 3 rectangles along the width because $38cm \times 3\ rectangles = 114cm$ but $38cm \times 4\ rectangles = 152cm$ which is longer than the width of $120cm$

So, he will still need to buy $30cm$ of length. This will cost £$2.20 \times 0.3 = 66p$

If Nathan chooses $160cm$ of width:

He will be able to fit all 4 rectangles along the width because $38cm \times 4 = 152cm$ which is less than the width of $160cm$

So, he will only need to buy 15cm of length.

Unfortunately, he needs to buy length in exactly multiples of 10cm, meaning that he must buy 20cm of length minimum.

This is still the cheapest option, costing him £$2.80 \times 0.2 = 56p$.

14. C

Steel baths:

Dalton – no side grips so does not fit his requirements

Europa - £126

Gamma – pre-drilled holes so does not fit his requirements

Polar – length only 1500mm so does not fit his requirements

Sierra – £128

Cheapest steel bath that fits his requirements is £126

Acrylic baths:

Balmoral – width is too long, 750mm does not fit his requirements

Carola – £130

Oporto – no side grips so does not fit his requirements

Rocca – no side grips so does not fit his requirements

Victory - £149

Cheapest Acrylic that fits his requirements is £130

He will save £4

15. E

Votes for Adventure Playground are no more than 25% of the total

This eliminates C

Votes for the Adventure Playground + Museum + Farm is less than 50% of the total

This eliminates A and B

Votes for the Farm are more than the Museum

This eliminates D

16. E

Total surface area per shed $= 2.5 + 2 + \frac{2.5+2}{2} \times 2 = 9m^2$

$9m^2 \times 4\,mins \times 3\,layers = 108\,mins\,per\,shed = 1hr\,48\,min\,per\,shed$

$1hr\,48\,min + 1hr\,48\,min + 20 - min\,tea\,break = 3hrs\,56\,mins$

17. A

The school party needs to buy 16 adult tickets and 8 child tickets in total.

3 group tickets will cost $525. This is the cheapest option given.

18. C

When the net folds, the 5 and the 6 should be positioned above the letter B. This eliminates A and B.

The numbers 5, 4 and 3 in option D are rotated the 180 degrees the wrong way.

The numbers in option E are rotated 90 degrees the wrong way.

19. D

550g of dough is needed

You start with 100g on Monday morning.

On Tuesday morning you have 76g (because 24g of water evaporated over the last 24hrs). You double this to 152g.

On Wednesday morning you have 128g. You double this to 256g.

On Thursday morning you have 232g. You double this to 464g.

On Friday morning you have 440g. You double this to 880g.

So only by Friday you have enough.

20. C

Almond was 20% of 250g = 50g.

200g of nuts are remaining.

If the peanuts were at their maximum, then $250g \times 0.4 = 100g$ of peanuts originally.

This is 50% of the remainder of the bag.

Section 1B

21. C

$$y = 3\left(\sqrt{\frac{x+1}{2}}\right) - 1$$

$$\frac{y+1}{3} = \sqrt{\frac{x+1}{2}}$$

$$2\left(\frac{y+1}{3}\right)^2 = x + 1$$

$$x = 2\left(\frac{y+1}{3}\right)^2 - 1$$

22. E

$0.9X = 28.80$

$0.1X = 3.20$

$X = 32$

$0.75Y = 28.80$

$0.25Y = 9.60$

$Y = 38.40$

Difference: $38.40 - 32 = £6.40$

23. F

$$1 + \frac{x^2 + 9x + 9}{x} > 0$$

We do not know if x is positive or negative. If we multiply through by x and it is negative, then the inequality will switch signs. First, we consider the case where x is positive:

$x + x^2 + 9x + 9 > 0$

$x^2 + 10x + 9 > 0$

$(x + 9)(x + 1) > 0$

Plotting the quadratic as normal and looking for the points for which the function > 0 would give the result $x < -9$ and $x > -1$. But we have already assumed that x is positive. Therefore solutions $x < -9$ and $-1 < x < 0$ are invalid. However, the solutions $x > 0$ are consistent with our assumption that x is positive.

Now consider the case where x is negative:

$x + x^2 + 9x + 9 < 0$

$x^2 + 10x + 9 < 0$

$(x + 9)(x + 1) < 0$

This gives $-9 < x < -1$. This is also consistent with our assumption that x is negative. Therefore, these are also valid solutions.

24. C

$$y = \frac{x^2 - 2}{x^{\frac{1}{2}}}$$

$$y = (x^2 - 2)(x^{-\frac{1}{2}})$$

$$y = x^{\frac{3}{2}} - 2x^{-\frac{1}{2}}$$

$$\frac{dy}{dx} = \frac{3}{2}x^{\frac{1}{2}} + x^{-\frac{3}{2}}$$

Subbing in $x = 2$:

$$\frac{dy}{dx} = \frac{3}{2}(2)^{\frac{1}{2}} + (2)^{-\frac{3}{2}}$$

$$= \frac{3}{2}\sqrt{2} + \frac{1}{\sqrt{2^3}}$$

$$= \frac{3}{2}\sqrt{2} + \left(\frac{1}{2\sqrt{2}} \times \frac{2\sqrt{2}}{2\sqrt{2}}\right)$$

$$= \frac{3}{2}\sqrt{2} + \frac{1}{4}\sqrt{2}$$

$$= \frac{7}{4}\sqrt{2}$$

25. B

$$\left(2\sqrt{p} + 3x\right)^5$$

$$= (2\sqrt{p} + 3x)(2\sqrt{p} + 3x)(2\sqrt{p} + 3x)(2\sqrt{p} + 3x)(2\sqrt{p} + 3x)$$

We are interested in the coefficient on x^3. There are $5C3 = 10$ ways to make an x^3 term. Thus, the coefficient on the x^3 term will be: $10 \times 3^3 \times \left(2\sqrt{p}\right)^2 = 10 \times 27 \times 4p = 1080p$

Solving $1080p = 8640$ gives $p = 8$

26. C

$$\log_3(k + \log_5 x) = 1$$

$$3^1 = k + \log_5 x$$

$$3 - k = \log_5 x$$

$$x = 5^{3-k}$$

27. B

The total number of marks Jenna scored is $1.15 \times 20 = 23$.

This is an odd number. Therefore, she must have correctly answered an odd number of 1-point questions.

Since the modal mark per question was 1, she scored 1 for a *minimum* of 7 questions. Combining this with the above, she either score 1 for 7 questions or 9 questions.

If she scored 1 for 7 questions, she would need to score 2 for 8 questions in order to get a total score of 23. This would make the modal mark per question equal to 2.

Therefore, she must have scored 1 for 9 questions exactly. She scored 2 for 7 questions. This means that she scored 0 for 4 questions.

28. A

For simplicity, let $z = x - 2$.

Our equation becomes:

$z^3 - 12z + k^2 = 0$

Consider the general shape of a cubic, $y = z^3 - 12z$

This cubic has 3-roots to the to the "= 0" equation

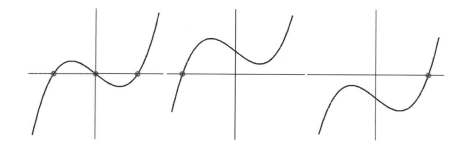

The cubic equation will have one root if either:

A. "k" is large enough to "lift the trough"

B. "k" is negative and "drops the peak"

We must therefore find the turning points:

$\frac{dy}{dz} = 3z^2 - 12 = 0$

$z^2 = 4 \quad z = \pm 2$

At these points

$y = z^3 - 12z = -16 \ or \ 16$

Looking back at the graphs, this means that:

$k^2 > 16 \ or \ k^2 < -16$

Therefore:

$k > 4 \ or \ k < -4$

($k^2 < -16$ has no real solutions)

29. E

25% of the students in the class are boys. The probability that the first student picked is a boy is $\frac{1}{4}$. The probability that the second student picked is also a boy is $\frac{(n-1)}{(4n-1)}$

Therefore, the probability that both students are boys:

$p = \frac{1}{4} \times \frac{(n-1)}{(4n-1)}$

$p = \frac{(n-1)}{4(4n-1)}$

$4p(4n - 1) = (n - 1)$

$16np - 4p - n + 1 = 0$

$n(16p - 1) = 4p - 1$

$n = \frac{4p-1}{16p-1}$

30. E

The sum of a geometric series is $\frac{a}{1-r}$ where a is the first term in the series and r is the geometric multiplier. In both series a is 1. In series R the multiplier is $\sqrt{0.3}$ and in series S the multiplier is $-\sqrt{0.3}$

The sum to infinity of R is $\frac{1}{1-\sqrt{0.3}}$ and the sum to infinity of S is $\frac{1}{1+\sqrt{0.3}}$.

$$R - S = \frac{1}{1-\sqrt{0.3}} - \frac{1}{1+\sqrt{0.3}}$$

$$= \frac{(1+\sqrt{0.3})}{(1-\sqrt{0.3})(1+\sqrt{0.3})} - \frac{(1-\sqrt{0.3})}{(1-\sqrt{0.3})(1+\sqrt{0.3})}$$

$$= \frac{2\sqrt{(0.3)}}{(1-\sqrt{0.3})(1+\sqrt{0.3})} = \frac{2\sqrt{0.3}}{1-0.3}$$

$$= \left(2\sqrt{\frac{1}{10} \times 3}\right) \times \frac{10}{7} = \left(2\sqrt{\frac{1}{10}} \times \sqrt{3}\right) \times \frac{10}{7}$$

$$= \left(\frac{2(\sqrt{10})}{10} \times \sqrt{3}\right) \times \frac{10}{7} = \frac{20\sqrt{10} \times \sqrt{3}}{70}$$

$$= \frac{2\sqrt{30}}{7}$$

31. A

We have negative parabola crossing the x-axis at $(0,0)$ and $(5,0)$. To find the area P, integrate the curve between 0 and 5.

$$\int_0^5 5x - x^2 \, dx$$

$$= \frac{5}{2}x^2 - \frac{1}{3}x^3 \Big|_0^5$$

$$= \frac{125}{2} - \frac{125}{3}$$

$$= \frac{375-250}{6} = \frac{125}{6}$$

The intersection of the two curves:

$$5x - x^2 = 2x$$

$$x(3-x) = 0$$

$$x = 0, 3$$

Coordinates: $(0,0), (3,6)$

To find the area Q, integrate the area between the 2 curves:

$$\int_0^3 3x - x^2 \, dx$$

$$= \frac{3}{2}x^2 - \frac{1}{3}x^3 \Big|_0^3$$

$$= \frac{27}{2} - 9 = \frac{9}{2}$$

Therefore:

$$Ratio \; Q : P = \frac{9}{2} : \frac{125}{6}$$

$$= \frac{54}{2} : 125 = 27 : 125$$

32. E

$f'(x) = 3p^{\frac{2}{3}}x^2 + 2px + p^{\frac{1}{3}}$

$f'(x) = 0$

$3p^{\frac{2}{3}}x^2 + 2px + p^{\frac{1}{3}} = 0$

Since there is exactly one point for which $f'(x) = 0$ the discriminant of the quadratic equation should be zero.

$4p^2 - 4 \times 3p^{\frac{2}{3}} \times p^{\frac{1}{3}} = 0$

$4p^2 - 12p = 0$

Since p is a positive constant (non-zero) we can divide through by p:

$4p = 12$

$p = 3$

33. E

$49^{2x} - 7^{x+1} + 12 = 0$

$(7^x - 4)(7^x - 3) = 0$

$7^x = 4 \text{ and } 7^x = 3$

$x = \dfrac{\log 4}{\log 7} \text{ and } x = \dfrac{\log 3}{\log 7}$

Sum of roots:

$\dfrac{\log 4 + \log 3}{\log 7} = \dfrac{\log 12}{\log 7}$

34. B

Statement 1 is true because $1 - 3 + 2 = 0$

Statement 2 is false because $(x - 2)(x - 1) = 0$. Therefore $x^2 - 3x + 2 = 0$ when $x = 2$ or $x = 1$. The "only" part of the statement is false.

Statement 3 is false, again, the "only" part of the statement is false.

Therefore, only statement 1 is true.

35. D

$P(balls\ of\ the\ same\ colour): q^2 + p^2$

$P(balls\ of\ different\ colours): 2qp$

$P(balls\ of\ the\ same\ colour) - P(balls\ of\ different\ colours) = \frac{1}{4}$

$q^2 + p^2 - 2qp = \frac{1}{4}$

$(1 - p)^2 + p^2 - 2(1 - p)p = \frac{1}{4}$

$1 - 2p + p^2 + p^2 - 2p + 2p^2 = \frac{1}{4}$

$4p^2 - 4p + \frac{3}{4} = 0$

$16p^2 - 16p + 3 = 0$

$16p^2 - 12p - 4p + 3 = 0$

$4p(4p - 3) - (4p - 3) = 0$

$(4p - 3)(4p - 1) = 0$

$p = \frac{1}{4}, \frac{3}{4}$

Since $q > p$, $p = \frac{1}{4}, q = \frac{3}{4}$

$\frac{q}{p} - \frac{p}{q} = 3 - \frac{1}{3} = \frac{8}{3}$

36. D

$(ax + b)(cx + d) = acx^2 + adx + bcx + bd = px^2 + q$

Therefore:

$ac = p,$

$ad = -bc,$

$bd = q$

Condition 1 is not sufficient because

$ad \neq -bc$

Condition 2 is sufficient. Condition 3 is also sufficient because if $a = c = 1$, then $d = -b$ for the condition $ad = -bc$ to hold, which is true.

END OF SECTION

Section 2

Read the article 'Global imbalances, a pre-crisis scourge, are back' taken from The Economist (October 26th, 2016). Based on this text, complete the task below.

Set out two ways in which global imbalances can cause problems for the development of the world economy.

Suggest possible reasons why an individual country might experience persistent current account surpluses or deficits.

Introduction:
- Define the current account, financial account, and the relationship between them. A current account deficit must be financed by a financial account surplus. Show the relationship between domestic savings, investments, and the current account:
  - $C + I + G + X - M = Y$
  - $Y - C - G = I + X - M$
  - $S = I + CA$ m
  - $CA = S - I$
- A very sophisticated answer might also mention the role of the current account in intertemporal consumption smoothing.

Reasons for which global imbalances can cause problems for the world economy:
- Savings glut can depress global interest rates and encourage risky borrowing and speculative or unproductive investment. This can lead to overleveraged financial institutions and asset bubbles. Can use the U.S. housing bubble in 2007 and the financial crisis that followed as an example
- Low global interest rates leave little leeway for central bank policy makers to respond to a crisis. Explain how a "liquidity trap" may emerge, as interest rates are pushed towards their effective lower bound.
- The article mentions "demand drain". Excessive global imbalances may result in lower domestic demand for goods and services, which will lower the countries growth (since they are importing rather than producing domestically).
- Vulnerability of surplus countries to future demand shocks. Rapid U.S. interest rate could suddenly reduce its demand for imports which could cause recession in exporting countries.
- Unemployment could increase within the deficit countries manufacturing sector (it is manufactured goods that are primarily imported). Possible economy wide productivity losses if manufacturing productivity growth stronger than other countries. Political consequences of unemployment – rising inequality and rise of populist politics

Why an individual country might experience persistent deficit?
- Looking at the equation in introduction - persistently low savings/high investment will result in persistent deficits
- Why might this occur? A rapidly growing developing economy may have very high investment rates, for example.

- Returns to investment in developing countries should be higher (because of diminishing marginal returns), so there should be capital outflows from advanced economies and capital inflows in developing ones, resulting in CA surpluses in advanced economies.
- The data in the article suggests the opposite
- This might be because investment in "highly financialised" economies in the West is seen as less risky so there are capital inflows, even if theory predicts the opposite
- This means that countries with large, persistent deficits can finance their CA deficit by attracting FDI and portfolio investment, meaning that they can persistently run a financial account surplus
- This is not "hot money", which can suddenly dry up, making it possible for persistent deficits to occur.

Conclusion:
- Summarise the 2 points that you gave for why global imbalances can present problem
- Summarise how advanced economies are able to persistently finance current account deficits by running financial account surpluses. This can occur as long as the political and economic situation remains stable, such that investment carries less risk than developing countries.

END OF PAPER

ECAA 2020 SOLUTIONS

Part A

1: D

The simultaneous equations are:

$$2a + 3c = 20$$

$$4a + 4c = 34$$

Doubling the first equation, the difference between the two is:

$$2c = 6$$

So, a child's ticket costs £3.

Substituting this back in, an adult's ticket costs £5.50.

Therefore, the cost for 6 adults and 2 children is £39.

2: G

Based on the options, only consider the 11th or 29th terms.

Substituting 11 in:

$$2(11) - 5 = 17$$

Checking the previous term:

$$2(10) - 5 = 15$$

Therefore, the difference is 2, so G is the correct row.

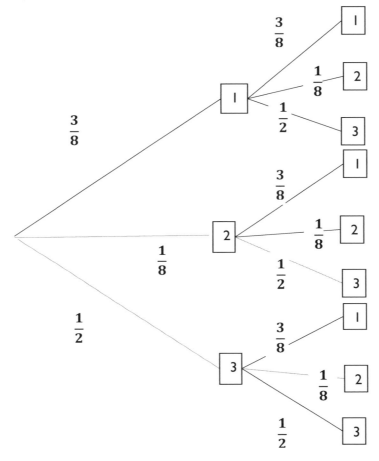

3: A

The two branches of the tree diagram in red indicate probabilities of the scores on the spinner adding to 5:

$$\frac{1}{8} \times \frac{1}{2} + \frac{1}{2} \times \frac{1}{8} = \frac{1}{8}$$

4: A

The area of the quarter-circle QPS is:

$$\frac{\pi x^2}{4}$$

The area of the semi-circle with M at the centre is:

$$\frac{\pi \left(\frac{x}{2}\right)^2}{2} = \frac{\pi x^2}{8}$$

Therefore, the shaded area is the difference:

$$\frac{\pi x^2}{4} - \frac{\pi x^2}{8} = \frac{\pi x^2}{8}$$

5: C

Reducing by 60% 3 times is equivalent to multiplying by 0.4^3:

$$5000 \times 0.4^3 = 320$$

6: B

The gradients of perpendicular lines are negative reciprocals of each other, so in the rearranged form:

1. $y = \frac{1}{2} - \frac{1}{3}x$
2. $y = \frac{1}{3}x - \frac{4}{9}$
3. $y = 3x + \frac{3}{2}$
4. $y = \frac{3}{2} - \frac{3}{2}x$

Lines 1 and 3 have perpendicular gradients.

$$-\frac{1}{3} \times 3 = -1$$

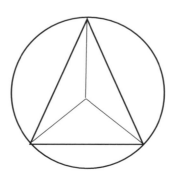

7: B

Each of the triangle's angles can be split into two 30° angles by a line to the centre – the radius.

The angles around the centre are 120°, so we use the sine rule to find the radius:

$$\frac{r}{sin30} = \frac{8}{sin120}$$

$sin120°$ is the same as $sin60°$ and $sin30° = 0.5$ so the circumference ($2\pi r$) can be expressed as:

$$2\pi \left(\frac{8 \times 0.5}{sin60}\right) = \frac{8\pi}{sin60}$$

8: F

Treat $\left(\frac{x}{4} + 3\right) = y$:

$$2y^2 - y - 36 = 0$$

$$(2y - 9)(y + 4) = 0$$

Hence:

$$y = \frac{9}{2} \, or - 4 = \frac{x}{4} + 3$$

Therefore:

$$x = 6 \, or - 28$$

So the sum of the solutions is -22.

9: A

Expand and collect like terms:

$$4x^2 + 12x + 9 - (x^2 - 6x + 9)$$

$$3x^2 + 18x$$

Factorise:

$$3[x^2 + 6x]$$

$$3[(x + 3)^2 - 9]$$

$$3(x + 3)^2 - 27$$

So $r = -27$.

10: E

The expression is equal to:

$$\frac{ac}{b} - \frac{a}{bc}$$

$$\frac{ac^2}{bc} - \frac{a}{bc}$$

$$\frac{ac^2 - a}{bc}$$

$$\frac{a(c^2 - 1)}{bc}$$

11: F

The mean will be equal to the total number of points scored divided by the total number of students across both groups:

$$\frac{10 \times 36 + 20 \times 48}{10 + 20} = 44$$

The range will be at least 21 because the scores in group Y were this spread out, and adding the other students' scores does not change this.

12: B

Let n be the number of boots sold:

$$n = \frac{k}{x^3}$$

Substitute in to find the constant, k:

$250 = \frac{k}{8^3}$ Therefore:

$k=128000$ Use the values for the following day to find the temperature:

$$250 \times \left(1 + \frac{700}{100}\right) = 2000 = \frac{128000}{x^3}$$

$$x = \sqrt[3]{64} = 4$$

13: E

Let x be the pre-sale price of the bike.

The sale price is $0.75x$

The customer calculated pre-sale price is:

$$0.75x \times 1.25 = 0.9375x$$

Which is £15 away from the true price, so:

$$(1 - 0.9375)x = 15$$

$$x = \frac{15}{0.0625} = 240$$

14: A

Summarise the information as follows:

Red	:	Blue	:	Yellow
18	:	5	:	
	:	p	:	3
12	:		:	5

Scale-up each ratio to the lowest common multiple:

Red	:	Blue	:	Yellow
36	:	10	:	
	:	5p	:	15
36	:		:	15

As the ratios are in the same proportion, 10 = 5p, so p = 2.

15: F

Line QS:

$$\sqrt{y^2 - x^2}$$

Triangle QSR:

$$\sin 61 = \frac{QS}{QR} = \frac{\sqrt{y^2 - x^2}}{z}$$

$$z = \frac{\sqrt{y^2 - x^2}}{\sin 61}$$

16: E

Each throw has a 50% chance of being even.

$$P(\text{at least one even}) = 1 - P(\text{all 4 are odd})\ 1 - \left(\frac{1}{2}\right)^4 = 1 - \frac{1}{16} = \frac{15}{16}$$

17: B

The equation $2x^2 - px - 4 = 0$ will factorise to an equation of the form $(2x - a)(x - b) = 0$

Also, as the two solutions differ by 6: $b - \frac{a}{2} = 6$

Expanding:

$$2x^2 - (a + 2b)x + ab = 0$$

Thus:

$$ab = -4 \text{ and } -(a + 2b) = -p$$

Substitute in to solve:

$$a\left(\frac{a}{2} + 6\right) = -4$$

$$a^2 + 12a + 8 = 0$$

$$a = -6 \pm 2\sqrt{7}$$

So:

$$b = 3 \pm \sqrt{7}$$

To find p:

$$p = (a + 2b) = 4\sqrt{7}$$

because it is positive

18: D

The solid square is the largest possible square and the dashed square is the smallest.

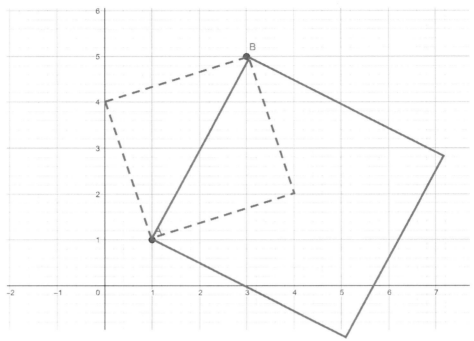

The length of the line AB is $\sqrt{(3-1)^2 + (5-1)^2} = \sqrt{20} = 2\sqrt{5}$ so the perimeter of the large square is $8\sqrt{5}$

As they are perpendicular to each other, the sides of the small square each stretch 3 units on the x-axis and 1 on the y axis, or vice versa. Therefore, their length is $\sqrt{3^2 + 1^2}$ so the perimeter is $4\sqrt{10}$

Thus, the difference in perimeters is:

$$4 \times 2\sqrt{5} - 4\sqrt{10} = 4\sqrt{5}(2 - \sqrt{2})$$

19: C

After the 90° rotation, the points R and S are $(-1, 3)$ and $(5, -2)$.

The midpoint of RS is $(2, 0.5)$.

Compared to the midpoint of TU, $(7, -2.5)$, the transformation is:

$$\begin{pmatrix} 5 \\ -3 \end{pmatrix}$$

20: D

Substituting in the radius and height into Volume of cone:

$$\frac{1}{3}\pi r^2 h = \frac{1}{3}\pi x^2 \left(\frac{5x}{2}\right) = \frac{5}{6}\pi x^3$$

Likewise, for Volume of hemisphere:

$$\frac{1}{2} \times \frac{4}{3}\pi r^3 = \frac{2}{3}\pi \left(\frac{y}{2}\right)^3 = \frac{1}{12}\pi y^3$$

So the answer is:

$$\frac{\frac{5}{6}\pi x^3}{\frac{1}{12}\pi y^3} = \frac{10x^3}{y^3}$$

Part B

21: F

Substitute in for g(x):

$$\int_4^9 2f(x) + 1\,dx = 2\int_4^9 f(x)\,dx + \int_4^9 1\,dx = 2 \times 3 + [9 - 4] = 11$$

22: B

Expanding $(x - 1)(x - 2)$, gives $x^2 - 3x + 2$

$x^4 + ax^3 + bx^2 - 12x + 4$ will therefore factorise to $(x^2 + px + 2)(x^2 - 3x + 2)$ because of the constant and x^4 terms.

Expanding gives:

$$x^4 - 3x^3 + 2x^2 + px^3 - 3px^2 + 2px + 2x^2 - 6x + 4$$

$$= x^4 + (p - 3)x^3 + (4 - 3p)x^2 + (2p - 6)x + 4$$

Comparing, $2p - 6 = -12$ so $p = -3$

Therefore $a = -6$ and $b = 13$

23: A

The area is $32\sqrt{2}$, so each isosceles triangle has an area of $4\sqrt{2}$.

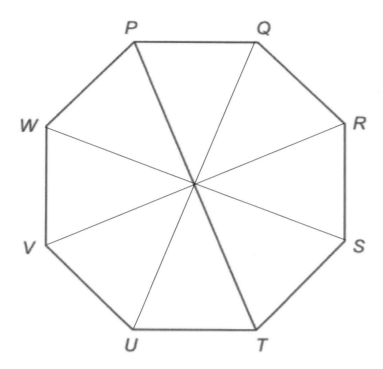

Set this equal to the formula for the area of a triangle, where a and b are the long sides, and angle C is 45° as angles around a point add to 360°, divided by 8:

$$4\sqrt{2} = \frac{1}{2}absinC = \frac{\sqrt{2}}{4}ab$$

So $ab = 16$ and since $a = b$, $a = 4$ as the lengths are positive. Therefore the length PT = 8cm.

24: E

To solve this, integrate:

$$\int_1^3 \frac{1}{2}x^2 - (-x)dx$$

$$\left[\frac{1}{6}x^3 + \frac{x^2}{2}\right] = \left(\frac{1}{6}(3)^3 + \frac{(3)^2}{2}\right) - \left(\frac{1}{6}(1)^3 + \frac{(1)^2}{2}\right) = \frac{25}{3}$$

25: B

Let length $WZ = a$ and $WX = 4b$

Hence:

$$\text{perimeter} = 260m = 8b + 5a$$

The area:

$$P = ab = a\left(\frac{260 - 5a}{8}\right) = \frac{65}{2}a - \frac{5}{8}a^2$$

To maximise:

$$\frac{dP}{da} = \frac{65}{2} - \frac{5}{4}a = 0$$

Therefore:

$$a = 26m$$

26: C

Consider that the gradient m means the line goes up y_0 for every x_0 it goes along. When it is reflected, it then travels x_0 vertically for every y_0 horizontally, so the new gradient is $\frac{1}{m}$

27: C

$$P(at\ least\ one\ red) = 1 - P(B \cap B) = 1 - \frac{1}{2} \times \frac{1}{3} = \frac{5}{6}$$

$$P(B|at\ least\ one\ red) = \frac{\frac{1}{2} \times \frac{2}{3} + \frac{1}{2} \times \frac{2}{3}}{\frac{5}{6}} = \frac{4}{5}$$

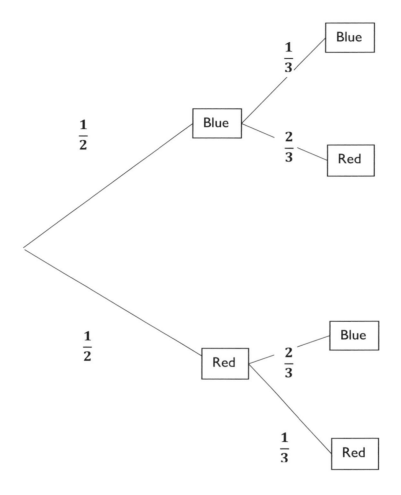

28: A

Using the sum of an arithmetic series:

$$S_{20} = 50 = \frac{n}{2}(2a + (n-1)d) = 10(2a + 19d) = 20a + 190d$$

$$S_{40} - S_{20} = -50 = 20(2a + 39d) - 10(2a + 19d) = 20a + 590d$$

Solving these, $d = -\frac{1}{4}$ and $a = \frac{39}{8}$

So:

$$S_{100} = 50(2a + 99d) = -750$$

29: E

Working backwards:

$$X_{50} = 6 = -\frac{12}{x_{49}} \text{ so } X_{49} = -2$$

$$X_{49} = -2 = -\frac{12}{x_{48}} \text{ so } X_{48} = 6$$

$$X_{48} = 6 = -\frac{12}{x_{47}} \text{ so } X_{47} = -2$$

And so on...

Since they alternate, the first 15 numbers will be made up of 8 lots of '-2' and 7 lots of '6'.

Therefore:

$$S_{15} = (8 \times -2) + (7 \times 6) = 26$$

30: D

The area of the triangle is found with the base on the y-axis and the height as the perpendicular distance to the point $(2, 4)$

$$\text{Area} = \frac{1}{2}bh = \frac{1}{2}(c_2 - c_1) \times 2 = 5$$

$$(c_2 - c_1) = 5$$

The equations of the two lines are:

$$y = mx + c_1 \text{ and } y = -\frac{1}{m}x + c_2$$

Substitute in $(2, 4)$:

$$4 = 2m + c_1, \, 4 = -\frac{2}{m} + c_2$$

With 3 equations and 3 unknown variables, it is possible to solve for m, giving $m = 2$

31: E

Let t_1 be the total of all the numbers when added up, and t_2 be the new total after two numbers are removed.

$$nm = t_1$$

$$(n-2)(m+2) = t_2$$

$$nm - 2m + 2n - 4 = t_2$$

For there to be a new mode after two numbers were removed, both of the numbers removed would have to be the modal number. Thus, half the difference between the two totals of all the numbers added up is equal to the number that was removed twice, which is the mode.

So, substituting for nm and rearranging:

$$\tfrac{1}{2}(t_1 - t_2) = m - n + 2$$

32: E

$$ar^2 = 4, ar^4 = 2$$

Dividing one by the other:

$$r^2 = \tfrac{1}{2} \text{ so } r = \pm\tfrac{1}{\sqrt{2}} \text{ and thus } a = 8$$

The sum to infinity is:

$$S = \frac{a}{1-r} = \frac{8}{1 \pm \dfrac{1}{\sqrt{2}}} = 16 \pm 8\sqrt{2}$$

Therefore, the modulus of the difference between the two sums to infinity is:

$$\left|16 + 8\sqrt{2} - \left(16 - 8\sqrt{2}\right)\right| = 16\sqrt{2}$$

33: D

Let the two points of intersection be A and B. The distances PQ, PA, PB, QA, QB are all equal to 1, as $r = 1$. Since PAQ is an equilateral triangle, angle A is 60°, so angle B is also 60° and angles P and Q must be 120°.

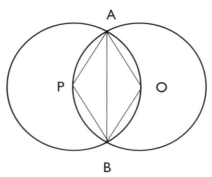

The area of the segment PAB is then just $\frac{120}{360}\pi r^2$, as is segment QAB. Adding these gives the area of overlap but has double-counted the two triangles in the middle.

$$\text{These have an area} = \frac{1}{2}absinC = \frac{1}{2} \times 1 \times 1 \times \sin 60 = \frac{\sqrt{3}}{4}$$

So, the area of overlap is:

$$(2 \times \frac{1}{3}\pi) - (2 \times \frac{\sqrt{3}}{4}) = \frac{2\pi}{3} - \frac{\sqrt{3}}{2}$$

34: A

$$y = x^3 + 3\sqrt{5}px^2 + 3px + 13$$

Differentiate:

$$\frac{dy}{dx} = 3x^2 + 6\sqrt{5}px + 3p = 0$$

For the curve to have two distinct turning points, the discriminant of the first derivative must be greater than 0 (so there are two solutions, which implies two turning points):

$$b^2 - 4ac > 0$$

$$\left(6\sqrt{5}p\right)^2 - 4 \times 3 \times 3p > 0$$

$$180p^2 - 36p > 0$$

$$p(5p - 1) > 0$$

So:

$$p < 0 \; or > \frac{1}{5}$$

35: G

Rearranging and factorising to solve:

$$x^4 - 13x^2 + 36 < 0$$

$$(x^2 - 9)(x^2 - 4) < 0$$

$$x = \pm 3 \; or \pm 2$$

As the curve is below 0 and it is a positive quartic, we know:

$$-3 < x < -2 \text{ and } 2 < x < 3$$

36: E

Using the trigonometric identity $\sin^2 x + \cos^2 x = 1$ and rearranging:

$$14\cos x(1 - \sin^2 x) + 10\sin^2 x \cos x = 13\cos x$$

$$14\cos x - 14\sin^2 x \cos x + 10\sin^2 x \cos x = 13\cos x$$

$$\cos x - 4\sin^2 x \cos x = 0$$

Factorising and solving:

$$\cos x(1 - 4\sin^2 x) = 0$$

So:

$$\cos x = 0 \text{ or } \sin^2 x = \frac{1}{4} \text{ which implies } \sin x = \frac{1}{2} \text{ or } -\frac{1}{2}$$

Each of these 3 will have 2 solutions in the range $0 \le x \le 2\pi$, so 4 solutions in the range $\qquad -2\pi \le x \le 2\pi$, which makes 12 in total.

37: F

This question uses log rules and rearranging:

$$2^x = 3^{2-x}$$

$$2^x = \frac{3^2}{3^x}$$

$$2^x \times 3^x = 9$$

$$\log(2^x \times 3^x) = \log 9$$

$$\log(2^x) + \log(3^x) = \log 9$$

$$x(\log 2 + \log 3) = \log 9$$

$$x(\log 6) = \log 9$$

$$x = \frac{\log 9}{\log 6}$$

38: D

Using log rules:

$$(logx + logx)^2 + logx = 3$$

$$4(logx)^2 + logx - 3 = 0$$

Factorising and solving:

$$(4logx - 3)(logx + 1) = 0$$

$$logx = \frac{3}{4} \, or -1$$

$$x = 10^{\frac{3}{4}} \, or \, 10^{-1}$$

So, the product of the roots is:

$$10^{\frac{3}{4}} \times 10^{-1} = 10^{\frac{-1}{4}}$$

39: D

The distance between two points is $\sqrt{(x - x_0)^2 + (y - y_0)^2}$

Substitute in $\left(0, \frac{9}{2}\right)$ and $y = x^2$:

$$\sqrt{\left(\sqrt{y} - 0\right)^2 + \left(y - \frac{9}{2}\right)^2}$$

Don't need $\pm$ as $y = x^2$ is a symmetric function

$$\sqrt{y + y^2 - 9y + \frac{81}{4}}$$

$$\sqrt{y^2 - 8y + \frac{81}{4}}$$

Completing the square to find the minimum:

$$\sqrt{(y - 4)^2 - 16 + \frac{81}{4}}$$

So, the distance is at its minimum when $y = 4$.

40: C

The gradient is:

$$\frac{dy}{dx} = -4 + 6x^{\frac{1}{2}} - 2x$$

Differentiate to find the maximum:

$$\frac{d^2y}{dx^2} = 3x^{-\frac{1}{2}} - 2 = 0$$

$$x = \left(\frac{2}{3}\right)^{-2} = \frac{9}{4}$$

The value of the gradient at its maximum is:

$$\frac{dy}{dx} = -4 + 9 - 4.5 = \frac{1}{2}$$

Section 2

- *Set out one reason why a wealth tax might discourage investments that result in technological innovations and one reason why such a tax might encourage them.*
- *Discuss the broader advantages and disadvantages of introducing a wealth tax in a rich developed economy.*

SUMMARY OF MAIN POINTS IN THE PASSAGE

- Thomas Piketty's 2014 "Capital in the Twenty-First Century" proposed a tax on wealth, which is an idea that has gained popularity in recent years.
  - He argues that concentrated wealth leads to the concentration of political power, undermining democracy.
- The top 0.1% of taxpayers accounted for 20% of the wealth in America in 2012, and the ratio of household wealth national income has nearly doubled over the past 40 years.
- Taxing wealth could also be justified on the basis of market failure.
- The traditional economic reasoning argues that wealth taxes are bad because they discourage the income-generating activities that created the wealth in the first place. Investment is an input into future growth, so it must not be discouraged, or the economy will be smaller in the future.
- A new paper argues that a tax on wealth would encourage people to spend their money. Hence, they invest in growing firms and grow the economy whilst reducing inequality and raising productivity.
- Another idea is taxes on land values. Land is valuable partly because it is a scarce resource, so owners should have to make improvements to the land itself to make a return on their investment.
- There is also a moral argument to be made as the taxes can be used to benefit society and encourage billionaires to put their money to good use.
- However, they may encourage more tax avoidance instead of more investment and could go too far. But the article suggests solutions such as exit taxes and mandated information sharing from banks to tax authorities.

SPECIMEN ANSWER

Plan

- Positive
    - Put the money to good use for return on investment instead of being taxed
        - Or lead to tax avoidance and other unintended consequences
- Negative
    - Less of an incentive to create the wealth in the first place as it would be taxed upon.
        - Though if set at a modest or optimal level, it should not discourage innovation and hard work since there will still be plenty of profit to be made.
- Broader advantages/disadvantages
    - (+) Moral considerations re inequality
    - (+) Less concentration of power (Piketty)
    - (-) If the country acts unilaterally, it may result in a 'brain drain' or similar emigration of workers and capital.

Wealth taxes are duties levied on the assets and capital that individuals own, as opposed to income taxes that are collected based on wages and other sources of income. They have recently become more widely debated in economics, with newer literature arguing for their merits instead of the established view that they would stunt economic growth. Their introduction could also yield broader advantages in the economy, such as less concentration of power among the wealthy and a better moral standing for society.

The proponents of wealth taxes argue that they would encourage wealthy individuals to seek out opportunities to invest rather than allow the value of their unused assets to be eroded by the annual tax. This should benefit firms that are seeking to improve productivity by expanding their capital stock. In turn, this improves the economy's productive capacity, which is good for society because living standards also rise as a result. It would reward the best investors, who seek out the investment opportunities that offer the highest return. This relies on the assumption that the free market operates sufficiently well to eliminate information asymmetries, which would distort the signals sent to investors about which are the most profitable investments.

On the other hand, wealth taxes may discourage investment and other wealth-generating economic activity because individuals would not be rewarded as highly, since some gain is taken away in tax. If the return is judged not to be great enough once the tax is accounted for, individuals may decide not to invest. However, there would still be significant incentives to earn more and create wealth due to the greater amount of goods and services consumed, which individuals derive utility from. Also, wealth taxes are not directly on labour supply or investment, so they are not as distortionary as they might be – they would only affect income from these sources if left unspent and become part of an individual's stock of assets.

There is also the moral argument that a tax on wealth would help reduce disparities in society so that there is greater equality, and more people can enjoy a better standard of living. This relies on the government redistributing the money to the right places so that it benefits society. Piketty (2014) argues that less concentration of wealth would mean less concentration of power, which would be good for society because the special interests of individuals would be considered less compared to the needs of society. However, the possibility of unintended consequences remains. Taxing wealth may lead to greater levels of tax avoidance and could even create such demand for investment opportunities that their price increases until they become no longer profitable. If a country acts unilaterally to impose a wealth tax, it might cause a 'brain drain' of workers and investment to other countries where their wealth will not be taxed so that they can gain greater utility.

Overall, the impact of a wealth tax on investment is likely to remain ambiguous until further research is carried out on the topic. While they may encourage wealthy individuals to put their funds to use, they may also reduce the incentive to create the wealth in the first place. Whilst they could have broader benefits to society in terms of greater equality and distribution of power, they may also have unintended adverse consequences like tax avoidance and the movement of capital and workers away from the country in question.

ECAA PRACTICE PAPERS
Revision Timetable

Still struggling to get organised? Then try filling in the example revision timetable below, remember to factor in enough time for short breaks, and stick to it! Remember to schedule in several breaks throughout the day and actually use them to do something you enjoy e.g., TV, reading, YouTube etc.

	8AM	10AM	12PM	2PM	4PM	6PM	8PM
MONDAY							
TUESDAY							
WEDNESDAY							
THURSDAY							
FRIDAY							
SATURDAY							
SUNDAY							
EXAMPLE DAY		School			Statistics	Pure Maths	Critical Thinking

> ***Top tip!*** Ensure that you take a watch that can show you the time in seconds into the exam. This will allow you have a much more accurate idea of the time you're spending on a question. In general, if you've spent >150 seconds on a section 1 question – move on regardless of how close you think you are to solving it.

Getting the most out of Mock Papers

Mock exams can prove invaluable if tackled correctly. Not only do they encourage you to start revision earlier, they also allow you to **practice and perfect your revision technique**. They are often the best way of improving your knowledge base or reinforcing what you have learnt. Probably the best reason for attempting mock papers is to familiarise yourself with the exam conditions of the ECAA as they are particularly tough.

Start Revision Earlier

Thirty five percent of students agree that they procrastinate to a degree that is detrimental to their exam performance. This is partly explained by the fact that they often seem a long way in the future. In the scientific literature this is well recognised, Dr Piers Steel, an expert on the field of motivation states that *'the further away an event is, the less impact it has on your decisions'*.

Mock exams are therefore a way of giving you a target to work towards and motivate you in the run up to the real thing – every time you do one treat it as the real deal! If you do well then it's a reassuring sign; if you do poorly then it will motivate you to work harder (and earlier!).

Practice and perfect revision techniques

In case you haven't realised already, revision is a skill all to itself, and can take some time to learn. For example, the most common revision techniques including **highlighting and/or re-reading are quite ineffective** ways of committing things to memory. Unless you are thinking critically about something you are much less likely to remember it or indeed understand it. Mock exams, therefore allow you to test your revision strategies as you go along. Try spacing out your revision sessions so you have time to forget what you have learnt in-between. This may sound counterintuitive but the second time you remember it for longer. Try teaching another student what you have learnt, this forces you to structure the information in a logical way that may aid memory. Always try to question what you have learnt and appraise its validity. Not only does this aid memory but it is also a useful skill for Oxbridge interviews and beyond.

Improve your knowledge

The act of applying what you have learnt reinforces that piece of knowledge. A question may ask you to think about a relatively basic concept in a novel way (not cited in textbooks), and so deepen your understanding. Exams rarely test word for word what is in the syllabus, so when running through mock papers try to understand how the basic facts are applied and tested in the exam. As you go through the mocks or past papers take note of your performance and see if you consistently under-perform in specific areas, thus highlighting areas for future study.

Get familiar with exam conditions

Pressure can cause all sorts of trouble for even the most brilliant students. The ECAA is a particularly time pressured exam with high stakes – your future (without exaggerating) does depend on your result to a great extent. The real key to the ECAA is overcoming this pressure and remaining calm to allow you to think efficiently.

Mock exams are therefore an excellent opportunity to devise and perfect your own exam techniques to beat the pressure and meet the demands of the exam. **Don't treat mock exams like practice questions – it's imperative you do them under time conditions.**

> ***Remember!*** It's better that you make all the mistakes you possibly can now in mock papers and then learn from them so as not to repeat them in the real exam.

Before using this section

Do the ground work

- Read in detail: the background, methods, and aims of the ECAA as well logistical considerations such as how to take the ECAA in practice. A good place to start is a ECAA textbook like *The Ultimate ECAA Guide* (flick to the back to get a free copy!) which covers all the groundwork.
    - It is generally a good idea to start re-capping all your GCSE and AS maths.
- Remember that calculators are not permitted in the exam, so get comfortable doing more complex long addition, multiplication, division, and subtraction.
- Get comfortable rapidly converting between percentages, decimals, and fractions.
- Practice developing logical arguments and structuring essays with an obvious introduction, main body, and ending.
- These are all things which are easiest to do alongside your revision for exams before the summer break. Not only gaining a head start on your ECAA revision but also complimenting your year 12 studies well.
- Discuss topical economics problems with others - propose theories and be ready to defend your argument. This will rapidly build your scientific understanding for section 2 but also prepare you well for an Oxbridge interview.
- Read through the ECAA syllabus before you start tackling whole papers. This is absolutely essential. It contains several stated formulae, constants, and facts that you are expected to apply - or may just be an answer in their own right. Familiarising yourself with the syllabus is also a quick way of teaching yourself the additional information other exam boards may learn which you do not. Sifting through the whole ECAA syllabus is a time-consuming process so we have done it for you. **Be sure to flick through the syllabus checklist** later on, which also doubles up as a great revision aid for the night before!

Ease in gently

With the ground work laid, there's still no point in adopting exam conditions straight away. Instead invest in a beginner's guide to the ECAA, which will not only describe in detail the background and theory of the exam, but take you through section by section what is expected. *The Ultimate ECAA Guide* is the most popular ECAA textbook – you can get a free copy by flicking to the back of this book.

When you are ready to move on to past papers, take your time and puzzle your way through all the questions. Really try to understand solutions. A past paper question won't be repeated in your real exam, so don't rote learn methods or facts. Instead, focus on applying prior knowledge to formulate your own approach.

If you're really struggling and have to take a sneak peek at the answers, then practice thinking of alternative solutions, or arguments for essays. It is unlikely that your answer will be more elegant or succinct than the model answer, but it is still a good task for encouraging creativity with your thinking. Get used to thinking outside the box!

Accelerate and Intensify

Start adopting exam conditions after you've done two past papers. Don't forget that **it's the time pressure that makes the ECAA hard** – if you had as long as you wanted to sit the exam you would probably get 100%. If you're struggling to find comprehensive answers to past papers then ECAA *Past Papers Worked Solutions* contains detailed explained answers to every ECAA past paper question and essay (flick to the back to get a free copy).

Doing every past paper at least twice is a good target for your revision. In any case, choose a paper and proceed with strict exam conditions. Take a short break and then mark your answers before reviewing your progress. For revision purposes, as you go along, keep track of those questions that you guess – these are equally as important to review as those you get wrong.

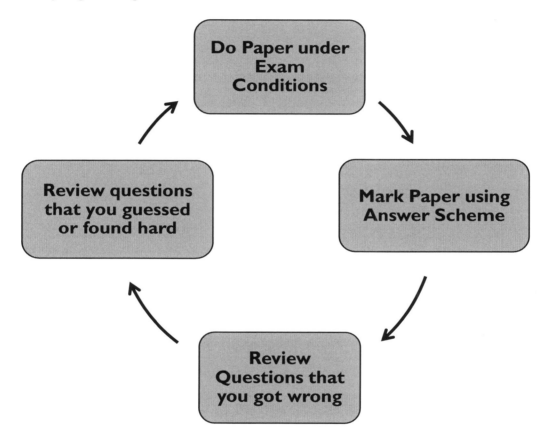

Once you've exhausted all the past papers, move on to tackling the unique mock papers in this book. In general, you should aim to complete one to two mock papers every night in the ten days preceding your exam.

Practice Papers

MOCK PAPER A

Section 1A

1. Calculate $4\frac{1}{5} - \frac{1}{2}$. Express your answer as a mixed number.

A. $3\frac{1}{10}$

B. $4\frac{1}{3}$

C. $4\frac{3}{10}$

D. $3\frac{7}{10}$

E. $4\frac{7}{10}$

2. Calculate the lowest common multiple of $3, 4, 5$ and 15.

A. 15

B. 900

C. 30

D. 600

E. 60

3. Put the following numbers in ascending order:

   I. 3×10^{20}

   II. 30×10^{-20}

   III. 3×10^{-4}

   IV. 300×10^{-5}

A. I, II, III, IV

B. II, III, I, IV

C. II, IV, I, III

D. I, IV, III, II

E. II, III, IV, I

4. Somebody rolls a fair six-sided die. Expressed in its simplest form, what is the probability that the result is prime?

A. $\frac{3}{6}$

B. $\frac{2}{3}$

C. $\frac{1}{6}$

D. $\frac{1}{2}$

E. $\frac{3}{4}$

5. Simplify as far as possible: $5(x-2)^2 + 2x^2 - 20$.

A. $2x^2 + 5x - 30$

B. $7x^2 - 20x$

C. $3x^2 - 20x + 40$

D. $7x^2 - 20$

E. $7x^2 + 20x$

6. Rationalize the following number: $\frac{9}{4 - \sqrt{2}}$.

A. $\frac{36 - 9\sqrt{2}}{14}$

B. $\frac{36 + 9\sqrt{2}}{4}$

C. $\frac{36 + 9\sqrt{2}}{14}$

D. $\frac{4 + \sqrt{2}}{4}$

E. $\frac{4 - \sqrt{2}}{4}$

7. Which integer is closest to $\pi\sqrt{10}$?

A. 8

B. 9

C. 10

D. 11

E. 12

8. A quarter of a drink is apple juice, a fifth is orange juice, and the rest is grape juice. Express the ratio of apple juice to orange juice to grape juice in the drink in its simplest form.

   A. $14:15:1120$
   B. $4:5:20$
   C. $5:4:11$
   D. $5:4:20$
   E. $4:5:11$

9. For the angle θ, we are told that $\sin \theta = \frac{3}{5}$. What is $\cos \theta$?

   A. $\frac{3}{4}$
   B. $\frac{\sqrt{2}}{2}$
   C. $\frac{4}{5}$
   D. $\frac{\sqrt{3}}{3}$
   E. 1

10. Given the following pair of equations, find x and y.
$$2x + 3 = 4y - 5$$
$$-3x + 7 = 9y + 1$$

   A. $x = -2$ and $y = 1$
   B. $x = 1$ and $y = 1$
   C. $x = \frac{8}{5}$ and $y = -\frac{6}{5}$
   D. $x = \frac{8}{5}$ and $y = \frac{6}{5}$
   E. $x = -\frac{8}{5}$ and $y = \frac{6}{5}$

11. Calculate $29.1 - 2.91$.

   A. 27.09
   B. 26.1
   C. 26.19
   D. 26.21
   E. 26.09

12. Fill in the blank: 36 is ____% of 30.

A. 1200
B. 120
C. 125
D. 130
E. $133.3\dot{3}$

13. Express the quadratic polynomial $x^2 - 5x + 6$ as a product of two linear polynomials.

A. $(x + 2)(x - 3)$
B. $(x - 2)(x - 3)$
C. $(x - 2)(x + 3)$
D. $(x - 6)(x + 1)$
E. $(x + 6)(x - 1)$

14. Determine the prime factorisation of 3,600.

A. $2^4 \times 3^2 \times 5^2$
B. $4^2 \times 3^2 \times 5^2$
C. $12^2 \times 5^2$
D. $3 \times 10^2 \times 12$
E. $6^2 \times 10^2$

15. In the Cartesian plane, a straight line contains the points $(-1, 10)$ and $(2, 1)$. Write the equation of that line in the form $y = mx + c$.

A. $y = 3x - 7$
B. $y = -x + 9$
C. $y = x + 11$
D. $y = 3x + 7$
E. $y = -3x + 7$

16. Find the interval on which it is true that $-2x + 10 \geq x + 4$.

A. $[-4, 5]$
B. $(-\infty, 2]$
C. $(-\infty, 2] \cup [5, \infty)$
D. $[5, \infty)$
E. $[2, 5]$

17. A circle has radius 1. Consider the largest square that fits inside that circle. What is the area of the part of the interior of the circle exterior to the square (shaded section of the diagram)?

  A. $\pi - 2$
  B. $\pi - 1$
  C. $\pi^2 - 1$
  D. $\pi^2 - 2$
  E. $\pi - \sqrt{2}$

18. In Country X, with a population of 1,000 people, 100 people have an annual income of $1,000 and 900 people have an annual income of $100. If the mean per capita annual income in Country X's population is called $MEAN$ and the median per capita annual income in Country X's population is called $MEDIAN$, what is $MEAN - MEDIAN$?

  A. $100
  B. $110
  C. $99
  D. $90
  E. $101

19. A box contains 3 red balls, 2 blue balls, and nothing else. Somebody draws out a random ball, replaces it, then draws out a random ball. What is the probability that that person drew out a red ball and then drew out a blue ball?

  A. $\frac{1}{25}$
  B. $\frac{1}{5}$
  C. $\frac{5}{6}$
  D. $\frac{6}{25}$
  E. $\frac{2}{3}$

20. A radius is drawn from the centre O of a circle to a point A on the circle. From another point B on the circle, the lines BA and BO are drawn. If the angle $O\hat{A}B$ is called θ, then what is the angle $O\hat{B}A$?

  A. $180^o - \theta$
  B. 2θ
  C. $360^o - \theta$
  D. $180^o + \theta$
  E. θ

END OF SECTION

Section 1B

21. Solve these simultaneous equations where a is a real value. Deduce the value or values of a for which there is only one real solution.

$$4x^2 + 6xy = 8$$
$$2x + y = 2a$$

A. $\dfrac{4}{3}$

B. $-\dfrac{4}{3}$

C. $\pm\dfrac{4}{3}$

D. $\dfrac{2}{3}$

E. $-\dfrac{2}{3}$

F. $\pm\dfrac{2}{3}$

22. In an arithmetic sequence, the sum of the first 10 terms equals the sum of the first 16 terms. Find the relationship between the values of a and d.

A. $a = -25d$

B. $a = -\dfrac{25}{2}d$

C. $a = \dfrac{25}{2}d$

D. $a = -\dfrac{75}{13}d$

E. $a = \dfrac{75}{13}d$

F. $a = \dfrac{16}{10}d$

G. $a = \dfrac{10}{16}d$

23. Solve the definite integral:

$$\int_{2}^{4} \frac{2x^3 + 15\sqrt{x}}{x^4} \, dx$$

A. $\ln 4 - \frac{1}{32} - 2^{\frac{3}{2}}$

B. $2\ln 2 - \frac{1}{16} - 2^{\frac{3}{2}}$

C. $\ln 2 - \frac{1}{16} + 2^{-\frac{3}{2}}$

D. $\ln 2 - \frac{1}{32} + 2^{-\frac{3}{2}}$

E. $\ln 4 - \frac{1}{16} - 2^{-\frac{3}{2}}$

F. $\ln 4 - \frac{1}{16} + 2^{\frac{3}{2}}$

G. $2\ln 2 - \frac{1}{32} + 2^{-\frac{3}{2}}$

24. In 2000, a car was valued at £3000, but when it was sold in 2002, it was said to be worth £9000. The value £V of the car can be modelled by the formula $V = Ak^t$, where t is the number of years since 2000 and A and k are constants. In what year will the value of the car first exceed £270,000

A. $2\log_3 90$

B. $\log_3 1800$

C. $\log 1800$

D. 2004

E. 2006

F. $2000 + \log_3 1800$

G. $2000 + 2\log_3 90$

25. Simplify the equation below.

$$\frac{12^{a-b} \times 36^{a+b}}{9^{3a+b} \times 16^a}$$

A. 4^{2a-b}

B. 4^{-2a-b}

C. 4^{-3a-b}

D. 3^{2a-b}

E. 3^{-2a-b}

F. 3^{3a-b}

G. $\frac{1}{3^{3a+b}}$

H. 3^{3a+b}

26. Which of the following graphs shows the equation $Y = 2x^3 - 5x^2 - 9x + 19$?

A.    B. 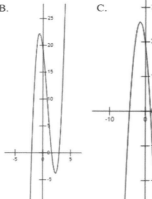   C.

D. 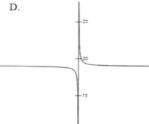   E.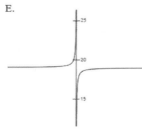

27. A quartic polynomial Y is given.

$$Y = 12x^4 + 5x^3 + 7x^2 + 3x + 1$$

By finding the equation of the tangent to the curve at the point where $x = 2$, what is the y intercept of the tangent:

A. $(0, -683)$
B. $(0, 267)$
C. $(0, -267)$
D. $(0, 475)$
E. $(0, -475)$
F. $(0, -341)$

28. f and g are two functions.

$f(g(x)) = \frac{x-3}{2}$ and $g(x) = 4x - 2$

Find $f(x^2 - 2)$:

A. $\frac{x-2}{8}$

B. $\frac{4x^2-2}{8}$

C. $\frac{x^2-5}{2}$

D. $\frac{x^2-12}{8}$

E. $\frac{x^2+12}{8}$

F. $\frac{x^2-8}{8}$

G. $\frac{(x+2)(x-2)}{8}$

29. Katie, Alex and Jennifer all tracked the number of biscuits they ate in a week. A biscuit box contains 6 biscuits. Katie ate 3 times as many biscuit boxes as Jennifer, but Alex ate 4 times as many biscuits as Katie. If Alex ate 33 more biscuits than Jennifer, how many biscuits boxes would they all eat in total if they were to all continue eating biscuits at the same rate for a whole month?

A. 4

B. 8

C. 12

D. 16

E. 32

F. 48

G. 192

30. A graph has coordinates in 3 out of 4 quadrants on an axis. Which of these equations could represent this graph?

A. $y = \frac{1}{x}$

B. $y = \frac{1}{x+2} - 5$

C. $y = \frac{2}{x}$

D. $y = \ln x$

E. $y = 3\ln x$

F. $y = \ln 3x$

G. $y = 5\sin(3x - 2) + 6$

31. John has a baguette that he is trying to store in his rectangular bread bin, shown below. If his baguette 17cm long (you may ignore the width/height). What is the length of baguette must he cut off to be able to fit his baguette in the bread bin exactly?

8cm 12cm 5cm

A. None, the baguette fits in the breadbin and could be longer.
B. None, the baguette fits in the breadbin exactly.
C. 2cm
D. $17 - 3\sqrt{3}$ cm
E. $17 - \sqrt{177}$ cm
F. $17 - \sqrt{233}$ cm

32. Cisco is trying to prove the circle theorem that angles from the same arc in the same segment are equal. Which of the following circle theorem rules should he use?

A. "The angle at the centre of a circle is twice the angle at the circumference of the circle from the same arc"
B. "The angle formed in a semicircle is always a right angle"
C. "Opposite angles of a cyclic quadrilateral add up to 180 degrees"
D. "Two tangents drawn from a point to a circle are equal"
E. "The angle between a tangent and a chord is equal to the angle at the circumference in the alternate segment"
F. "The perpendicular line from the centre of a circle to a chord bisects the chord"

33. In a tropical country:
• the probability of it not being hot is 0.42
• the probability of it being hot and not raining is 0.15
• the probability of it raining is 0.55

What is the probability, given that it has rained and been hot for the last 3 days, that it is currently not hot and not raining?

A. 0.12
B. 0.43
C. 0.55
D. 0.42
E. 0.3
F. 0.15
G. 0.45
H. 0.42

34. A Pythagorean triple is where 3 positive integers, a, b and c fit the equation $a^2 + b^2 = c^2$. The 2 smallest integers of a Pythagorean triple are 20 and 21. Find the third integer. Comparing this to the smallest Pythagorean triple, what is the highest common factor of the sum of the integers in both equations and the integer formed by the two largest numbers plus the 2 smallest numbers from both equations.

A. 1
B. 2
C. 3
D. 5
E. 7
F. 11
G. 13
H. 17

35. Below are 2 box plots, A and B.

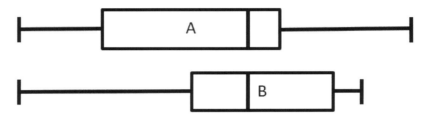

The student makes the following deductions:
   I.   A has a larger range than B
   II. A has a larger IQR than B
   III. B has a larger mode than A
   IV. B has a larger median than A

Which of these are true?
A. I only
B. II only
C. III only
D. IV only
E. I, II
F. II, III
G. I, III, IV
H. I, II, IV

36. A swimming pool is filled with water such that the volume of the pool in gallons (G) over time in minutes (T) is given by:

$$G = 30t - 12t^3 + 9$$

At what fraction of time (T) in minutes is the water flowing at the maximum rate?

A. $\sqrt{\dfrac{30}{12}}$

B. $\dfrac{1}{12}$

C. $\sqrt{\dfrac{30}{6}}$

D. $\sqrt{\dfrac{6}{6}}$

E. $\sqrt{\dfrac{30}{16}}$

F. $\sqrt{\dfrac{6}{36}}$

37. A cubic polynomial satisfies the following conditions
- $f(3) = 0$
- Can be expressed in the form $(x - a)(x - 1)(x + 1)$

Find the total area under the curve between $x = -1, x = 1$

A. $-\dfrac{1}{12}$

B. $\dfrac{1}{2}$

C. 16

D. 0

E. 4

38. Solve:

$$2^{x+1} - 2^{-x} = 0$$

A. $x = 0$

B. $x = 1, -1$

C. $x = 1, 2$

D. $x = -1, 2$

E. $x = \log 2$

$$2 \cdot 2^x - \frac{1}{2^x} = 0$$

$$2^x = y$$

$$2y - \frac{1}{y} = 0$$

$$2y^2 - 1 = 0$$

39. A series has a first term a and a common difference d
The sum of the first 10 terms is 1075
The 3rd term of the sequence is 15
Find the values of a and d

A. $a = 5$, $d = -4$
B. $a = 7$, $d = 3$
C. $a = -24$, $d = 19.5$
D. $a = -59$, $d = 37$
E. $a = 3$, $d = 6$
F. $a = -2.5$, $d = 8.75$

40. The circle above has a centre P and contains a square with 2 vertices on the diameter of the circle, and 2 vertices on the circumference of the circle. The diameter of the circle is 4cm.

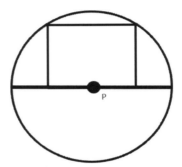

Calculate the area of the square.

A. $\frac{4}{5}$

B. $\frac{16}{5}$

C. 4

D. $\frac{7}{2}$

E. $\frac{9}{2}$

F. $\frac{17}{4}$

G. $\frac{64}{5}$

END OF SECTION.

Section 2

Read the extract taken from Neal Reaich's *What price honesty?* (2014, Bized) and then answer the question below in the space provided in this booklet.

Your answer will be assessed taking into account your ability to construct a reasoned, insightful and logically consistent argument with clarity and precision.

QUESTION

To what extent can prices be considered a true reflection of value, and to what extent should governments regulate price-setting behaviours such as reference pricing? Discuss with reference to the passage above.

What price honesty?

Pricing seems to be mentioned quite a lot in recent news headlines. The latest is the investigation by the Office of Fair Trading (OFT) into just how genuine the advertised price cuts in some large furniture stores really are. The OFT use the term reference pricing. They've found cases in shops under investigation where not a single product had, in reality, been sold at the, supposedly original, higher price. The argument goes that since 95% of sales were at the lower or 'now' price then the stated original prices cannot be really genuine.

Are we really so stupid as to be misled by reference pricing? When my wife buys some clothes in a sale and I ask how much it cost, she always responds by saying how much money she has saved. Well, unless she had the definite intention of buying it in the first place, she hasn't saved anything: in fact, she has spent it. The question is whether or not the reference pricing made a difference to her decision to buy the product. It must do, otherwise why is it so commonly used?

Heuristics suggests that people are not as rational as the standard economic model implies. Instead, they use rules of the thumb, educated guesses or short cuts in decision-making. Anchoring refers to people making decisions based upon something they know to start with. For example, the anchor price of a jumper was £40 and there is 20 per cent discount offer making the new price £32 a saving of £8. If I decide to buy, I might be thinking of the £8 saved because I didn't have to pay the full price, when I should be thinking logically about the actual price I am paying. In this case there is too much focus on the anchor price, which is at A level that I wouldn't have purchased the item anyway.

In some cases, reference pricing is part of a strategy of price discrimination over time. Clothes shops attempt to capture consumer surplus by charging a high initial price for a few weeks for the 'must have and will pay' customers. The shops then give a discount which increases over time. New potential customers must now weigh up whether to buy now and get a 25 per cent discount or wait longer for a 5per cent saving and risk losing the deal because they have run out of their size.

Another tactic is to use time-limited offers where notice is given that the offer ends soon: buy now or miss out. Double glazing sales were notorious for using this tactic, encouraging customers to 'sign up today to will get an extra 20 per cent off'.

Supermarkets are always giving volume offers, such as three for the price of two or get the second purchase for half the price. The supermarkets know we will pay more for the first item than we would for a second or third one. This tactic must lead to food waste as we are tempted to buy some products that we cannot possibly use before the sell-by date.

The OFT also look at baiting sales where only a very limited number of products are available at the most discounted price. This sounds a little like discounts given for advanced booking train tickets.

The OFT always makes mention of portioned 'drip' pricing where price increments drip through the buying process. It's those little add-ons that all add-up. Booking certain airline tickets comes to mind here.

Restaurants often make an offer of a free second main course meal after buying one main course at full price. Now add on the fact that we may have full priced deserts, order drinks at a high mark up and then add the tip. Get your calculator out and the deal doesn't seem so good.

All these examples of price framing seek to alter a consumer's perception of the value of the offer. But there is more: have you purchased a printer at a ridiculously low price only to be stung on purchasing printer ink cartridges? Some businesses operate at a loss or low profit margin on certain items, to entice customers to part with more money on higher-profit goods. They bundle items together.

Some advice then:
➢ Bring a calculator with you when shopping
➢ When buying clothes divide the total by 50 to give you the average cost of wearing something once a week for a year: a shirt costing £25 will work out at 50 pence for every day worn;
➢ Avoid impulse buying on larger-ticket items;
➢ Only purchase multi-buys with long sell by dates;
➢ Ignore the original price: it's only the current price you need to know about;
➢ Avoid time limited offers.

END OF PAPER

MOCK PAPER B

Section 1A

1. Somebody rolls a fair 20-sided die with faces numbered from 1 to 20. What is the probability that the result is a factor or a multiple of 8?

A. $\frac{1}{5}$

B. $\frac{1}{4}$

C. $\frac{1}{3}$

D. $\frac{1}{2}$

E. $\frac{3}{5}$

2. The mean of a set of fifteen numbers is 15. A new set is created by taking the original numbers and adding a sixteenth number, the number 31. What is the mean of this new set of sixteen?

A. 16

B. $15\frac{1}{31}$

C. $15\frac{1}{15}$

D. $15\frac{1}{16}$

E. $15\frac{1}{30}$

3. Express the following ratio in its simplest form: $\frac{2}{9} : \frac{16}{27}$.

A. $3:8$

B. $6:16$

C. $2:16$

D. $1:3$

E. $9:16$

4. Circle C_1 is centred at the point $(0,0)$ in the Cartesian plane and has radius 2. Circle C_2 is centred at $(0,1)$ and has radius 1. What is the area of the part of the interior of C_1 which is exterior to C_2?

A. π

B. 2π

C. $4\pi - 1$

D. 3π

E. $4\pi - 2$

5. Out of which of the following is it possible to construct a triangle?
    I.   Three line segments with respective lengths 3, 4 and 5.
    II. Three line segments with respective lengths 3, 4 and 6.
    III. Three line segments with respective lengths 3, 4 and 7.
    IV. Three line segments with respective lengths 3, 4 and 8.

A. (I), (II), (III) and (IV)
B. (I), (II) and (III) only
C. (I) and (II) only
D. only (I)
E. none of (I), (II), (III) or (IV)

6. What is the maximum value of $\sin 4\theta$ for positive θ?

A. 1
B. 2
C. 4
D. 16
E. the function is not bounded above.

7. At which x-value does the parabola given by $y = x^2 - 7x + 9$ have its turning point?

A. $-\dfrac{13}{4}$
B. $-\dfrac{7}{2}$
C. $\dfrac{13}{4}$
D. 7
E. $\dfrac{7}{2}$

8. Jane runs at a constant speed from midnight to the following midnight and covers a distance of 100 miles. How many miles did Jane cover from 8 o' clock in the morning to 5 o'clock in the afternoon?

A. $\dfrac{75}{2}$
B. $\dfrac{800}{3}$
C. $\dfrac{25}{2}$
D. 50
E. $\dfrac{25}{6}$

9. Find all the x-values for which $x^2 - 4x = 7$

A. There are no real solutions for x.

B. $x = \dfrac{4 + \sqrt{7}}{2}$ and $x = \dfrac{4 - \sqrt{7}}{2}$

C. $x = \dfrac{2 + \sqrt{13}}{2}$ and $x = \dfrac{2 - \sqrt{13}}{2}$

D. $x = 2 + \sqrt{11}$ and $x = 2 - \sqrt{11}$

E. $x = 4 + 2\sqrt{7}$ and $x = 4 - 2\sqrt{7}$

10. Express $3 \times 3^{-3} \times 27^2$ as a power of 3.

A. 3^4

B. 3^3

C. 3^2

D. 3^1

E. 3^0

11. Simplify and rationalise the following.

$$\frac{3}{2 + \sqrt{5}} + 1$$

A. $\sqrt{5} - 2$

B. $\sqrt{5} - 2$

C. $3\sqrt{5} - 6$

D. $3\sqrt{5} - 5$

E. $3\sqrt{5} + 5$

12. Find the highest common factor among the following: $10, 12, 20$ and 100.

A. 5

B. 4

C. 10

D. 2

E. 600

13. Find $8\big(4 \times (9 \div 3)\big) - 6 \div 3$.

A. 30

B. 6

C. 94

D. 26

E. $10\frac{2}{3}$

14. Consider the circle C of radius 1 centred at $O = (0,0)$ in the Cartesian plane. Let A denote the intersection of C and the x-axis and let B denote the intersection of C and the y-axis. What is the perimeter of the triangle AOB?

A. 4
B. $1 + \sqrt{2}$
C. $2 + \sqrt{2}$
D. $2 + \frac{\sqrt{2}}{2}$
E. 3

15. Calculate the distance in the Cartesian plane between the points $(-5, -10)$ and $(2, 4)$ expressed in its simplest form.

A. 21
B. $7\sqrt{5}$
C. 35
D. $\sqrt{245}$
E. $7\sqrt{3}$

16. A linear sequence has first term 19 and common difference -4. For an arbitrary positive integer n, give an expression for the nth term in the sequence.

A. $-4n + 23$
B. $-4n + 19$
C. $-4n + 15$
D. $19n - 4$
E. $23n - 4$

17. For any positive integer n, the nth term in a sequence is given by $n^2 - 10n - 5$. Which entry in the sequence is the first positive entry?

A. the first
B. the fifth
C. the fifteenth
D. the tenth
E. the eleventh

18. John has a bag of marbles containing 8 blue marbles, 4 red marbles, and nothing else. At random, John draws out a marble. Without replacing that marble, John draws out another. Then without replacing either of the two marbles he has so far drawn out, John draws out a third marble. What is the probability that John drew out three blue marbles?

A. $\frac{165}{314}$

B. $\frac{8}{27}$

C. $\frac{14}{55}$

D. $\frac{41}{55}$

E. $\frac{19}{27}$

19. Bilal flips a fair coin five times. What is the probability that it comes up heads at least once?

A. $\frac{1}{10}$

B. $\frac{1}{32}$

C. $\frac{31}{32}$

D. $\frac{9}{10}$

E. $\frac{5}{32}$

20. Consider the following data set:

$$1, 2, 2, 3, 3, 3, 4, 4, 4, 4, 5, 5, 5, 5, 5, 6, 6, 6, 6, 6, 6, 7, 7, 7, 7, 7, 7, 7$$

If we denote by MODE the mode of this data set and by IQR its interquartile range, what is $MODE - IQR$?

A. $\frac{5}{2}$

B. 3

C. $\frac{7}{2}$

D. 4

E. $\frac{9}{2}$

END OF SECTION

Section 1B

21. The figure shows a semicircle on-top of an isosceles triangle. The equal sides of the triangle are both 7cm long, and the angle between them is 30 degrees. Calculate the perimeter of the composite shape.

It is given that $\sin 75 = \frac{\sqrt{6}+\sqrt{2}}{4}$

A. $14 + \frac{7\pi}{12}(\sqrt{6} - \sqrt{3})$

B. $7 + \frac{7\pi}{12}(\sqrt{6} - \sqrt{2})$

C. $14 + \frac{7\pi}{8}(\sqrt{6} - \sqrt{2})$

D. $\frac{7\pi}{24}(\sqrt{6} - \sqrt{2})$

E. $\frac{7\pi}{12}(\sqrt{6} - \sqrt{2})$

F. $\frac{7\pi}{12}(\sqrt{6} - \sqrt{3})$

G. $14 + \frac{3\pi}{8}(3\sqrt{2} - \sqrt{3})$

H. $\frac{3\pi}{8}(3\sqrt{2} - \sqrt{3})$

22. How many values satisfy the following equation between -2π and $2\pi s$
$$2 \sin x \cos x = \cos x$$

A. 4

B. 2

C. 1

D. 8

E. 16

F. 3

G. 6

23. Calculate the exact solution to the equation:
$$log_6(4x + 3) = log_6(9x - 5) + 2$$

A. $\frac{578}{693}$

B. $\frac{653}{855}$

C. $-\frac{896}{146}$

D. $-\frac{203}{5}$

E. $\frac{183}{320}$

F. $\frac{219}{34}$

24. The function $f(x)$ has a stationary point at $(5, 12)$ and $f''(x) = 18x + 12$. Find $f(x)$

A. $3x^3 + 3x^2 - 316x + 1142$
B. $6x^3 + 3x^2 - 189x + 132$
C. $3x^3 + 6x^2 - 285x + 912$
D. $x^3 + 12x^2 - 128x + 227$
E. $2x^3 + 14x^2 - 336x + 1242$
F. $9x^2 + 12x - 273$

25. Find the coefficient of x^3 in the binomial expansion of:
$$y = (2x - 1)^9$$

A. 8
B. -8
C. 72
D. -72
E. 112
F. -112
G. 672
H. -672

26. On a cheese farm, the mass of cheese produced and measured on the scales, T minutes after the cheese machine has started is G grams. For any time, the rate of cheese production is proportional to the mass of cheese formed. However, cheese is removed from scales at a constant rate of 10 grams per minute. When the mass of cheese on the scales was 150g, and the rate of change of cheese weight on the scales was 90g/minute. Create a differential equation to show this. When the rate of change of mass of cheese was 50g/m, what was the mass of cheese formed?

A. 150
B. 50
C. 40
D. 90
E. 150
F. 60

27. The graph of $y = \sqrt{5x - 2}$ undergoes the below transformations in the given order.
- Translated horizontally left by 4
- Translated vertically down by 6
- Vertical reflection in the axis $y = 0$
- Stretch factor $\frac{1}{3}$ in the y-axis
- Stretch factor 2 in the x-axis

Which of the following equations describes the transformed graph?

A. $y = \sqrt{2 - \frac{5x}{18}} - 2$

B. $y = \frac{\sqrt{-10x-6}-4}{3}$

C. $y = -\frac{\sqrt{\frac{5}{2}x-22}-6}{3}$

D. $y = -\frac{\sqrt{\frac{5}{2}x+18}-6}{3}$

E. $y = \frac{\sqrt{\frac{5}{2}x-22}-6}{3}$

F. $y = -\frac{\sqrt{\frac{5}{2}x+22}-6}{3}$

G. $y = \frac{\sqrt{\frac{5}{2}x+14}}{3}$

28. A circle has the equation $x^2 - 12x + y^2 - 10y + 12 = 0$, and is tangent to 2 sides of the triangle. Some coordinates on the triangle are labelled. Find the exact value of the shaded area.

A. 305

B. $528 - 49\pi$

C. $552 - 49^2\pi$

D. $4290 - 36^2\pi$

E. $276 - 49\pi$

F. $169 - 36\pi$

$(-10, y)$

$(x, -12)$

29. A baker believes that the amount of bread (B) and the number of muffins (M) produced are related by the equation $M = aB^n$. She collects the data from a day at the bakery and creates a scatter graph with log B as the x axis, and log M on the y axis. The results have a straight-line gradient of 5 and y intercept -1. What are the exact values for a and n?

A. $a = \log 5, n = -1$
B. $a = -5, n = -1$
C. $a = \log 5, n = 1$
D. $a = 5, n = 100$
E. $a = -5, n = -0.1$
F. $a = 5, n = 0.1$
G. $a = 5, n = 10$
H. $a = \log 5, n = 10$

30. Given that $\sin x = \frac{1}{3}$, find the product of all possible exact values of $\cos x + \tan x$.

A. 0
B. $\pm \frac{5\sqrt{2}}{12}$
C. $\frac{\sqrt{2}}{2}$
D. $\frac{5\sqrt{2}}{12}$
E. $\frac{55}{72}$
F. $\frac{1}{3}$
G. $\frac{-1}{3}$

31. Study the equation below:

$$16^{0.5(x+1)} + 6 = 4^{2x+1}$$

What is the value of 4^x

A. 16
B. 64
C. $\log_4 \frac{-4\pm\sqrt{112}}{-8}$
D. $\frac{4\pm\sqrt{112}}{8}$
E. $\frac{1}{2}\log_4 7$
F. $\frac{-8\pm\sqrt{113}}{-6}$
G. $\log_4 \frac{-8\pm\sqrt{113}}{-6}$
H. $\log_4 \frac{-2\pm\sqrt{115}}{-6}$

32. Consider the following statement: "No cube of an integer, n, has a units' digit that is a multiple of 3". Which of these is not a counterexample of the statement?

A. $n = 6$
B. $n = 7$
C. $n = 8$
D. $n = 9$
E. $n = 16$

33. Which of the following is the correct sketch of the graph $y = 4k^x$ where k is a positive integer?

A.
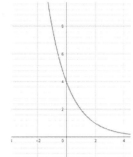

B.
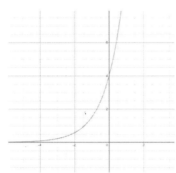

C.
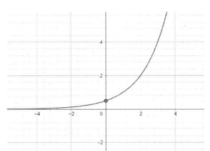

D.
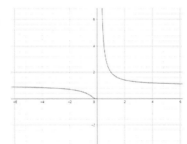

E.
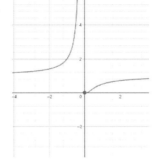

34. Solve the definite integral:

$$\int_1^5 \frac{5x^6 + 3}{x^4}\, dx$$

A. $\dfrac{623}{3} - \dfrac{1}{125}$

B. $2\ln 2 - \dfrac{1}{16} - 2^{\frac{3}{2}}$

C. $\dfrac{625}{3} - \dfrac{1}{125}$

D. $\dfrac{627}{3} - \dfrac{1}{127}$

E. $\dfrac{125}{3} - \dfrac{1}{125}$

F. $\dfrac{625}{6} - \dfrac{1}{125}$

G. $\dfrac{613}{3} - \dfrac{1}{115}$

35. The cuboid shown above has a volume of 150cm³. Find the value of x which gives the minimum surface area.

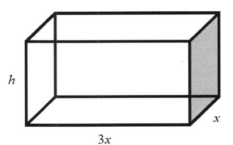

A. $\sqrt[2]{\dfrac{10}{3}}$

B. $\sqrt[2]{\dfrac{100}{3}}$

C. $\sqrt[3]{\dfrac{100}{30}}$

D. $\sqrt[3]{\dfrac{100}{3}}$

E. $\sqrt[3]{\dfrac{10}{3}}$

F. $\sqrt[2]{\dfrac{1}{3}}$

G. $\sqrt[3]{\dfrac{1}{3}}$

H. $\sqrt[3]{\dfrac{1}{30}}$

36. The gradient of a curve is $\frac{dy}{dx} = 6\sqrt{x-1}$, the curve passes through the point $(3, 5)$. Find the equation of the curve.

A. $2(x-1)^{0.5} + \frac{1.25}{2^{1.5}}$

B. $\frac{3}{(x-1)^{0.5}}$

C. $\frac{3}{(x-1)^{0.5}} + \frac{10-3\sqrt{2}}{2}$

D. $\frac{3}{(x-1)^{0.5}} - \frac{10-3\sqrt{2}}{2}$

E. $4(x-1)^{1.5} + \frac{1.25}{2^{1.5}}$

F. $4(x-1)^{1.5} + \frac{1.5}{2^{0.5}}$

37. The following graph is shown.
Which of the below equations represents the   inverse
equation?

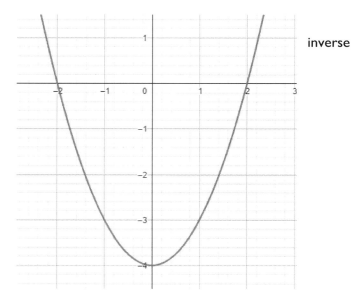

A. $y = x^2 - 2$

B. $y = x^2 + 2$

C. $y = x^2 - 4$

D. $y = x^2 + 4$

E. $y = \sqrt{x^2 - 4}$

F. $y = \sqrt{x^2 + 4}$

G. $y = \sqrt{x^2 - 2}$

H. $y = \sqrt{x^2 + 2}$

38. The graph of $y = lnx$ undergoes the below transformations in the given order.
- Reflection in the y axis
- Stretch factor $\frac{1}{3}$ in the x axis
- translation in the positive x direction by 3 units

Find the resulting equation:

A. $-\ln(3x - 3)$
B. $-\ln(\frac{1}{3}x - 1)$
C. $\ln(-\frac{1}{3}x - 1)$
D. $\ln(-\frac{1}{3}x - 3)$
E. $\ln(-3x + 9)$
F. $-\ln(3x - 9)$
G. $\ln(-3x - 9)$

39. A baker is testing different versions of a recipe, by increasing the amount of sugar in each batch. In the first batch, she uses 60g of sugar, but in the second she uses 100g. The amount of sugar used in each batch forms a geometric progression. The baker only has three 500g bags of sugar. Calculate the greatest number of batches she can make.

A. $log_{\frac{5}{3}}\left(\frac{53}{3}\right)$
B. $log_3\left(\frac{53}{3}\right)$
C. 105
D. $log_5\left(\frac{53}{3}\right)$
E. $log_2\left(\frac{53}{3}\right)$
F. $log_3\left(\frac{51}{2}\right)$

40. What is the correlation for the above data? *(you may use the axis to help)*

x	y
0.2	0.2
0.3	0.2
1	0.1
0.1	1
1	1
2	1.8
1.9	2.1
3	0.1
−1	−0.8
−0.9	−1.9
−0.9	−0.8

A. no correlation
B. slight positive correlation
C. strong positive correlation
D. slight negative correlation
E. strong negative correlation

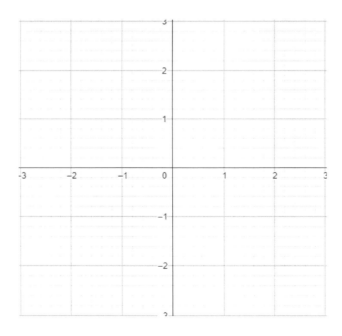

END OF SECTION

Section 2

Read the extract taken from Simon Tait's *Maria Miller: thank you and goodbye* (2014, *The Stage* - edited) and then answer the question below in the space provided in this booklet.

Your answer will be assessed taking into account your ability to construct a reasoned, insightful and logically consistent argument with clarity and precision.

To what extent does art and culture merit public funding?

Maria Miller: thank you and goodbye

She "has done an effective job in making the case for the value of public funding" Bazalgette says in response to the news that the arts are to get a ring-fenced 5% cut when ACE had been told to model for 10% and 15% scenarios for 2015/16.

But it is rather damning with faint praise. He goes on to say: "It is hugely encouraging that the Chancellor and the Treasury have listened to the argument that the arts and culture makes such a valuable contribution to our quality of life and the economy".

The argument made by the arts and culture, note, not the secretary of state.

DCMS (Department for Culture, Media and Sport) as a whole has got a less generous cut of 8%, and the deal for the arts appears to have been negotiated separately by the likes of Bazalgette and national museum directors like Nicholas Serota who, three weeks ago, went to George Osborne directly with economic arguments for a more lenient treatment of the sector. It was at this point that Osborne and the Treasury finally "got it" and realised how damaging a bigger arts cut would be to the economy for negligible saving.

It means that Mrs Miller cannot simply pass on to the arts the 8% cut as she and her predecessor, Jeremy Hunt, have done in the past because there is no fat in the DCMS, having been cut to the bone already, to absorb a new reduction itself. As it is, she will have to find the saving from elsewhere in her budget.

Nevertheless, she has hung out and got a better settlement than most other government departments who are suffering at least 10% reductions as the government tries to find more savings, but it seems the knives are out not for culture or the arts but for Miller herself.

The knives appear to be out for her in government for a number of reasons, including not dealing decisively with Leveson. The culture secretary has also been the subject of unprecedented vilification in the Tory press, with the Daily Mail's drama critic Quentin Letts declaring a couple of weeks ago that <u>"Culture is the department where a country can assert its character. If only its Secretary of State had one"</u>. In May, she made her first speech on the arts, calling for the economic argument to be made, Letts conceded, but "Where was the question of morality in Mrs Miller's approach to the arts? Where was the vision that the arts can civilise us? Where was an idea of the arts as the most meritocratic of gifts, a route which can offer talented and aspiring youngsters a route to self-fulfilment...? There is not even much impression she is an arts lover. It was a speech that could have been given by any one of her departmental officials".

Her desperate attempts to grab a positive headline culminated last week in a damp squib of an announcement about the First World War centenary commemoration, in which nothing new was announced (except that 600-odd streets in England were to be renamed after VC winners from the Great War), and the major news about the cultural element cannot be revealed before August. On Friday, The Times's normally gentle columnist Richard Morrison wrote that "Some (culture secretaries) have been bores; some bluffers. But not one has depressed me as Maria Miller does.

As for the arts, the triumph is substantial and this might be a sea-change in the way governments see the sector. The Arts Council, as fuel for the Bonfire of the Quangos, has taken an enormous battering since 2010 and the sector has correctly acknowledged that there is no case for "special treatment" while cuts amounting to 33% have been meted out, and of 50% to ACE itself. But now culture has established the principle that it is a special case after all, and with sense and imagination much of the effect of the new 5% cut might be ameliorated through the National Lottery.

The question now is whether that principle will be accepted by the other great subsidisers of the arts, the local authorities in whose hands the futures of dozens of theatres lie and whose extreme economic pain is even greater than Osborne's.

END OF PAPER

ANSWERS

ANSWER KEY

Paper A		Paper B	
1	D	1	B
2	E	2	A
3	E	3	A
4	D	4	D
5	B	5	C
6	C	6	A
7	C	7	E
8	C	8	A
9	C	9	D
10	E	10	A
11	C	11	D
12	B	12	D
13	B	13	C
14	A	14	C
15	E	15	B
16	B	16	A
17	A	17	E
18	D	18	C
19	D	19	C
20	E	20	E
21	C	21	C
22	B	22	D
23	C	23	B
24	G	24	C
25	G	25	G
26	B	26	D
27	A	27	D
28	D	28	E
29	E	29	F
30	B	30	E
31	F	31	D
32	A	32	C
33	E	33	B
34	A	34	A
35	E	35	D
36	C	36	E
37	E	37	F
38	A	38	F
39	D	39	A
40	B	40	B

MOCK PAPER A ANSWERS

Section 1A

1. D

$$4\frac{1}{5} - \frac{1}{2} = \frac{21}{5} - \frac{1}{2} = \frac{42}{10} - \frac{5}{10} = \frac{37}{10} = 3\frac{7}{10}$$

2. E

15 is a multiple of 3 (and of 5), so we only need the lowest common multiple of $3, 4$ and 5. Since those three numbers share no common factors greater than 1, their lowest common multiple is the product of the three, that is, 60.

3. E

(I) has 20 zeros and is the largest; (II) is smaller than billionths and is the smallest; (IV) is ten times larger than (III), and both (III) and (IV) are larger than (IV).

4. D

Of the numbers from 1 to 6, the following are prime: 2, 3, and 5. That is three outcomes out of a possible six, so the probability is $\frac{3}{6} = \frac{1}{2}$ in its simplest form.

5. B

$5(x - 2)^2 + 2x^2 - 20 = 5(x^2 - 4x + 4) + 2x^2 - 20$
$= 5x^2 - 20x + 20 + 2x^2 - 20$
$= 7x^2 - 20x$

6. C

$$\frac{9}{4 - \sqrt{2}} = \frac{9}{4 - \sqrt{2}} \times \frac{4 + \sqrt{2}}{4 + \sqrt{2}} = \frac{9(4 + \sqrt{2})}{(4 - \sqrt{2})(4\sqrt{2})} = \frac{36 + 9\sqrt{2}}{14}$$

7. C

$\pi \approx 3.142$ and $\sqrt{10} \approx 3.2$. Multiply the two together and a fairly accurate answer is 9.9, thus 10.

8. C

First calculate how much of the drink is grape juice: $1 - \frac{1}{4} - \frac{1}{5} = 1 - \frac{9}{20} = \frac{11}{20}$.

So, the ratio we need is: $\frac{1}{4} : \frac{1}{5} : \frac{11}{20} = \frac{5}{20} : \frac{4}{20} : \frac{11}{20} = 5 : 4 : 11$

9. C

Consider the right-angled triangle with side lengths $3, 4$ and 5. If $\sin\theta = \frac{3}{5}$, then since $\sin\theta$ measures the ratio of the side opposite θ and the hypotenuse, the side opposite θ has length 3. Thus the side adjacent to θ has length 4, so by definition $\cos\theta = \frac{4}{5}$.

10. E

First multiply the equations by appropriate numbers to get the x-coefficients to match up. That is, multiply the first by 3 and the second by 2. We get:

$6x + 9 = 12y - 15$

$-6x + 14 = 18y + 2$

Then add the two equations to eliminate x:

$23 = 30y - 13$

This gives $y = \frac{6}{5}$.

Substitute this into the first equation:

$2x + 3 = \frac{24}{5} - 5$

$2x + 3 = -\frac{1}{5}$

$2x = -\frac{16}{5}$

$x = -\frac{8}{5}$

11. C

To make the calculation easier, add 0.09 to the first number and take away 0.09 from the second. This gives $29.19 - 3 = 26.19$.

12. B

$\frac{36}{30} = 1\frac{6}{30} = 1\frac{1}{5}$, and since $\frac{1}{5} = 20\%$, 36 is 120% of 30.

13. B

We need a pair of numbers that add up to -5 and multiply to give 6. Those two numbers are -2 and -3. So the product decomposition is $(x - 2)(x - 3)$.

14. A

Use the ladder method:

3600 | 2
1800 | 2
900 | 2
450 | 2
225 | 3
75 | 3
25 | 5
5 | 5
1|

And read off the solution $2^4 \times 3^2 \times 5^2$

15. E

The x-difference between the given points is 3 and the y-difference is -9. Thus $m = -3$. The first point tells us that $10 = (-3)(-1) + c$, so $c = 7$.

16. B

We manipulate the inequality:

$-2x + 10 \geq x + 4$

$-3x \geq -6$

$x \leq 2$

Alternatively, draw the graph of each linear function and note that they cross when $x = 2$.

17. A

The line from the centre of the square to one of its vertices is a radius of the circle, so that line's length is 1. This line is half of the square's diagonal, so the square's diagonal has length 2. By Pythagoras's theorem, each side of the square therefore has length $\sqrt{2}$. Thus, the area of the square is $\sqrt{2}^2 = 2$. Finally, the area of the circle is $\pi(1)^2 = \pi$. So the 'leftover' area we're looking for is $\pi - 2$.

18. D

The total amount earned annually in Country X is $\$(100 \times 1,000) + \$(900 \times 100)$, which is $\$190,000$. Since there are 1,000 people in the country, we have $MEAN = \$190$. Meanwhile, the middle entry in an ordered list of incomes will clearly be $\$100$, which is MEDIAN. So $MEAN - MEDIAN = \$190 - \$100 = \$90$.

19. D

There are 5 balls total, so the probability of drawing out a red ball first is $\frac{3}{5}$. And the probability of drawing out a blue ball second is $\frac{2}{5}$. Since the events are independent, the probability of both occurring is the product of the two probabilities, that is, $\frac{3}{5} \times \frac{2}{5} = \frac{6}{25}$.

20. E

Since the triangle OAB is an isosceles triangle (since both OA and OB are radii and therefore they have the same length), $\theta = O\hat{A}B = O\hat{B}A$.

END OF SECTION

Section 1B

21. C

$2x + y = 2a$ can be rearranged to $y = 2a - 2x$

Sub into equation 1:

$4x^2 + 6x(2a - 2x) = 8$

$4x^2 + 12ax - 12x^2 = 8$

$-8x^2 + 12ax - 8 = 0$

Using the discriminant,

$b^2 - 4ac = 0$ if there is only one real root

$(12a)^2 - (4 \times -8 \times -8) = 0$

$144a^2 - 256 = 0$

$a^2 = \frac{16}{9}$

$a = \pm \frac{4}{3}$

22. B

Using the equation for the sum of an arithmetic sequence $= \frac{n}{2}(2a + (n-1)d)$

Sum of the first 10 terms $= \frac{10}{2}(2a + (10-1)d) = 5(2a + 9d)$

Sum of the first 16 terms $= \frac{16}{2}(2a + (16-1)d) = 8(2a + 15d)$

Thus,

$10a + 45d = 16a + 120d$

$-6a = 75d$

$a = -\frac{25}{2}d$

23. C

$\int_2^4 \frac{2x^3 + 5\sqrt{x}}{x^4} \, dx$

Separate out variables

$\int_2^4 2x^{-1} + 5x^{-\frac{7}{2}} \, dx$

$\left[2lnx - 2x^{-\frac{5}{2}} \right]_2^4$

$\left(2ln4 - 2\left(4^{-\frac{5}{2}}\right) \right) - \left(2ln2 - 2\left(2^{-\frac{5}{2}}\right) \right)$

$\left(ln16 - 2\left(\frac{1}{32}\right) \right) - \left(ln\,4 - 2^{-\frac{3}{2}} \right)$

$ln\,4 - \frac{1}{16} + 2^{-\frac{3}{2}}$

24. G

$V = Akt$

When $t = 0$, then $V = A = 3000$

When $t = 2$, then $9000 = 3000k^2$

$3 = k^2$

$k = \sqrt{3}$

When $V = 270000$,

$270,000 = 3000\sqrt{3}^t$

$90 = 3^{t/2}$

$8100 = 3^t$

$t = \log_3 8100 = 2\log_3 90$

The year will be $2000 + t$, so the answer is option G, $2000 + 2\log_3 90$

25. G

Split each number into its factors:

$$\frac{12^{a-b} \times 36^{a+b}}{9^{3a+b} \times 16^a} = \frac{(3\times4)^{a-b} \times (3^2\times4)^{a+b}}{(3^2)^{3a+b} \times (4^2)^a}$$

$$= \frac{3^{a-b} \times 4^{a-b} \times 3^{2a+2b} \times 4^{a+b}}{3^{6a+2b} \times 4^{2a}}$$

$$= \frac{3^{3a+b} \times 4^{2a}}{3^{6a+2b} \times 4^{2a}}$$

$$= \frac{1}{3^{3a+b}}$$

26. B

B.

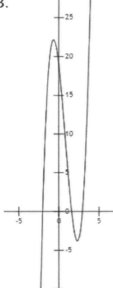

The y intercept is at 19

The gradient is positive at first, so positive x^3

A is a negative cubic graph, C is a quadratic, D and E are reciprocal graphs, therefore B is the only graph that fits the equation.

27. A

$\frac{dy}{dx} = 48x^3 + 15x^2 + 14x + 3$

Where $x = 2$, $\frac{dy}{dx} = 475$ and $Y = 267$

Thus, the tangent has a gradient of 475 and passes through the point $(2, 267)$

Therefore, the y-intercept $= 267 - 2 \times 475$

The equation of the tangent is $y = 475x - 683$

28. D

$$f(g(x)) = f(4x - 2) = \frac{x-3}{2}$$

Find the transformation that takes $(4x - 2)$ to $\frac{x-3}{2}$

Divide by 8,

$$\frac{4x-2}{8} = \frac{2x-1}{4}$$

Then $-\frac{5}{4}$,

$$\frac{2x-1}{4} - \frac{5}{4} = \frac{2x-6}{4} = \frac{x-3}{2}$$

Therefore,

$$f(x) = \frac{x}{8} - \frac{5}{4}$$

So,

$$f(x^2 - 2) = \frac{x^2-2}{8} - \frac{5}{4} = \frac{x^2-12}{8}$$

29. E

$K : A : J$

For biscuit boxes:

$3x : 12x : x = 3 : 12 : 1$

For biscuits, the ratio remains the same, therefore:

$12x = x + 33$

$x = 3$

Therefore, there were $36 + 9 + 3 = 48$ biscuits in total, 8 boxes. Therefore, in a month they would eat 32 boxes.

30. B

Candidate must identify that any stretch or reflection of the reciprocal graph will only fill 2 quadrants, eliminating options A and C. Likewise with the lnx graph, hence options D, E and F are eliminated. For option G, the minimum y coordinate is usually -1, which would be translated to 1 (by a translation 6 upwards, and then squashed by a factor of 5 in the vertical direction), thus the whole graph will be above the x-axis. The only remaining option is B, where the graph is translated by 2 in the negative x direction and by 5 in the negative y direction and thus is has co-ordinates in all quadrants apart from quadrant 1.

31. F

This is a 3D Pythagoras Question

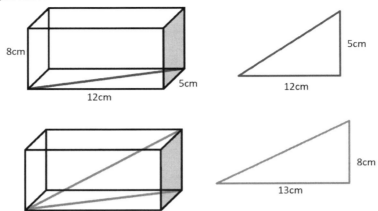

Use Pythagoras' theorem to see that:

$12^2 + 5^2 = 13^2$

Therefore, the hypotenuse is 13cm long

$Hypotenuse = \sqrt{13^2 + 8^2} = \sqrt{233}$

The candidate should recognise that this is just over 15cm. The answer is $17 - \sqrt{233}$

32. A

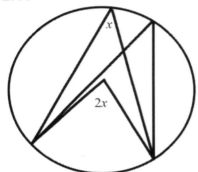

33. E

The fact that it has rained and been hot for 3 days is not important, the probability is still the same for each day. The easiest way to see the answer is to draw a probability table.

	Hot	Not Hot	Total
Raining	0.43	0.12	0.55
Not Raining	0.15	**0.3**	0.45
Total	0.58	0.42	1.0

From this we can see the probability of it being hot will be $1.0 - 0.42 = 0.58$

- the probability of it raining and being hot must be $0.58 - 0.15 = 0.43$
- the probability of it raining and not being hot must be $0.55 - 0.43 = 0.12$
- the probability of it not raining $1.0 - 0.55 = 0.45$
- the probability it is not raining and not hot must therefore be 0.3

34. A

$20^2 + 21^2 = 29^2$

The smallest triple is $3^2 + 4^2 = 5^2$

If this is not known, it can easily be worked out by writing down all the square numbers until you see 2 that will add to make another one.

Sum of the integers in both equations $= 20 + 21 + 29 + 3 + 4 + 5 = 82$

Product of the two largest numbers plus the 2 smallest numbers from both equations

$= (29 + 21) + (3 + 4) = 57$

HCF of 57 and 82:

82 factors: $1, 2, 41, 82$

57 factors: $1, 3, 19, 57$

$HCF = 1$

35. E

3 is incorrect, because you cannot determine the mode from the box plot. 4 is also incorrect, because the middle line is the median and the median of A is the same as the median of B. Thus only 1 and 2 are correct and the answer is E.

36. C

To find the rate, we differentiate $G = 30t - 12t^3$, giving us

$f'(G) = 30 - 36t^2$

Minimum / Maximum where $f'(G) = 0$,

$30 = 36t^2$

$T = \sqrt{30/6}$

37. E

$f(3) = 0$ thus,

$3 - a = 0$

$a = 3$

The correct polynomial is $(x - 3)(x - 1)(x + 1)$

Correct expansion is $x^3 - 3x^2 - x + 3$

Integrated form: $\frac{x^4}{4} - x^3 - \frac{x^2}{2} + 3x$

Need to sub in from 0 to 1, and then from -1 to 0, and add the positive values together

$\left[\frac{x^4}{4} - x^3 - \frac{x^2}{2} + 3x \right]_{-1}^{0} = \left(0 - \left(-\frac{9}{4} \right) \right) = \frac{9}{4}$

$\left[\frac{x^4}{4} - x^3 - \frac{x^2}{2} + 3x \right]_{0}^{1} = \frac{7}{4}$

$\frac{9}{4} + \frac{7}{4} = 4$

38. A

This is a hidden Quadratic equation:

Separate 2^{x+1} into $2^x \times 2$

$2^x \times 2 - 2^{-x}$

Multiply everything by 2^x:

$2(2^{2x}) - 2 = 0$

Let $u = 2^x$:

$2u^2 - 2 = 0$

$2(u + 1)(u - 1) = 0$

$2^x = \pm 1$

$x = 0$

39. D

$Sn = \frac{10}{2}[2a + 9d] = 1075$

$2a + 9d = 215$

$Un = a + 2d = 15$

$a = 15 - 2d$

Sub this into the other equation:

$2(15 - 2d) + 9d = 215$

$30 - 4d + 9d = 215$

$5d = 185$

$d = 37$, sub back in for $a, = -59$

40. B

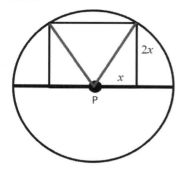

You can form 2 triangles, using 2 radii, each of length 2cm.

We can label the length of each side of the square as $2x$, so the distance from P to the vertex is x

Using Pythagoras' theorem:

$2^2 = x^2 + (2x)^2$

$4 = 5x^2$

$x^2 = \frac{4}{5}$

Area of square:

$4 \times x^2 = 4 \times \frac{4}{5} = \frac{16}{5}$

END OF SECTION.

Section 2

Introduction:

- Define "value". Provide a provisional definition, describing value in terms of the benefit that is generated for consumers by a particular product. In this passage, we described the phenomenon of 'price framing', which is the practice of setting prices such that the consumer perceives something as valuable as a result of the price that is offered, although this value need not directly correspond to an objective dollar valuation, as we have seen in the case of the crafty seller.

- The key question: To what extent does price reflect value to a consumer, should perception of value in and of itself be taken as value in and of itself? Who is qualified to speak of 'value' and how can this be regulated, if at all?

Paragraph 1:

- You can suggest that pricing reflects value insofar as it corresponds to a dollar sacrifice that is made in order to obtain a particular product. Prices in a free market are set by the interactions of buyers and sellers, who set prices on the basis of their business requirements – Insofar as we are consumers, we do not actually know what a business's private valuation of the good they are selling is, and therefore we can leave reason to things that reason deserves. Even if we were to take issue with a particular discount, this is the word of the consumer against the word of the seller, and the seller privately knows the price that they wanted to sell at, unless a specific rule for pricing was determined beforehand, it was known, and it was clear that it was deviated from.

- Passage Example:
  Price may reflect value insofar as it corresponds to a dollar sacrifice that a consumer makes in order to purchase or obtain a product. Economic theory suggests that if the price were set wrongly, then people would simply not pay. On some level, consumers 'get what they pay for', which suggests that things are priced fairly, but it depends on how you define 'value', because no matter what the promotion was set at, if the consumer paid, then there is no problem.

- Suppose we define value as what consumers are willing to pay. If we abide by what we observe from consumer behaviour in response to misleading pricing, there are two possible explanations, one of which is that consumers are irrational and unable to distinguish value accurately or with certainty save for through heuristics and hence are easily deceived, and the second of which is that consumers place a valuation not just on the product in and of itself, but on the nature of price cut displays or the limited time promotion, which can provide the psychological reassurance that the consumer is getting a good deal or affect how much they value the deal, which is priced into their decision when considering different alternatives.

- In this line of argument, perception equals value, and the good is priced correctly. Government need not do anything.

Paragraph 2:

- You can suggest that price can be used deceptively, as in the examples that have been given in the text. It is completely possible that businesses can use prices in order to deceive, mislead, to suggest that something is worth more than it actually is, or to imply that something has a value that it never had – But subsequently note that that is based on a specific definition or designation of value, which may not in fact have an objective basis.

- <u>Passage Example:</u>
  Suppose that we define value in absolute dollar terms, and suggest therefore that there is an absolute valuation for a good that consumers misperceive. Behavioural economics suggests that humans are not completely rational in determining price, and pricing strategies play into the systematic biases that they have, suggesting that humans can systematically misperceive the absolute value of a product if they fail to consider their biases. For example, suppose the example of a single product that is marketed differently, one presenting the benefits of the good alone, and the other presenting the potential loss that a customer might sustain if they did not purchase that good. Kahneman and Tversky write that human beings exhibit loss aversion, which suggests that if they had the opportunity to pass up what has been presented as a good discount, they may consider it to be more favourable relative to the scenario in which they had been presented with a good deal, even though there was a true absolute valuation, and the consumer was wrong on every count.

- Point out that the role of government, if viewed as protecting consumers, suggests that if this view is held, then the government should regulate.

Paragraph 3:

- To what extent regulating price-setting makes sense, and some possible regulatory schemes.

- <u>Passage Example:</u>
  How governments treat 'value' affects how they in turn treat the question of whether they should regulate at all, that is, if you even consider the free decisions of consumers to purchase and sellers to set prices to be a domain in which the government should interfere in the first place. Supposing you do, then your decision may be moderated by whether you believe value is solely determined by perception of the consumer, or there is an objective price for a specific good that should be arrived at independently by different individuals, free markets should theoretically allow for people to set price in accordance to their desires, and to have businesses live or die depending on whether they set the price too high and subsequently receive no customers, or set it too low.

- Make some possible arguments for regulating the information that sellers provide in their prices, and outline their implications. What would happen if we implemented a 'no reference pricing' policy? Would outcomes be fairer, less fair, would they be better? According to what dimension? If 'value' is simply defined as what consumers are willing to pay in dollars, what is better and what is worse? If it is defined as something that is absolute but that consumers routinely misperceive, what is the implication?

Conclusion

Summarize the main points:

- How you treat 'value' affects the particular way you consider a particular price.
- You may consider 'value' to reflect just the perception of the consumer, in which case there may not be a problem.
- On the other hand, you may consider there to be an objective 'value' that consumers misperceive, in which case then perhaps there is an issue.
- How you treat value affects how you will regulate, if at all you believe that regulation should be implemented.
- Zoom out and say why the question really matters.
- Price reflects value, but whether this value is solely contingent on perception or showcases something absolute, is something that is up in the air.
- This should affect our decisions and views concerning whether to regulate or not to regulate accordingly.

MOCK PAPER B ANSWERS

Section 1A

1. B

The factors of 8 on faces of the die are $1, 2, 4$ and 8. The multiples are 8 and 16. There are therefore five numbers out of 20 giving the desired outcome, so the probability is $\frac{5}{20} = \frac{1}{4}$.

2. A

We can take 1 away from 31 fifteen times, 'giving' 1 to each of the original numbers and increasing each, on average, to 16, while 31 has been decreased to 16. So, without changing the total of our numbers or the number of data points, we have 'changed' the new set into a set of sixteen numbers which are all 16, and that set clearly has mean 16.

Alternatively, calculate $\frac{15(15) + 31}{16}$ and find that it is equal to 16.

3. A

$$\frac{2}{9} : \frac{16}{27} = \frac{6}{27} : \frac{16}{27} = 6 : 16 = 3 : 8$$

4. D

C_1 has area $\pi \times 2^2 = 4\pi$. Meanwhile C_2 has area $\pi \times 1^2 = \pi$. Now C_2 is entirely contained in C_1 (and touches the larger circle at the point $(0, 2)$), so the area we're looking for is $4\pi - \pi = 3\pi$.

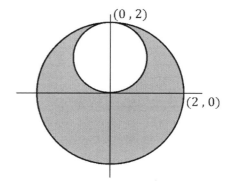

5. C

It is possible to construct a triangle out of three line segments if and only if the shortest two segments have a combined (i.e. added) length greater than the longest length. That is true of (I) and (II) only.

6. A

The factor of 4 in the function's argument only increases the function's frequency – that is, it makes the function repeat itself more quickly, in other words reduces its period. It does not affect its range on an unbounded interval, so the function has the same range, and the same maximum, as $sin\theta$, thus the answer is 1.

7. E

At the turning point the gradient of the curve is 0, thus $\frac{dy}{dx} = 0$, therefore:

$\frac{dy}{dx} = 2x - 7 = 0$

$x = \frac{7}{2}$

Thus, the answer is E.

Alternatively, completing the square allows us to express the function as $y = (x - \frac{7}{2})^2 - \frac{13}{4}$, which means the parabola's lowest point is $(\frac{7}{2}, -\frac{13}{4})$.

8. A

From 8 o' clock in the morning to 5 o'clock in the afternoon is a period of 9 hours. Jane runs at $\frac{100}{24}$ miles per hour, so in those 9 hours she travels $\frac{100}{24} \times 9$ miles, which is $\frac{75}{2}$ miles.

9. D

We need to solve the quadratic equation $x^2 - 4x - 7 = 0$, which we can do by applying the quadratic formula:

$x = \frac{-(-4) \pm \sqrt{(-4)^2 - 4(-7)}}{2} = \frac{4 \pm \sqrt{44}}{2} = \frac{4 \pm 2\sqrt{11}}{2} = 2 \pm \sqrt{11}$

giving $x = 2 + \sqrt{11}$ and $x = 2 - \sqrt{11}$ as solutions.

10. A

Note that $27 = 3^3$, so $27^2 = (3^3)^2 = 3^{3 \times 2} = 3^6$, and thus

$3 \times 3^{-3} \times 27^2 = 3 \times 3^{-3} \times 3^6 = 3^{1-3+6} = 3^4$

11. D

$\frac{3}{2 + \sqrt{5}} + 1 = \frac{3(2 - \sqrt{5})}{(2 + \sqrt{5})(2 - \sqrt{5})} + 1$

$= \frac{6 - 3\sqrt{5}}{4 - 5} + 1$

$= -6 + 3\sqrt{5} + 1$

$= 3\sqrt{5} - 5$

12. D

The only factors of 10 greater than 1 are $2, 5$ and 10. Of these, only 2 is a factor of 12. 2 is also a factor of the other two numbers, so the answer is 2.

13. C

Apply all division and multiplication before subtraction to obtain $32(3) - 2 = 96 - 2 = 94$.

14. C

$A = (1, 0)$ and $B = (0, 1)$. The distance AB is the hypotenuse of the triangle AOB and, by Pythagoras, has length $\sqrt{2}$. So, the total perimeter is $1 + 1 + \sqrt{2}$.

15. B

By the distance formula, that is, Pythagoras's theorem, the distance is

$$\sqrt{(-5-2)^2 + (-10-4)^2} = \sqrt{7^2 + 14^2} = \sqrt{7^2}\sqrt{1^2 + 2^2} = 7\sqrt{5}$$

16. A

Call the nth term $T_n = an + b$. Since the common difference is -4, we must have $a = -4$. Then since $T_1 = 19 = -4(1) + b$, we deduce $b = 23$.

17. E

The first entry is clearly negative and this is a quadratic sequence which grows arbitrarily large, so if we can find a positive value of x for which the function $x^2 - 10x - 5 = 0$, then any n greater than that x-value will produce a positive entry. Now by the quadratic formula, the solutions to our equation are

$$x = \frac{10 \pm \sqrt{100 - 4(-5)}}{2}$$
$$= \frac{10 \pm \sqrt{120}}{2}$$

Now $\sqrt{120}$ is almost exactly 11. Approximating, then, we write

$$x \approx \frac{10 \pm 11}{2}$$

The positive solution to which is $x = 10\frac{1}{2}$. So we have excellent reason to think $n = 11$ is the entry we are looking for. This can be confirmed by checking that the tenth entry is negative.

18. C

The probability of a blue marble on the first draw is $\frac{8}{12} = \frac{2}{3}$. Then there are 11 marbles left, of which 7 are blue. So, the probability of a blue marble on the second draw is $\frac{7}{11}$. Similarly, the probability of a blue marble on the third draw is $\frac{6}{10} = \frac{3}{5}$. Since all of these events need to occur, we multiply the probabilities:

$$\frac{2}{3} \times \frac{7}{11} \times \frac{3}{5} = \frac{2}{5} \times \frac{7}{11} = \frac{14}{55}.$$

19. C

If P is the probability of no flip coming heads, then the probability we seek is $1 - P$. Note that P is also the probability that every flip comes up tails. Since the probability of a single flip coming up tails is $\frac{1}{2}$, the probability of five consecutive flips coming up tails is $(\frac{1}{2})^5 = \frac{1}{2^5} = \frac{1}{32}$. So, the probability we seek is $1 - \frac{1}{32} = \frac{31}{32}$.

20. E

$$1, 2, 2, 3, 3, 3, 4, \qquad 4, 4, 4, 5, 5, 5, 5, \qquad 5, 6, 6, 6, 6, 6, 6, \qquad 7, 7, 7, 7, 7, 7, 7$$

If we denote by MODE the mode of this data set and by IQR its interquartile range, what is $MODE - IQR$?

Solution: Split the data into four groups of seven. This allows us to see that $Q_1 = \frac{4+4}{2} = 4$ and $Q_3 = \frac{6+7}{2} = \frac{13}{2}$. So $IQR = \frac{13}{2} - 4 = \frac{5}{2}$. Meanwhile 7 is the most common entry, so $MODE = 7$. Thus $MODE - IQR = 7 - \frac{5}{2} = \frac{9}{2}$.

END OF SECTION

Section 1B

21. C

Calculate diameter, d, of semicircle

The other 2 angles in the triangle are 75 degrees each

Using sin rule:

$$\frac{d}{\sin 30} = \frac{7}{\sin 75}$$

$$d = 7 \div \frac{\sqrt{6}+\sqrt{2}}{4} \times \sin 30$$

$$d = 7 \times \frac{4}{\sqrt{6}+\sqrt{2}} \times \frac{1}{2}$$

Rationalise the denominator:

$$\frac{4}{\sqrt{6}+\sqrt{2}} \times \frac{\sqrt{6}-\sqrt{2}}{\sqrt{6}-\sqrt{2}} = \frac{4\sqrt{6}-4\sqrt{2}}{6-2} = \sqrt{6} - \sqrt{2}$$

Thus,

$$d = \frac{7}{2}\left(\sqrt{6} - \sqrt{2}\right)$$

Therefore, the radius = $\frac{7}{4}\left(\sqrt{6} - \sqrt{2}\right)$

Thus, the arc length is $\frac{1}{2}\pi d = \frac{7}{8}\pi\left(\sqrt{6} - \sqrt{2}\right)$

Perimeter = $14 + \frac{7\pi}{8}(\sqrt{6} - \sqrt{2})$

22. D

$2\sin x \cos x = \cos x$

$2\sin x \cos x - \cos x = 0$

$\cos x\,(2\sin x - 1) = 0$

$\cos x = 0$ and $\sin x = 1/2$

Between -2π and 2π,

There are 4 solutions for $\sin x = 1/2$ and 4 solutions for $\cos x = 0$

23. B

$\log_6(4x + 3) = \log_6(9x - 5) + 2$

$\log_6(4x + 3) - \log_6(9x - 5) = 2$

$\log_6\left(\frac{4x+3}{9x-5}\right) = 2$

$6^2 = \frac{4x+3}{9x-5}$

$36(9x - 5) = 4x + 3$

$x = \frac{183}{320}$

24. C

We are told that $f(5) = 12$, and $f'(5) = 0$

Integrate $f''(x)$ to $f'(x)$

$= 9x^2 + 12x + c$

$f'(5) = 9(25) + 12(5) + c = 0$

$c = -285$

Integrate $f'(x)$ to $f(x)$

$= 3x^3 + 6x^2 - 285x + c$

$f(5) = 12$

$3(125) + 6(25) - 285(5) + c = 12$

$c = 912$

$f(x) = 3x^3 + 6x^2 - 285x + 912$

25. G

The expansion coefficients for $n = 9$ are unlikely to be known, so instead the formula $\frac{n!}{r!(n-r)!}$ Must be used

Expansion coefficients $= 1, 9, 36, 84, 126, 126, 84, 36, 9, 1$

Expansion: $(2x)^9 + 9(2x)^8(-1) + 36(2x)^7(-1)^2 + 84(2x)^6(-1)^3$ .....

Coefficient for x³ will be $(84)(2x)^3(-1)^6 = 672$

26. D

The rate of change of cheese mass equals the rate of formation – rate of removal of cheese from the scales

$dG/dt = kG - 10$

$90 = 150k - 10$

$k = 2/3$

$dG/dt = 50, G = 90.$

27. D
Translated horizontally left by 4
Replace x with $(x + 4)$
$y = \sqrt{5(x + 4) - 2}$
$y = \sqrt{5x + 18}$
Translated vertically down by 6
Replace y with $y + 6$
$y + 6 = \sqrt{5x + 18}$
Vertical reflection in the axis $y = 0$
Replace y with $-y$
$-y = \sqrt{5x + 18} - 6$
Stretch factor $\frac{1}{3}$ in the y axis
Replace y with $3y$
$-3y = \sqrt{5x + 18} - 6$
Stretch factor 2 in the x axis
$-3y = \sqrt{5(\frac{1}{2}x) + 18} - 6$
Thus,
$$y = -\frac{\sqrt{\frac{5}{2}x + 18} - 6}{3}$$

28. E
Find the equation of the circle by completing the square:
$x^2 - 12x + y^2 - 10y + 12 = 0$
$(x - 6)^2 - 36 + (y - 5)^2 - 25 + 12 = 0$
$(x - 6)^2 + (y - 5)^2 = 49$
Radius $= 7$, centre $(6, 5)$

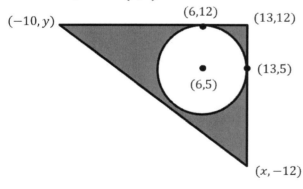

Area of triangle $= \frac{1}{2} \times 23 \times 24 = 276$
Circle area $= 49\pi$
Shaded area $= 276 - 49\pi$

29. F

$M = aB^n$

$\log M = \log a + n \log B$

Thus, the gradient is n therefore, $n = 5$, and the y-intercept is $\log a$ therefore, $a = 10^{-1} = 0.1$

30. E

Given that $\sin x = \frac{1}{3}$, $\sin^2 x = \frac{1}{9}$

$\cos^2 x = 1 - \sin^2 x$

$\cos^2 x = \frac{8}{9}$

$\cos x = \pm\frac{2\sqrt{2}}{3}$

$\tan x = \frac{\sin x}{\cos x} = \frac{1}{3} \times \frac{3}{2\sqrt{2}} = \pm\frac{\sqrt{2}}{4}$

$\cos x + \tan x = \pm\frac{11\sqrt{2}}{12}, \pm\frac{5\sqrt{2}}{12}$

$\frac{11\sqrt{2}}{12} \times \frac{5\sqrt{2}}{12} = \frac{55}{72}$

31. D

This is a hidden quadratic

$16^{0.5(x+1)} + 6 = 4^{2x+1}$

$0 = (4 \times 4^{2x}) - \left(\sqrt{16}^{(x+1)}\right) - 6$

$0 = (4 \times 4^{2x}) - (4 \times 4^x) - 6$

$0 = 4(4^{2x}) - 4(4^x) - 6$

Substitution $u = 4^x$:

$4u^2 - 4u - 6 = 0$

using the quadratic equation:

$u = \frac{-b \pm \sqrt{b^2 - 4ac}}{2a}$

$u = \frac{-(-4) \pm \sqrt{(-4)^2 - (4 \times 4 \times -6)}}{2 \times 4}$

$u = \frac{4 \pm \sqrt{4^2 - (4 \times 4 \times -6)}}{8}$

$4^x = \frac{4 \pm \sqrt{112}}{8}$

32. C

$8^3 = 512$, has 2 as the units' digit, which is not a multiple of 3

33. B

It has an intersection at (4,0) and shows exponential growth.

34. A

$$\int_1^5 \frac{5x^6+3}{x^4}\, dx$$

Separate out variables

$$\int_1^5 5x^2 + 3x^{-4}\, dx$$

$$\left[\frac{5}{3}x^3 - x^{-3}\right]_1^5$$

$$\left[\frac{625}{3} - \frac{1}{125}\right] - \left[\frac{5}{3} - 1\right]$$

$$\frac{625}{3} - \frac{1}{125} - \frac{2}{3} = \frac{623}{3} - \frac{1}{125}$$

35. D

$$3x^2 h = 150$$

$$h = \frac{150}{3x^2} = \frac{50}{x^2}$$

Surface area formula $= 2(3xh) + 2(3x^2) + 2xh = 6x^2 + 8xh$

$$A = 6x^2 + 8x\left(\frac{50}{x^2}\right) = 6x^2 + \frac{400}{x}$$

$$\frac{dA}{dx} = 12x - \frac{400}{x^2}$$

$$0 = 12x - \frac{400}{x^2}$$

$$400 = 12x^3$$

$$x = \sqrt[3]{\frac{100}{3}}$$

Test in

$$\frac{d^2 A}{dx^2} = 12 + \frac{800}{x^3}$$

$$\frac{d^2 A}{dx^2} = 12 + \frac{800}{\left(\frac{100}{3}\right)} = 36 \text{ is positive therefore, it is a minimum.}$$

36. E

Integrate the equation.

$$\int 6(x-1)^{0.5}\, dx$$

$$= 4(x-1)^{1.5} + c$$

when $x = 3, y = 5$

$$5 = 4(2^{1.5}) + c$$

$$c = \frac{1.25}{2^{1.5}}$$

37. F

The shown graph represents the equation $y = x^2 - 4$, as it has a y intercept of -4, and roots 2 and -2.

Find the inverse function by swapping x and y, then rearranging to get y.

$$x = y^2 - 4$$

$$y^2 = x + 4$$

$$y = \sqrt{x^2 + 4}$$

38. F

$y = lnx$

Reflection in the y axis:

$y = -lnx$

Stretch factor $\frac{1}{3}$ in the x axis:

$y = -ln3x$

Translation in the positive x direction by 3 units:

$y = -ln3(x-3) = -ln(3x-9)$

39. A

$a = 60, \ r = \frac{100}{60} = \frac{5}{3}$

$Sn = \frac{a(r^n-1)}{r-1} = \frac{60\left(\frac{5^n}{3}-1\right)}{\frac{5}{3}-1} = \frac{60\left(\frac{5^n}{3}-1\right)}{\frac{2}{3}} = 1500$

$\frac{60\left(\frac{5^n}{3}-1\right)}{\frac{2}{3}} = 1500$

$60\left(\frac{5^n}{3}-1\right) = 1000$

$\frac{5^n}{3} - 1 = \frac{50}{3}$

$\frac{5^n}{3} = \frac{53}{3}$

$n = log_{\frac{5}{3}}\left(\frac{53}{3}\right)$

40. B

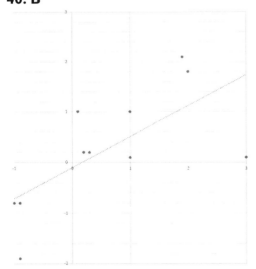

END OF SECTION

Section 2

Introduction:

- Raise the point about how art and culture are hotly debated in the national sphere, and about the possible reasons as to why they should or should not receive funding – Or, in the case of austerity, lesser budget reductions amongst a host of various possible alternatives. Consider your case in light of the possible economic implications of reductions in funding for arts and culture, and other points of view as well.

- The key question: To what extent is art and culture something that deserves public funding, and by whom and for what purpose? What are the potential benefits of funding the arts, and what might the potential tradeoffs be?

Paragraph 1:

- Highlight the economic argument for funding the arts, with a specific example that is of relevance.

- Passage Example:
  A possible reason to support art and culture is that these are economically beneficial industries to a certain extent. The economic impact of arts funding may be direct, insofar as artists who otherwise would not have been able to perform the tasks that allowed them to generate valuable works, or it may be indirect, insofar as these works may have in turn stimulated ideas within others, causing them to create things of value to the economy. Some economic developments may be contingent on arts and culture, or specifically the individuals who are involved in art and culture who would not otherwise be able to take part in a life of art. Art and culture represents a host of ideas and cultural expressions that might not otherwise exist if not for art and culture funding: To the extent that art is considered valuable to individuals and can facilitate the transfer of ideas within a society, one might consider the provision of art and culture funding to be a public good or an investment.

- Example: Artists in Italy after World War II – Italy supported their designers and artists, and the nation was able to bolster its economy by exporting their products, such as Italian leather, etc, which lends credence to the idea that we should support people with the ideas but not the means. National arts grants, that allow artists to make a living.

Paragraph 2:

- Consider including a counterargument – Although the arts can be economically beneficial, it is hard to assess the impact of funding the arts relative to other industries, and this should be factored into the decision of whether to fund or not to fund.

- Passage Example:
  Though we see that the arts account for ___% of GDP in the current scenario, the impact of retracting arts funding can be hard to measure, and it is questionable who exactly it will impact, in what scenarios. In a situation in which a government must consider questions of what it will cut from the budget, it must think about what is relatively more important to preserve. Other examples: Example of say, a scenario in which a government must debate between cutting pensions vs. cutting art, followed by justifications concerning why it is that one scenario might have more clear-cut benefits than the other.

Paragraph 3:

- To question the approach of making the decision of whether to fund the arts or not on the basis of economic considerations, and what the implications of several possible approaches may be.

Passage Example:

- On the one hand, making the decision to fund or not fund the arts on the basis of economic considerations may potentially be problematic altogether. If a decision to fund art is made on the basis of economic considerations alone, then a government risks funding only very specific forms of art, not others, which in turn may be justification for governments not to focus on the absolute amount of funding that they provide to art and culture in general, but to zero in on the distribution of those funds in particular. On the other hand, perhaps an economic approach to decision-making on behalf of funding the arts is inappropriate altogether. Funding arts and culture might be more of a moral consideration than an economic one, as the value lost might be greater than what economic impact might otherwise suggest.

Conclusion

Summarize the points:

- Art can be treated as something economically valuable to a country, whether directly or indirectly. These might be considered as justifications to fund or not to fund.
- On the other hand, assessing the economic impact of that funding is difficult, and a government should assess the potential tradeoffs that it is making when attempting to assess how and whether to fund.
- It may be the case that economic considerations may not be the best way to make a decision on whether to fund or not to fund art, as there may be moral considerations that are involved in that process above and beyond our immediate economic ones.

END OF PAPER

FINAL ADVICE

Arrive well rested, well fed and well hydrated

The ECAA is an intensive test, so make sure you're ready for it. Ensure you get a good night's sleep before the exam (there is little point cramming) and don't miss breakfast. If you're taking water into the exam then make sure you've been to the toilet before so you don't have to leave during the exam. Make sure you're well rested and fed in order to be at your best!

Move on

If you're struggling, move on. Every question has equal weighting and there is no negative marking. In the time it takes to answer on hard question, you could gain three times the marks by answering the easier ones. Be smart to score points- especially in the maths section where some questions are far easier than others.

Make Notes on your Essay

You may get asked questions on your essay at the interview. Given that there is sometimes more than four weeks from the ECAA to the interview, it is really important to make short notes on the essay title and your main arguments after the essay. You'll thank yourself after the interview if you do this.

Afterword

Remember that the route to a high score is your approach and practice. Don't fall into the trap that *"you can't prepare for the ECAA"*– this could not be further from the truth. With knowledge of the test, some useful time-saving techniques and plenty of practice you can dramatically boost your score.

Work hard, never give up and do yourself justice.

Good luck!

Acknowledgements

I would like to express my sincerest thanks to the many people who helped make this book possible, especially the Oxbridge Tutors who shared their expertise in compiling the huge number of questions and answers.

Rohan

About Us

We currently publish over 100 titles across a range of subject areas – covering specialised admissions tests, examination techniques, personal statement guides, plus everything else you need to improve your chances of getting on to competitive courses such as medicine and law, as well as into universities such as Oxford and Cambridge.

Outside of publishing we also operate a highly successful tuition division, called UniAdmissions. This company was founded in 2013 by Dr Rohan Agarwal and Dr David Salt, both Cambridge Medical graduates with several years of tutoring experience. Since then, every year, hundreds of applicants and schools work with us on our programmes. Through the programmes we offer, we deliver expert tuition, exclusive course places, online courses, best-selling textbooks and much more.

With a team of over 1,000 Oxbridge tutors and a proven track record, UniAdmissions have quickly become the UK's number one admissions company.

Visit and engage with us at:

Website (UniAdmissions): www.uniadmissions.co.uk

Facebook: www.facebook.com/uniadmissionsuk

YOUR FREE BOOK

Thanks for purchasing this Ultimate Collection Book. Readers like you have the power to make or break a book – hopefully you found this one useful and informative. *UniAdmissions* would love to hear about your experiences with this book. As thanks for your time we'll send you another ebook from our Ultimate Guide series absolutely <u>FREE</u>!

How to Redeem Your Free Ebook
1) Find the book you have on your Amazon
purchase history or your email receipt to help find the book on Amazon.

2) On the product page at the Customer Reviews area, click 'Write a customer review'. Write your review and post it! Copy the review page or take a screen shot of the review you have left.

3) Head over to www.uniadmissions.co.uk/free-book and select your chosen free ebook!

Your ebook will then be emailed to you – it's as simple as that!
Alternatively, you can buy all the titles at

UNIADMISSIONS

53%

UNIADMISSIONS 3-Year Oxbridge Engineering Programme Success Rate

14%

The Average Cambridge Engineering Success Rate

300+
Students successfully placed at Oxbridge in the last 3 years

50
Places available on our Oxbridge Engineering Programme

BOOK YOUR **FREE** INTENSIVE COURSE

VISIT: uniadmissions.co.uk/exam-course/

WHY STUDENTS SEE SUCCESS ON OUR INTENSIVE COURSE

1
EXPERT TUTORS.
The course is designed and led by an expert course instructor who has scored in the top 10% of their admissions cycle for this exam. You'll only be taught by the best.

2
GUIDED THROUGH ALL SECTIONS.
You'll be taken through each section of the exam in-depth with a tutor who truly knows the test inside out. They will teach you how to effectively approach each section of the test.

3
LEARN KEY STRATEGIES & TIME-SAVING TIPS.
Throughout the course, you will learn vital strategies to apply when sitting the exam. You will also be taught valuable time-saving tips that help you gain marks most students won't.

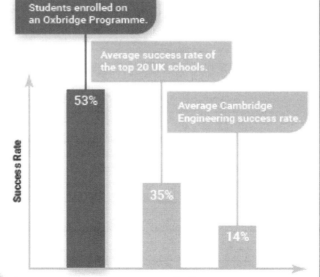

Students enrolled on an Oxbridge Programme.

Average success rate of the top 20 UK schools.

Average Cambridge Engineering success rate.

53%

35%

14%

Success Rate

UNIADMISSIONS Oxbridge Engineering Programme Average Success Rate

Printed in Great Britain
by Amazon

64589592R00203